P9-APR-326

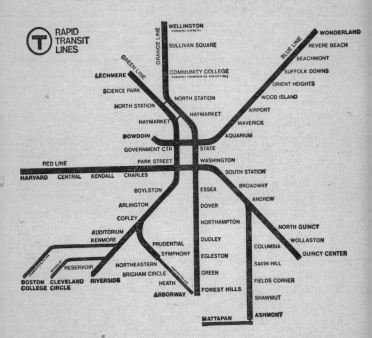

(T) RAPID TRANSIT LINES

WELLINGTON (FORMERLY EVERETT)
SULLIVAN SQUARE
COMMUNITY COLLEGE (FORMERLY THOMPSON SQ. AND CITY SQ.)
ORANGE LINE

WONDERLAND
REVERE BEACH
BEACHMONT
SUFFOLK DOWNS
ORIENT HEIGHTS
WOOD ISLAND
AIRPORT
MAVERICK
AQUARIUM
BLUE LINE

GREEN LINE
LECHMERE
SCIENCE PARK
NORTH STATION
NORTH STATION
HAYMARKET
HAYMARKET
BOWDOIN
GOVERNMENT CTR
STATE

RED LINE
HARVARD CENTRAL KENDALL CHARLES
PARK STREET WASHINGTON
SOUTH STATION
BROADWAY
ANDREW

BOYLSTON
ARLINGTON
COPLEY
AUDITORIUM
KENMORE
RESERVOIR
BOSTON CLEVELAND
COLLEGE CIRCLE
RIVERSIDE
NORTHEASTERN
BRIGHAM CIRCLE
HEATH
ARBORWAY

ESSEX
DOVER
NORTHAMPTON
DUDLEY
EGLESTON
GREEN
FOREST HILLS

MATTAPAN

PRUDENTIAL
SYMPHONY

NORTH QUINCY
WOLLASTON
QUINCY CENTER
COLUMBIA
SAVIN HILL
FIELDS CORNER
SHAWMUT
ASHMONT

MASSACHUSETTS
BAY
TRANSPORTATION
AUTHORITY

500 ARBORWAY
JAMAICA PLAIN, MASS.

– – – – – – – – – 722-5000

Boston

The Official Bicentennial Guidebook

A Sunrise Book
E. P. Dutton & Co., Inc.
New York
1975

In November, 1972, Mayor Kevin H. White established the Mayor's Office of the Boston Bicentennial to coordinate city-wide activities commemorating the Bicentennial of the American Revolution. The Mayor's Office of the Boston Bicentennial then created The Boston 200 Corporation, a nonprofit corporation, to operate those Bicentennial programs known as "Boston 200."

The downtown map of Boston with points of interest is the property of the National Survey of Chester, Vermont.

Development of the Neighborhood Discovery Trails was supported by a grant from the National Endowment for the Arts in Washington, D.C., a Federal agency.

This guidebook is available in Braille and on tape cassettes, thanks to the National Braille Press, a nonprofit service organization for the blind. Inquire at a Boston 200 Visitor Information Center.

ISBN: 0-87690-146-1

Dutton-Sunrise, Inc., a subsidiary of E. P. Dutton & Co., Inc.

Printed at the Colonial Press, Clinton, Massachusetts.

STAFF

Editors: Susan Okie and Donna Yee
Boston 200 Coordinator: J. Mark Schuster
Managing Editor: Steven P. Motenko
Consultants: Paul Silver and Kit Haspel
Director of Advertising Sales: Jo Anne La Sala
Advertising Sales Representatives: D. Thomas Abbott, James J. Lopes
Researchers: James J. Lopes, Lisa Perry, Annette Sanderson, Dorothy Smith and Stanley A. Twarog

MAPS AND ILLUSTRATIONS

Neighborhood Discovery Trail Maps: Michael & Susan Southworth/ City Design & Architecture
Black Heritage Trail and Activities Map: Geneva Printing and Publishing, Inc.
Cover Photograph: Fay Foto Service, Inc.
Exhibit Representations: Deenie Yudell

ACKNOWLEDGMENTS

The editors wish to thank Katharine D. Kane, Director of Boston 200, and all the members of her staff for their unlimited cooperation in producing this book. They also thank Jane Reed, Jill Norton and the board of the Cambridge Bicentennial Corporation for their assistance with the Cambridge Discovery Trail. Special thanks to Michael and Susan Southworth, Marcia Myers and Judy McDonough of the Boston Redevelopment Authority, and to those members of historical societies, neighborhood groups and city agencies who helped with the trail research.

The staff is also grateful to Katharine D. Kane, to Thomas A. Sampson, Chairman of the Board of Directors of The Boston 200 Corporation, and to Timothy E. Feige for their help with the advertising campaign. We also thank Jack Macrae, Michael L. Ryan and David Zable of E. P. Dutton.

Grateful acknowledgments to Francis W. Hatch for permission to reprint portions of "Bestir ye! Peter Faneuil" and "Some coward/Closed the Old Howard."

TABLE OF CONTENTS

A GUIDE TO THE GUIDEBOOK

The guidebook is divided into five sections. The first, Boston Background, is a presentation of the city by three prominent Boston writers. Read it at your leisure before or during your stay to get an overall view of Boston history and the flavor of the town.

The second section, Getting Settled in Boston, is designed to orient you to the city and its visitor services. It opens with instructions for getting to and from the airport, lists train stations and bus terminals, and acquaints you with the locations and uses of Boston 200 Visitor Information Centers. These centers, and the Boston 200 information numbers (338-1975 or 338-1976) are at your service during your stay, and can both answer questions and inform you of events and tourist facilities. Be sure to inquire at one of the centers when you arrive about special Bicentennial shuttle buses and parking facilities. The rest of the section provides emergency telephone numbers, a comprehensive hotel list, ways to enjoy a short visit, and a mine of practical information for solving any problem from exchanging currency to getting your child treated for measles. If you have trouble finding what you need, look up your problem in the index.

The Transportation section is short because your best and most reliable means of getting around this city is your own two feet. Boston is a city for walking. You will be aided in your progress by the MBTA, Boston's public transportation system. An explanation here supplements the map in the front of the book, and subway stations are included in our listings, preceded by the symbol "T." If you *must* drive in Boston—which we strongly suggest you avoid—the rest of the section offers what advice it can.

The Citygame section is the focus of the guidebook. It contains exciting new ways for visitors to discover Boston—not only in terms of the city's past, but in terms of its present. Three major Boston 200 exhibits await your participation, each concentrating on a century of Boston history. For visitors with limited time, these exhibits are the best way to get a sense of Boston's unique character. For further exploration, the section presents eight new walking trails through Boston neighborhoods, including the world-famous Freedom Trail. A ninth trail, the Black Heritage Trail, traces the history and contributions of Boston's black population. The section ends with short histories of other Boston neighborhoods, and advice for visitors interested in special areas of Boston's past—medicine, literature, architecture, women's history, and others.

The final section of the guidebook suggests ways to have fun in Boston. The Festival American Calendar lists events and festivals occurring in the city during each month of the Bicentennial. Museums and Attractions is a detailed guide to the city's sightseeing possibilities. Entries on shopping, restaurants and nightlife are grouped by location within the city, while those on outdoor activities and cultural entertainment are arranged by category. The restaurant and shopping sections are done geographically in order to complement the neighborhood trails, but if you are searching for a specific item or type of cuisine, you can consult the index. Keep in mind that the entertainment section is only meant to give you an idea of what Boston offers—the city's attractions are inexhaustible, and we urge you to find your own favorite places to eat, shop and enjoy yourself.

In 1843 Benjamin Stevens was a cabin boy on the Constitution. In 1865 he was New England Life's second president.

To this very day, our clients enjoy first cabin service.

BOSTON IN THE "PROPER" SPIRIT

By Cleveland Amory

Say New York or Chicago or Los Angeles or San Francisco or even Philadelphia—and you think of place. But say Boston and you think, first, of people. Dozens of names start rolling like a drumbeat.

And this is as it should be. For Boston is the place where, after all, America began. Without Sam Adams there would have been no Revolution—without John Adams, no Declaration of Independence.

And one war was not enough for Boston. From the pulpits of Boston—from William Ellery Channing and Theodore Parker and Lyman Beecher and William Lloyd Garrison and all the rest—was launched the crusade against slavery, and Mr. Lincoln himself gave the final accolade to the daughter of one of those clergymen. Meeting Harriet Beecher Stowe, author of *Uncle Tom's Cabin,* Lincoln called her, "the little woman who started the great war."

Boston is, first of all, Presidents—John Adams, John Quincy Adams, John Fitzgerald Kennedy—but Boston is also men far greater than all but a handful of our Presidents—Ben Franklin, the godlike Dan Webster, and that magnificent Yankee and great dissenter, Oliver Wendell Holmes.

Boston gave America its greatest philosopher, Ralph Waldo Emerson; its greatest free thinker, Henry David Thoreau; and its first great novelist, Nathaniel Hawthorne.

But Boston too is a portrait—by painters like Gilbert Stuart, John Singleton Copley, and John Singer Sargent. And if Boston is poetry by historians—historians like Francis Parkman, William Hickling Prescott, and John Lothrop Motley—it is also, surely, history by poets—poets like Henry Wadsworth Longfellow, John Greenleaf Whittier and James Russell Lowell, and still another, Oliver Wendell Holmes, the father of the Justice.

Boston's great women, too, seem to have their own special

11

three-name ring—Mary Baker Eddy, founder of the Christian Science Church; Julia Ward Howe, author of "The Battle Hymn of the Republic;" Louisa May Alcott, and of course, Rose Fitzgerald Kennedy.

The home of the bean and the cod, where the Lowells—not the Lodges, please—speak only to Cabots and the Cabots speak only to God; Boston even has its very own accent, one that is a strange combination of English, Irish, and Yankee. And to go with its accent it has its very own pronunciation. Quinzy for Quincy, Louisburg Square and not Faneuil but Fun'l. Even the gravestone cutter of Old Granary, burying Peter Faneuil, wanted to make sure no outlander got it wrong. He lettered the grave "P. Funel."

One thing Boston was, and perhaps ever will be, is Puritan. The *Mayflower* took Pilgrims to Plymouth, but the *Arabella* and the *Ambrose*, the *Jewell*, and the *Talbot* took Puritans to Boston. Led by John Winthrop, whom they had elected governor, they landed in Salem, but they did not like it and soon moved to Charlestown. Here they were visited by a minister named Reverend William Blackstone. He lived on what is now Beacon Hill, in what was then called Shawmut. He had come over with a shipload of adventurers, all of whom, he told his visitors, were both wicked and, worst of all, lazy. In any case, they had gone back to England and had left him all alone.

Reverend Blackstone took his new friends over to look at Shawmut and told them that if they liked it, they could stay. Since the foul water sources in Charlestown were felling Puritans at an alarming rate, Winthrop was more than happy to accept Blackstone's hospitality—and his fresh water. Blackstone soon had reason to regret his offer, for in short order Governor Winthrop and his people had changed Shawmut's name to Boston, after the little town in England from which many of them had come, and had promptly claimed all the land as their own.

Being charitable men, of course, they didn't completely forget the Reverend. They voted him fifty acres of land.

Blackstone wasn't entirely enamored with the idea of being given, as a generous donation, fifty acres of what was formerly all his. But Bostonians are realists—and merchants at heart. He sold back to Winthrop "their fifty acres" for $150—a princely sum in those days—and moved to Rhode Island.

Since each of Winthrop's men had chipped in to buy Blackstone's land, it was recognized as common property, set aside for public use. The "Common" remains today one of the oldest public parks in the world.

One of Governor Winthrop's first acts in regard to the Common was to order a carpenter to build a set of "stocks"—the typical Puritan punishment. And the first customer was typical, too—the carpenter who built the stocks. He had, Governor Winthrop declared, charged too much for them.

One historian has thoughtfully provided a list of "stock" offenses in the first twenty years of the Colony:

> Eavesdropping
> Meddling
> Neglecting work
> Scolding
> Naughty speeches
> Pulling hair
> Pushing his wife
> Riding behind two fellows
> Selling dear
> Sleeping in meeting
> Repeating a scandalous lie
> Selling strong water by small measure
> Spying into the chamber of his master and mistress
>   and reporting what he saw
> Dissenting from the rest of the jury

Good ruled all, of course. And sometimes they could get you coming and going. One sea captain, for example, home from a voyage, kissed his wife on the Sabbath—and compounded the felony by doing it in public, on his own doorstep. Obviously, he had to be taught a lesson, so he was publicly whipped. A year later he was back before the court again. This time his offense was "neglecting his wife and living apart from her." Once again he was whipped.

Boston was not Salem—only four women were executed for witchcraft and of these one wanted to be hanged and, having

13

been rescued, came back and surrendered to the gallows. Another was executed not only for witchcraft but also for murder, and in the case of a third, witchcraft was used for an excuse to get rid of a formerly wealthy widow who had become "a common scold."

It was a Boston judge, Samuel Sewall, who presided over most of the Salem witchcraft trials, but he later confessed the error of his ways. The public confession was made on the site of the Old South Meeting House—later made famous when 5,000 patriots rallied there in 1773, then marched off to dump the King's tea into the waters of Boston harbor.

Even though Boston didn't execute witches, neither was it, in those early days, a picnic. Witness *The Diary of Cotton Mather* of 1698:

I took my little daughter Katy into my Study and there I told my child That I am to Dy Shortly and Shee must, when I am Dead, Remember Every Thing, that I now said unto her. I sett before her the sinful condition of her Nature, and I charged here to pray in secret places every day. That God for the sake of Jesus Christ would give her a new Heart. I gave her to understand that when I am taken from her, she must looke to meet with more Humbling Afflictions than she does now she has a tender Father to provide for her.

At this time, bear in mind, Miss Katy Mather was exactly four years old. Somehow, though, out of all the blue laws and blue noses, burnings and bannings came, by the time of the Revolution, a city that could produce in one family alone not only Sam Adams, "the man who made the Revolution," but also his cousin John, the man most responsible for the Declaration of Independence and the separation from England. And, over and over again, the Boston woman was as responsible as the Boston man. The mother of Boston's Burnhams watched four sons go off to war. "Never let me hear," she shouted after them, "that one of you was shot in the back." Needless to say, none of them was. Coming from such a home, the army must have seemed, for the Burnham Boys, the life of Riley.

There were Bostonians on the village green of Lexington, where Captain John Parker, commanding less than sixty men, saw row after row of the advancing redcoats and said calmly, "Stand your ground, men. Don't fire unless fired upon. But if

14

they want to have a war, let us begin right here." There were Bostonians, too, by the "rude bridge that arched the flood" at Concord, when Major Buttrick, who had still not heard what had occurred at Lexington, first the shot heard 'round the world. And finally, of course, there were almost all Bostonians at Bunker Hill, in reality Breed's Hill, where a "ragtag and bobtail" army of Americans, with no uniforms, no flags, not even enough ammunition punished the well-groomed, well-armed British redcoats. George Washington's first question when he heard of the battle was whether or not the militia had stood firm. Told they had, he exclaimed, "Then the liberties of the country are safe!"

Bostonians loved a good fight. And, on many an eighteenth-century tombstone, there are words that tell of battles carried on even beyond the grave. Witness Mrs. Ameney Hunt's epitaph at the Copp's Hill Burying Ground:

> A sister of Sarah Lucas lieth here,
> Whom I did love most dear;
> And now her soul hath took its flight,
> And bid her spiteful self good night.

Whatever else old Boston was, it was America's Family City. A small handful of families placed their stamp on it so securely that the personality of the city remains less the city's than theirs. In no other city does this exist to the extent it does in Boston. Once upon a time it used to be said that socially speaking Philadelphia asked who a person is; New York, how much is he worth; and Boston, what does he know. In fact, Boston was asking Philadelphia's question—with a venegence; not only who somebody *is*, but also who he *was*—and not just has parents either, or even his grandparents, but 'way back. Ask a Bostonian such a question as, "How long have you been in Boston?" and he is likely to reply, "I've been here since 1730," or "1700"—and he really thinks he has. As late as the middle of the nineteenth century, Dr. Holmes, father of the chief justice, issued a remarkable manifesto on the subject. Asked by an anxious Boston mother when her child's education should begin, Dr. Holmes replied, "About a hundred years, Madam, before he was born."

Children were given a strong sense of their family's "place" in the Boston social hierarchy. In college, Dr. Holmes pointed

15

out, students "took rank on the (college) catalogue from their parent's condition." By 1749, the ranking was strictly official: it determined not only the order of chapel seating and marching in college processions but also precedence for classroom reciting and serving oneself at table. While all ranking was done in what was to become the great Boston Society tradition —according, it was recorded, "to the Dignity of the Familie where to the students severally belonged"—there can be no doubt that it caused a certain amount of hard feeling. In a noted essay on the subject, the late New England historian Franklin Bowditch Dexter, a Yale man, put the matter of these early day Harvard rankings as tactfully as possible but made clear that it was usually some time before each newly ranked class was "settled down to an acquiescence in their allotment," and that often the parents of the young men were "enraged beyond bounds." Dexter blamed most of the trouble on the "intermediate" members of the class, claiming that the highest and the lowest rankings were more "comfortably ascertained" than theirs. He cited the case of one Bostonian who, piqued to note his son was ranked fourteenth in a class of thirty-seven, went off and tried unsuccessfully to found a new college in western Massachusetts.

The most notable case of dissatisfaction with the rankings was no matter of the "intermediates" or Harvard bourgeoisie, however, but concerned the distinguished Phillips family, noted for their connection with Andover and Exeter academies. It took place in the summer of 1769 with the publication of the rank list for the following fall. Searching the list, Samuel Phillips, wealthy merchant, discovered that his son Samuel, Jr., later founder of Andover Academy, was well down the line, and in time-honored Proper Bostonian manner, he complained directly to Harvard's president. He felt particularly strongly about his son's being placed below a boy named Daniel Murray, but it is worth noting that he did not make his complaint on the grounds that he was a wealthy merchant and that Murray's father was not. The merchant era had not yet come into its nineteenth-century own in Boston Society; this was the magistrate era, and Phillips rested his case solely on the point that while both he and Murray, Sr., were justices of the peace, he had been a justice longer than Mr. Murray, and therefore Phillips, Jr. deserved precedence over Murray, Jr.

16

Harvard's president was a man named Edward Holyoke, distinguished in the college's social history largely through the fact that it was in his reign—1759—that an edict was passed forbidding the wearing of nightgowns by students. At the time of Phillips's complaint he was in the last of his thirty-two years on Harvard's throne and had apparently little stomach for a quarrel over a social point. In any case, he promptly reranked his entire student body, elevating young Phillips not only the number of notches demanded by his parent but also a few extra ones for good measure. Phillips never troubled to thank Holyoke for this, but upon noting the new ratings, under date of 29 August 1769, he wrote his son a letter which remains—more for what it does not say than for what it says—a sharp commentary on Proper Bostonian father-to-son protocol:

> You are now in the most difficult situation & the eyes of all, above and below you, will be upon you, & I wish it might be that you could be at home till the talk about the change was a little over. Every word, every action, and even your countenance, will be watched, particularly by those who envy you, and perhaps by those who do not. If any difficulties should arise with any of your classmates that now fall below you, treat them with all possible tenderness. If Murray is uneasy and manifests it to you, say nothing to irritate him. On the whole, say as little as possible.

Even in the nineteenth century, Harvard's president Kirkland was, as he put it, "finding it convenient" to keep a method of placing his students "other than alphabetical." As for Edmund Quincy, who was at one time mayor of Boston and at another president of Harvard, he seemed to regard all Harvard students as a special breed. "If a man's in there," he used to say, tapping his Harvard Triennial Catalogue, "that's who he is. If he isn't, who is he?" The feeling carried over to the twentieth century when, during the Taft Administration in Washington, a visitor to Harvard sought to see Lawrence Lowell, then president of the university. Lowell, however, had been called to the nation's capital on a matter of business. The visitor was stopped by a secretary in the outer office. "The President is in Washington," the secretary said, "seeing Mr. Taft."

One thing is certain. The dynastic proportions of Boston's first families are staggering. The Saltonstall family, for example, are currently sending to Harvard the eleventh successive generation of Saltonstalls, all descendants in the male line, to attend the college, as follows: Nathaniel, 1659; Richard, 1695; Richard, 1722; Nathaniel, 1766; Leverett, 1802; Leverett, 1844; Richard, 1881; Leverett, 1914; Leverett, 1931; Leverett, 1952; and Leverett, 1975.

The First Families have indeed always been noted not only for the recurrence of the same first name, but also for the recurrence of the same profession. In the Lowell family there were three generations of Judge Johns, beginning with one appointed by George Washington. Among the Cabots there have been seven successive generations of Samuels, the last three of whom have been manufacturing chemists.

First Families in Boston have tended toward marrying each other in a way that would do justice to the planned marriages of European royalty. Historian John Gorham Palfrey, commenting on the homogeneousness of New England life, once declared that a purer strain of English blood existed in New England than in any English county. Boston's best have determined to keep it that way. With the exception that no Saltonstall has ever yet married a Lowell, intermarriage among First Families has occurred in large proportion in almost every generation. In one Cabot family, out of seven children who married, four married Higginsons. In a Jackson family of five, three married Cabots.

Yet even this intimate marriage circle has often proved too large. There is scarcely a First Family in Boston without a record in its background of a marriage of cousins. When George Cabot, the first great Cabot merchant, married a Higginson, it was a double-first-cousin alliance. Nathaniel Bowditch, rated one of the most illustrious ancestors on any First Family tree, married a first cousin of his second wife. Charles Bulfinch, Boston's greatest architect, Helen Choate Bell, Boston's best-known society wit, Lawrence Lowell and Endicott Peabody, Boston's two outstanding educators, all chose cousin spouses.

Recently, when two young First Family cousins become engaged, a Boston matron put her official stamp of approval on the young girl's intention. "Isn't it nice," she said, "Faith isn't marrying out of the Family."

18

At an early age, the late Henry Cabot Lodge was once moved to ask his grandfather about his ancestors. "My boy," he was told sharply, "we do not talk about Family in this country. It is enough for you to know that your grandfather was an honest man." The remark had such a profound effect on Lodge that he never forgot it. He was soon to find, however, that his grandfather was almost alone in Boston in such ancestral impiety. When Lodge became a senator, his Massachusetts colleague, Senator Samuel Hoar, told him—"with great satisfaction," Lodge recalled—that he had discovered that through a mutual ancestor, the pastor of Salem's first church, they were both descended from a sister of Chaucer.

No Boston First Family party is complete without some discussion of genealogy. One of these parties, traditionally a Thanksgiving or Christmas affair, is apt to be so large that many of the guests, though relatives, will be strangers to each other; if afterwards one speaks of not connecting with someone, he means, in the Boston manner of speaking, that though he saw the person and even may have spoken with him, he did not place him on the family tree.

The Bowditch Family met the problem squarely as recently as 1936 by supplying every guest present with a ten-generation genealogy, a pamphlet designed in a loose-leaf form with extra space provided for keeping the work up to date. Occasionally a crisis occurs at one of these parties, as when Calvin Coolidge was elected president and a Boston Coolidge dinner was thrown into an uproar of discussion to determine what exact relation was this man from far-off Vermont. To get this distinguished family talking about anything was in itself no mean achievement—the society journal *Town Topics* once described Boston Coolidge as "scions of silence"—but fortunately among those present was Julian Coolidge, professor of mathematics at Harvard, who is a very precise man. After a moment's thought, he came up with his answer, "Calvin is my seventh cousin once removed," he said. He was later proved correct.

In one way the personality—or family—of Boston is easy to laugh at. In another way, however, it is not. Earl Derr Biggers, who later became famous as the author of the Charlie Chan mystery stories, recalled that his first newspaper job was writing a column in Boston. "Writing a humorous column in Boston," he said, "was a good deal like making faces in

church. It offended a lot of nice people and wasn't much fun."
The late *New Yorker* cartoonist Gluyas Williams put it another
way. Although born in California, he made his home in Boston
for some thirty-five years. "Your Bostonian will laugh, all
right," he declared, "only not when you expect him to."
"I came," wrote the novelist William Dean Howells, of his
first visit, "as the passionate pilgrim from the West approached his holy land in Boston." Howells, of course, was
welcome. Less so, in California, was the Proper Bostonian
woman who, asked how she had come, replied, "Via Dedham."
The same woman was also asked if she really liked Boston.
"Like it?" she said. "Why, I never thought of it that way.
Liking Boston is like saluting the flag."

The evidence is strong that even the "Improper Bostonian,"
as the late Fred Allen once called himself, "rather looks up
to the Proper Bostonian and is not inclined to laugh at him."
Referring to the least endearing of Boston's First Family traits
—such as the bluntness of Cabots, the frostiness of Lowells,
the tactlessness of Adamses, the perversities of Forbeses, the
irascibility of Higginsons and Amorys, the frugality of Lawr-
ences, etc.—the late James Byrne, a lawyer, once said that to
him there was nothing humorous about it. The son of an Irish
contractor, Byrne worked his way through Harvard tutoring
sons of First Families and became the only man of his background and religion up to that time ever honored with membership on the Harvard Corporation. "It is strong stock," he
said, "that can produce the same traits of character in generation after generation. No, I don't laugh at it."

Strong stock indeed. When British soldiers were accused of
murder in the Boston Massacre, John Adams and Josiah Quincy
volunteered to defend the men in court—hardly a popular
position in revolutionary Boston. The story is told that after
the verdict was announced, Adams, gathering up his papers,
walked to the prisoners' room. They crowded around him.
"God bless you, Mr. Adams," they cried. "We owe our lives
to you and Mr. Quincy. You are an honest man and a clever
one." "And by God," someone said roughly, "a brave one."

Another Adams, John Quincy, returned from the White
House virtually penniless, his real estate in both Boston and
Quincy mortgaged to pay his debts. Almost immediately, how-
ever, he returned to Washington, and for eight successive
Congresses—a period of seventeen years—he sat humbly in

the House of Representatives, which he had once addressed as President. The patrician Henry Clay sneered at him. He was beginning again, Clay said, like a boy. For all those years he did his duty as he saw it, "refusing," says one historian, "with tart asperity, to sacrifice his judgement to ministers, kings, or people."

The present Charles Francis Adams, sixth in the "royal" Adams line, recalls what his father once told him. "My father," he says quietly, "never talked much about family. But the day I went to work, he told me, 'I believe you have a reputation for honesty—God help you if you lose it.' That is all he said." Such a story had added poignancy when, in 1958, the story burst upon the country of the relationship between Sherman Adams, Eisenhower's right-hand man, and certain free hotel rooms and vicuna coats, and an Oriental rug accepted from the Boston industrialist Bernard Goldfine. This writer's own father was particularly disturbed by the story and scurried to his genealogy. He sent me a letter containing good news:

> The news about Adams is bad, Son, and Sherman is an Adams, it is true. But your Mother and I looked it up last night, and it is quite clear that Sherman is, after all, a New Hampshire Adams. There are very many of these, as I am sure you know, and they are only very distantly related to the Boston Adamses. Some of them have never even established any connection at all, and certainly in Boston nobody who knows anything about it at all would ever for a moment consider Sherman one of *the* Adamses.

The women of Boston were also a special breed. In the golden clipper ship days, married early, girls often went to sea side by side with their husband ship captains. At the age of nineteen one wife, sailing from Boston to San Francisco, had her husband suddenly stricken blind with brain fever, and with no other officer on board who understood navigation, was forced to take charge of the ship. Calmly studying in spare moments out of books brought to her from the ship's cabin, not only navigation but also medicine—so that she could care for her husband—she brought the ship around Cape Horn and put into Frisco on time to discharge the cargo. For fifty nights, it is recorded, she never left the deck.

Her physical hardihood established, the Boston woman of the nineteenth century went on to greater things. It seems impossible to realize now, but there was a time in Boston when females were not admitted to lectures. When the Boston Lyceum series of lectures was inaugurated early in the nineteenth century, however, its promoter had an idea. "I will attach a *locomotive* to this Lyceum," he declared, "'which shall *make it go*." His locomotive was the Boston woman, and it is doubtful if anyone has even given a more accurate description of the female of the Proper Bostonian species.

Women, not men, were the moving spirit of one nineteenth-century meeting which had as it object no less a goal than Universal Reform. If the Proper Boston merchant held sternly aloof from Brook Farm, the country's most distinguished experiment in communal living—what else could he do with an organization which had Nathaniel Hawthorne for head of its finance committee, a man who had never met a payroll in his life?—his sisters, and in some cases, even his wife, did not. First Family women were from the start a real force in the experiment, and if foredoomed to general failure, the Farm succeeded in giving women one ultra-modern landmark in emancipation—the establishment of the first nursery school known in America.

As a general thing, wife-reformers of the nineteenth century did not disturb the tranquillity of the Proper Boston marriage as they have been know to do in later days. This seems to have been at least partly due to the remarkable equanimity of the merchant-husbands involved, who were evidently able to take such things, along with their occasional financial reverses, in stride. One of these merchant-husbands, asked how he felt about the manifold activities of his wife, a well-known reformer of her day, replied briefly that he attended the closer to his own business the more his wife attended to other people's. But the question seems also to have been solved by the fact that many a First Family woman, feeling the urge for reform at an early age, chose for her mate, not a merchant at all but a very different type of man. A young Cabot girl with a reforming bent, for example, married Theodore Parker, a veritable firebrand of reform. Parker, who once devoted an entire sermon to the topic "The Temptations of Milkmen," and who ate no breakfast, but instead started each day by reading five books of the Bible, would have been a match for any wife-reformer. So, too, would have been his friend, George Ripley, founder of Brook Farm. Ripley once stated with some pride that his marriage was "founded not upon any romantic or sudden passion" but instead "upon great respect for her [his wife's] intellectual power, moral worth, deep and true Christian piety and peculiar refinement and dignity of character." Wendell Phillips, the abolitionist, though a son of Boston's first mayor and a First Family man, was still another young bridegroom far removed from the merchant-husband when he admitted that his wife invariably preceded him in the adoption of the various causes he advocated. Leaving his London boardinghouse one day to attend a convention where he was to deliver an address, he went out the door with the parting words of his young wife ringing in his ears: "Wendell, don't shilly shally." Wendell did not. Though the convention was a World Anti-Slavery meeting and had nothing to do with women at all, Phillips ended by delivering the first speech ever made by a man in advocacy of the rights of women.

Margaret Fuller caught the spirit of Boston women when, as far back as 1843, she sounded the clarion cry of what would come to be known as women's rights. "It is a vulgar error," she said, "that love, *a* love, is to woman her whole existance. She was also born for Truth and Love, in their universal energy." This came at a time, mind you, when another leading essayist of the day was posing the question: "Should women learn the alphabet?"

Miss Fuller is remembered today not so much for her writings or criticism as for the power of her personality—a remarkable distinction for a plain woman who spoke in a nasal voice, had remarkably poor health and the disconcerting habit of closing her eyes when she talked. The daughter of a historian and member of Congress, she was taught Latin as soon as she knew English and Greek at the age of four.

She became the first woman war correspondent, covering the Mazzini Revolution in Italy. While there, she married a young *marchese*. She was shipwrecked with him off New York harbor when she returned to the United States. Thoreau himself walked the beaches for days in a vain search for her body.

The Proper Boston woman has a busy day on Friday. She has a Chilton Club lecture and a Chilton Club lunch. But she is never late, and seldom early, for Symphony. For three quarters of a century, attired in her sensible coat, her sensible hat, and her sensible shoes, she has entered the hall promptly

23

at 2:25 and has then swept serenely to her seat in a manner that defies description. If she forgets her ticket, it is no tragedy. A large proportion of patrons regularly do this. But they have been so resolutely marching toward the same seat for so many years that no usher, even in a packed hall, would dare attempt to stop them.

Boston's powerful sense of tradition is some times mistaken for hidebound conservatism. It is not. The groundbreaking opinions of the great dissenter Mr. Justice Holmes symbolize Boston's concern for progress and the rights of the individual. One by one, as Catherine Drinker Bowen noted, his dissents become law—*Hammer* v. *Dagenhart,* "Child labor can be regulated by Congress," *Lochner* v. *New York,* "The liberty of the citizen to do as he pleases does not mean he can force other men to work twelve hours a day"; *Coppage* v. *Kansas, Truax* v. *Corrigan,* and *Vegelahn* v. *Buntner,* "I think the strike a lawful instrument in the universal struggle for life."; *Abrams* v. *The United States* and *The United States* v. *Rosika Schwimmer,* "Free thought—not free thought for those who agree with us but freedom for the thought that we hate."

Somehow the spirit of Holmes seemed present in 1954, during the Army-McCarthy hearings, when another great Boston lawyer, Joseph Welch, was faced with a personal breach of trust—when the late Senator McCarthy, in front of a nationwide television audience, first slandered a young man in his office and then turned to Welch for forgiveness. "I am a forgiving man, Senator," Welch said in his clipped Bostonian accent, "but you will have to find your forgiveness somewhere else than from me."

In 1843, Charles Dickens, in his *American Notes,* paid Boston a compliment in a book that contained few of them.

The golden calf they worship at Boston is a pygmy compared to the giant effigies set up in other parts of that vast counting-house which lies beyond the Atlantic, and the almighty dollar sinks into something comparatively insignificant amidst a whole pantheon of better gods.

In 1871, E. L. Godkin put it in simpler terms. "Boston," he said, "is the one place in America where wealth and the knowledge of how to use it are apt to coincide." Retail penury

24

but wholesale charity was ever the watchword, and yet there was always the question of making money. The Lowell family might have three generations of poets—James Russell Lowell, Amy Lowell, and Robert Lowell—but Lawrence Lowell was too wise not to be nervous. "I'm getting worried about the Lowell Family," he confided to a friend. "There is nobody in it making money anymore." And yet Bostonians did not put all their stock in making money. "The successful man," my father once told me, "is successful three times out of five. The failure is successful two times out of five."

Present-day Boston families like the Appletons and the Coolidges treasure statements of merchant integrity as issued by their family-founding forebears. An Appleton compared the mercantile honor of the day with the honor of a woman. It was "as delicate and fragile," he said, and it would not "bear the slightest stain." A filial Coolidge, speaking of his merchnt father, writes:

> Mr. Coolidge never went astray . . . did not content himself with obeying the rules of the technical code of mere mercantile honesty but preferred rather to carry downtown with him the honorable spirit of a gentleman. . . . The result was that not so much as even a mark of interrogation was ever set against any act of his.

The "spirit of a gentleman" remains of great importance to the Proper Bostonian. He wishes no truck with the modern idea of "deals" carried on with the aid of a few drinks and a hotel suite. "A Boston gentleman," said the late Rodman Weld, "never takes a drink before 3 o'clock or east of Park Street," by which he meant before the time of the stock-market closing or anywhere in the business district. West of Park Street, in the club and residential district, it was all right, of course, for gentlemen to get together "after hours." A nephew of Weld's once came to him claiming that in the law office where he was working, he was being made the butt of jokes by an officious partner of the firm and disliked it so much he was determined to leave the office. Weld looked at his nephew without sympathy. He asked him only. if he was learning something where he was. When the nephew admitted as much, Weld declared, "If you are getting what you want, why do you care whether you get it from a gentleman or a cad? You are not going to his office for his society but to be a better lawyer. You can associate with gentlemen after six o'clock."

The inherited religion of Boston's First Families was Episcopalian—a kind of Episcopalianism once defined by Emerson as "the best diagonal line that could be drawn between the life of Jesus Christ and that of the Boston merchant, Abbott Lawrence." Boston was also Unitarian—the kind once defined by the mother of Harvard's famed "Five-Foot Shelf," President Eliot. "Eliza," she asked a friend, who had just become a Unitarian, "do you kneel down in church and call yourself a miserable sinner? Neither I nor any member of my family will ever do that."

As might be expected, this attitude toward religion has made for some notable departures. Aunt Sara Palfrey, for example, at the age of eighty-eight, during her final illness, took up the study of Hebrew. When a friend remonstrated with her for the effort this involved, she said that she had always intended to take up the language and had put it off far too long as it was. "I wish to be able," she said with some finality, "to greet my Creator in his native tongue."

The younger Colonel Perkins, son of Boston's greatest merchant, Thomas Handasyd Perkins, provided an equally exemplary male departure. Once called Boston's best-dressed man—a small compliment—he had been rather a gay blade in his time. On his deathbed, he was approached by a friend who gave him, understandably hesitantly, the advice that he would do well to repent his sins if he wanted to go to Heaven. Perkins thought little of the idea. In two sentences he delivered what will undoubtedly remain as the all-time Proper Bostonian statement on the question of the hereafter.

"I am about as good," he declared, "as Gus Thorndike, Jim Otis or Charlie Hammond, and almost as good as Frank Codman. I shall go where they go, and that is where I wish to go."

CHANGING BOSTON

By Alan Lupo and Caryl Rivers

The gold hands on Boston's Custom House tower stand at 6 P.M., and the face of the clock peers impassively down on the cars that clog the streets below, filled with commuters rushing to leave the city. The tower climbs out of the torso of a fine old Doric structure, which once had a dome and stood by the edge of the water. But now so much of the harbor has been filled in that you can't even see the water from the ground floor, and the tower, an afterthought, spoils the lines of the building. The Custom House, like the city, changed and grew in haphazard fashion.

By the time the hands have moved to 6:30, the rush hour below is nearly over. Half the city's daytime people have gone, packed together three cars abreast on the expressway that slices through the city, or jammed together face to sweaty face, hands grabbing for leverage on one of the four subway lines that snakes its way through the city.

In the dusk, the neighborhoods are at their peak of life. The corners are busy. Outside, in front of houses, in folding chairs and on stoops, the people of the dusk sit, sometimes to talk, sometimes just to sit. A door opens, and everybody in a ten-yard radius knows what that household served for dinner. Unlike the embarrassed lady on the television commercial, no one here cares that the kitchen smells like a kitchen and that the parlor—that's parlor, not living room—also smells like the kitchen. These are good smells, the smells of life and suste-nance, of foods transplanted from Europe and Russia, from Jamaica and Hong Kong, from Mississippi and Aguadilla, all simmering in American-made pots.

At dusk, part of the city dies.

In the financial and insurance district, there is little activity now. There are no outward manifestations of the power that is generated every day in those offices, power carried by the vehicles of stocks, bonds, annuities, cash, investments. It is here, in this daytime neighborhood of conservatively dressed people—commuters often, men usually, white usually, Yankee often—that decisions are made that may guarantee life or death for other neighborhoods, other communities.

But at dusk, there is nothing here. An occasional late worker with briefcase tucked neatly under an arm. A scrubwoman, more likely Irish than black.

There are ghosts downtown at dusk, memories of earlier times guarded over by the new high rises, themselves shadowing the old office buildings that line the little streets that crisscross back and forth and weave about and change names from corner to corner. This is the heart of an earlier Boston, built up from the shoreline and paved over a hundred times. Its very pattern defies traffic and tourists, challenging the Bostonian to pick his way in and out of the asphalt underbrush, the brick and granite woods.

The Tremont Temple, dark this evening, locking in the echoes of a more turbulent political era, echoes of the Reverend P. S. Henson. The year 1907, the subject under discussion, John F. "Honey Fitz" Fitzgerald, then mayor and someday to be grandfather of a President, a candidate for President and a U.S. Senator: "I tell you, when a honey-tongued Democrat holds the highest place and regards the city over which he rules as if it were meant to be looted by him and the gang of which he is the leader—what is to be expected?"

Across town, in the environs of the Prudential Center, across town in the nightspots around Kenmore Square, in the watering holes for swinging singles, athletes, students, nurses, secretaries, junior executives, there is talk, heady talk, of more current matters. For that too is Boston, a Boston of no definable ethnic persuasion, whose major commodity is youth.

The action, as some call it, is no longer here. Part of it has moved to the newer Boston, the New Boston of Kenmore Square and the Pru. Another part of it, a more tawdry slice that once flourished in Scollay Square—long ago demolished for the creation of Government Center, daytime abode for federal, state and local bureaucrats—now lives in the Combat Zone, a half-dozen city blocks south of the Tremont Temple and the Park Street church. . . .

The morning comes in gray and cool with a promise of heat later in the day. The tide is full in the harbor, with a current from the southwest, a mild one. Early in the mist, there were foghorns and then the squawk of gulls. Then, a quiet period, before the big jets began lining up for the departures from Logan Airport, before the traffic jams and the backups of buses bringing their carrion into the subway terminals.

So, as with the dusk of yesterday, the city has a moment of peace before the cycle resumes. The menhaden and striped bass swim under the Belle Isle Bridge unmolested; the oysters, clams and mussels await the clamdiggers.

A city truck washes the streets. Laundry still hangs on lines strung between the porches of the three-deckers. As polluted as the air might be, the wash will still feel and smell fresher than what comes out of a dryer. Real food and real air. Outside, you can see things you don't see in the dusk of yesterday —one house after another being renovated with aluminum siding, people staying in the city.

In the warmth of daylight, an old lady walks out of the dark doorway of the three-story row house in East Boston, out onto the unshaded sidewalk. The old lady wears the black stockings and shoes and kerchief of the old people. She is of the old style, those who sit near the open windows and act as community radar. They see and know all, the old-timers. They are the seers of the second story. When you play in the street, every once in a while, you check back and up over your shoulder to see if she's still there. Your mother. Somebody else's mother. Somebody's grandmother. Somebody's aunt. Somebody. The somebody doesn't nod in recognition. She doesn't have to. You know she's there; she knows you're there. All's right with the neighborhood. That's what it means generally. What it means specifically is that you are not going to take your bat and smash in the neighbor's car headlight, because such action triggers the radar system.

On this warm day, the woman, maybe tired of a winter of looking out the window, is now out on the sidewalk. She walks with difficulty. Life is not getting easier for the greenhorns of eighty years or more. They draw strength from the sun and from the neighborhood. In the suburbs, where some of their offspring have traded Stations of the Cross for pink flamingos, the corners sprout grass. Back here, in the city, they sprout people. The corners are for people. Here, in East Boston, for Italians. In Roxbury, for blacks. In Charlestown, for the Irish. In the South End, for Puerto Ricans.

The corners are training grounds for a variety of occupations. They have bred boxers, ballerinas, barristers, bookies, bandits and bartenders. Collected together, they are the heart of the neighborhood. And the neighborhoods are the heart of Boston. Somehow, confronted with wrenching change, they endure.

Old-timers die, and old-timers shrug and move to the suburbs, where the dishwashers and garbage disposals automate them out of business, where they sit and watch the crabgrass from the first-floor window and dream less of the old country than of the old neighborhoods.

In the heart of the city, in Dorchester, a black family moves next door to a white family. Sometimes, they form a common alliance. Sometimes, they rub against each other and make sparks. Washington turns its head, tells America that "the hour of urban crisis has passed," speaks of benign neglect and cuts off funds that allow white and black families to fix and paint their houses.

Yet, somehow they hold on, the neighborhoods. They hold on, knowing that if they do not, Boston, for all its new imagery, for all its skyscrapers and rock clubs and alternative newspapers and university affiliations and medical reputation, will wither and die.

The neighborhoods have contributed their own distinctive architectural form to the city. It is a form that has none of the aristocratic grace of the Bulfinch houses, nor the curlicued elegance of the old civic buildings, nor the vaulting grace and arrogance of the skyscrapers. The three-decker is a structure that might be called, in the argot of the present day, "people's architecture." You can see three-deckers all over this city. They are, like their builders, solid and eminently practical: three floors, each housing one spacious apartment, and on the front of each house, a railed porch. The Irish may not have invented the form, but in the neighborhoods where they have come and gone, three-deckers sprouted like toadstools. The classic Irish success story can be explained in a phrase: from three-deckers to three toilets.

"Boston Irish" has a meaning all its own, or more appropriately, a dozen contradictory meanings. The Irish in America are not all clustered in the city by the sea, but one never speaks of "Milwaukee Irish" or "Newark Irish." Boston's Irishness is pervasive but hard to grasp, like the fog that rolls in from the ocean on warm September nights. Ask anyone on a

Boston street, "Where do you find the Irish?" and they will at first look thoughtful and then perplexed, as if they should know the answer but inexplicably do not. When the Chamber of Commerce was asked that question, there was a perplexed silence from a secretary on the other end of the line. Finally she said, "There's a man here who's Irish, I'll ask him." Silence. Finally she returned and announced, "He says they've all moved to the suburbs."

Not quite. The mayor's name is Kevin Hagan White. The five-member school committee is often completely Irish, as are two thirds of the city council, half the city's delegation to the State House and both its congressmen. The Irish constitute the city's largest ethnic group, with the Italians about 7000 behind. Some 186,000 persons in Greater Boston told the U.S. Census Bureau that they, their parents or grandparents came from Ireland. That's more Irishmen than the combined population of Cork and Limerick.

In 1846, in Ireland, a spreading rot took hold of the potato crop. The crop failed, as had so many things before it on that green and windy island embraced by the sea.

The Irish poured into the port of Boston, arriving at the Cunard terminal in East Boston. At first, they were a welcome source of cheap labor, working fifteen hours a day at un-skilled construction jobs, leveling the hills of Boston and filling in parts of the harbor, hauling bricks, tending the horses. But as the green tide began to push the natives out of some of the city neighborhoods, the hostilities emerged. "No Irish Need Apply" signs were hung on the doorways of the shops. When the new immigrants clung together, rejected and scorned by their Yankee neighbors, they were described as clannish.

The native Americans, themselves children of alien soil not so many years before, did not exactly open their arms in brotherly embrace to the "huddled masses yearning to breathe free." As early as 1831, a nativist mob attacked and burned the Ursuline Convent in Charlestown, where the battle of Bunker Hill had been fought fifty-four years earlier.

By the turn of the century, there was a new kind of Irish politician up and about in Boston. Unlike the city's first two Irish mayors, Hugh O'Brien and Patrick Andrew Collins, these men were born in Boston and were more familiar with the struggles of their precincts than The Struggle in Ireland. These were brash men, whom the Yankees accepted only as a prag-

31

matic means of currying favor and retaining whatever power they could.

The Yankees could count more than receipts and coupons. They could count election returns and voting lists as well. By the mid-1890s, 32 percent of the registered voters in Boston were foreign-born, and about half of them were Irish. Where once a Yankee mayor got in trouble by appointing Irish to the police force, now a mayor would commit political suicide by not doing so. And while some wards in Boston were electing people named Lowell and Emerson to the legislature, others were sending forth Kelly, Tague, McCarthy, Leary, Mahoney, Rourke, Falvey, Clancy, Toomey, McManus and O'Toole.

By the twentieth century, a flamboyant Irishman named Curley became the symbol of Irish political power.

James Michael Curley was born in 1874 in a cold-water tenement in Roxbury, where his parents paid six dollars a month rent and the bathroom was an outhouse in the yard. His father got a job as a hod carrier at ten cents an hour, eleven hours a day, through the good efforts of one "Pea Jacket" Maguire, boss of Ward 17. The father died when James Michael was ten, and the mother went to work as a scrubwoman to support her family.

Young Curley went on to learn political tricks from the best in the business, including Martin Lomasney, the leader of the West End and perhaps the most successful ward boss in Boston's history. When a rival politician set up roadblocks to keep Lomasney's men from arriving at a nominating convention in East Boston, Lomasney rented a hearse and sent his delegates through as a funeral procession. Because of his influence with the Naturalization Bureau, Lomasney arranged for illiterate youngsters to become American citizens. He sent them into the voting booths carrying combs with certain teeth extracted in a peculiar pattern. The illiterate voter simply placed the comb over the ballot, and the teeth covered all the names except the Lomasney candidates.

Because many illiterate voters were apt to put a cross by the first name they saw, first position on the ballot was important to a politician. Curley's first race, for common council, was in 1898, when he was twenty-four years old. He lost it, and was determined to win the following year.

Position on the ballot was determined by the order in which candidates filed nomination papers. Curley, his brother and a "score of brawny friends" barricaded the door to the election office the night before filing date. "It was some siege," he later recalled. "Several times that night, flying wedges of rowdies tried to crash our lines, but we plugged them as they came in. John suffered a broken jaw, and my cohorts and I took a pounding, but when the clerks and registrars arrived the following morning, we still held the fort and my name topped the ballot."

Curley formed his own political organization, and among his services to his constituents was job hunting. By his own estimate, he secured positions for more than 700 men and women in one two-year period, often filling out the job applications himself. He was arrested for taking a civil service exam for a position as a postman for one needy constituent. He served a sixty-day sentence in the Charles Street Jail, and while he was behind bars, he was elected to the board of Aldermen. "I felt then, as now," Curley wrote, "that I had done a charitable thing for a man who needed a job so he could support a wife and four children." For years afterward, Curley's political opponents liked to dredge up the jail sentence. The fraud charge cut little ice with Boston's immigrant voters who saw him as something of a Gaelic Robin Hood.

Curley served as mayor of Boston four times and was beaten in an attempt to do so six other times. He served on the old common council, the old board of aldermen, the city council, in Congress and once as governor of Massachusetts. In his lifetime, the transfer of political power from the Yankees to the Irish was begun and completed. He became the archetype of the Irish politician and achieved a particularly American form of immortality. He was played on screen by Spencer Tracy in "The Last Hurrah" as a shrewd, sentimental, roguish but loveable man of the people. To his critics, Curley was the machine pol who bent the political process to his own ends, who used favoritism, demogoguery and dirty tricks as the machinery of government; who was a self-inflated egomaniac who left no successors because he wanted no rivals. William Shannon says, "For thirty years he kept the population half-drunk with fantasies, invective and showmanship." Shannon sees Curley as a man unable to break free of the fierce Yankee-Irish antagonism that molded him, "a self-crippled giant on a provincial stage."

His admirers would point out that Curley's style of government was responsive to his constituents, the "new" Americans, in a way that the good-government reformers ("the goo-goos") could never be. As governor, he oversaw the passage of an impressive body of social legislation. William Green, president of the American Federation of Labor, wrote: "More progressive laws were enacted under Curley in two years than under all previous administrations in any ten-year period in the history of the state."

By the time the Italians, Jews, Poles and Slavs got serious about settling in Boston, the Irish were firmly in control, and the reactions from these new groups ran the gamut from street fighting to registering as Republicans to joining the local Irish machine.

The Italians were assaulted not only by those Brahmins who wrote of "fumes of garlic" or who waxed patronizingly about such "quaint Mediterranean" folk, but also from an Irish-dominated church and political structure. For years it was unthinkable than an Italian-American pastor would be in charge of an Irish parish. The church in Boston was not just Catholic. It was Irish Catholic. As for politics, the Irish were smart enough not to hang out any "No Italians (Jews, Slavs, etc.) Need Apply" signs, but the application process was fairly well controlled.

For the Jews, there was not even the common bond of the Church. The largest bloc of immigrants arriving between 1900 and 1914 were Russian and Polish Jews, and they found little in common with the small and fairly well-assimilated German Jews. "Yankee Jews," the newcomers would call them.

So intense was the impact of immigration that a Yankee school committeeman moaned, "We have in one of our schools 280 boys from Russia and Italy. The teachers in some of these schools who are trying to rescue and save these boys from ruin are engaged in a mission almost as holy as the ministers of religion." These boys, whom the Yankees were hell-bent on "saving," were sleeping in the streets, assaulting the teachers, refusing to be assimilated.

The boys he referred to were Jews and Italians living in the North End. In March, 1899, architects reporting on tenements in the North and West Ends of the city found "dirty and battered walls and ceilings, dark cellars with water standing in them, alleys littered with garbage and filth, broken and leaking drain-pipes. . . dark and filthy water-closets, closets long frozen or otherwise out of order. . . and houses so dilapidated and so much settled that they are dangerous."

For the first thirty years of this century, Yankees, blacks, hyphenated Americans all jostled about, elbowing, pushing, picking up and moving, one group forcing out another, until they all found their own turf, their own neighborhoods, until enough years of living in the same city had brought about at least an uneasy coexistence, if not friendships.

To the east, across the harbor, East Boston, the ward that John F. Kennedy's paternal grandfather had delivered faithfully to the Irish mayor-makers in the early 1900s, had turned Jewish and Italian, and during the 1930s became almost completely Italian.

A similar pattern was taking shape in the old North End, home of the other Kennedy grandfather, "Honey Fitz" Fitzgerald. There the Brahmins held onto their red brick historic churches and the Catholic churches retained Irish names, but the language of the street was the language of Abruzzi, Avellino and Calabria.

To the north, Charlestown, keeping to itself, retained its Irish character.

The West End looked like an old "Dead End Kids" movie scene. Jews, Irish, Italians, Lithuanians, Albanians, Poles lived in tenements, hung wash out the back and front windows, grew plants in every inch of available dirt, washed down the stairs on their hands and knees and made sure the streets were safe for West Enders. There would always be a West End, would there not?

In the South End, Syrians, Lebanese, Jews, Greeks, the ever-present Irish, Italians were all packed into one square mile living in the brick row houses that once had promised to be the chic residence for nineteenth-century Yankee merchants. They lived in what seemed to be harmony with the city's black population, still relatively small in number, including the descendants of the earliest of America's freedom fighters. Their numbers would burgeon.

Some of those blacks were moving next door to Roxbury, once a strong Irish ward, but now a Jewish ghetto rapidly spreading south: down Blue Hill Avenue through Dorchester and into Mattapan, a *shtetl* transplanted from Eastern Europe and Russia by way of the North and South and West Ends, East Boston and nearby Chelsea. No one would predict then, in those years when duplex houses were transformed into instant synagogues, that three decades later there would be no crowds of young Jews playing, fighting, loving at Franklin Field, that no Jews would be found gathered at the G & G Delicatessen to *shmooz* and read the *Daily Forward*, that only the echoes of that civilization would linger—and these only in the hearts of those who had known what it was to be an urban Jew.

But in the 1920s and 1930s, the Jewish wave rolled relentlessly like the tides in the outer harbor, pushing away both Irish and Yankees and establishing a territory. Elsewhere in Dorchester, the upwardly mobile Irish were settling in. "Lace Curtain," they were called and called themselves. But "Lace Curtain" didn't mean there weren't plenty of pols who played the game as rough as they and their fathers had learned it in the North End and Roxbury and South Boston.

South Boston.

Another neighborhood, but more, really. It was becoming a symbol of Boston, a place where Irish politics was practiced without a break, without quarter. Lithuanians, Italians and Poles would move into South Boston, but it would always be known as Irish. More than that, Southie would become the symbol of "neighborhood," with all the poetry and parochialism inherent in the word.

Southie had power. Southie was home for boxers, ballplayers, hoods, priests. It sent John McCormack to Congress, where he became Speaker of the House. It sent Richard Cushing to the church, where he became cardinal of the archdiocese, a man who did more with his raspy humor to calm down the religious wars than any brotherhood conference or governmental commission. Southie bred Louise Day Hicks, who became a national symbol of resistance to the busing of students.

For the brothers Kennedy, none of whom lived there, Southie became a reference point to document the national press image of Boston politics, and every political observer became fond of repeating, "There's an old saying in South Boston. Don't get mad. Get even."

Southie became more than a neighborhood. It was, and remains, a state of mind. In Catholic colleges around the country, Massachusetts kids who rarely left the confines of the Irish Riviera on the South Shore, who may have visited South Boston only on an occasional St. Patrick's Day, warble "Southie Is My Home Town."

There is the mystique of Southie, good ole Southie, the friendly neighborhood, I was born down on A Street, brought up on B Street, priests who look and act like Pat O'Brien and "Dead End Kids" who talk tough and punch tough but deep down are swell guys, and cooking broth for the sick neighbor's boy. And there is stereotyped Southie, bigoted, racist, parochial, narrow-minded, politically potent, grease-my-palm Southie.

There is truth and fiction to both sets of myths, for Southie, like the rest of Boston's neighborhoods, is not all Irish. Nor is it all one big happy urban neighborhood family collectively cooking soup all day for its sick relatives, nor is it all full of hate and prejudice. Like the other neighborhoods, white and black, Southie feels persecuted, pushed, threatened.

The neighborhoods could live with faulty zoning decisions that left red brick industrial buildings flush up against three-decker wooden houses. They could survive fuel storage tanks and noisy truck routes. But what came close to killing Boston's neighborhoods was a combination of urban neglect, subsidized suburbia and changing lifestyles. Such grand and sweeping trends were beyond the reach of the ward leaders. It was one thing to get the boys on the corner on the civil service list, but how did you keep them out of the suburbs?

In the mid-1960s, a white businessman who had stayed in his Jamaica Plain neighborhood looked around at a particularly desolate scene, swept his hand across the vista of neglect and said, "A whole generation of leadership moved away."

In the 1950s, the Eisenhower grin stretched across America from horizon to horizon, a smiling aperture that was a cornucopia of good things. Progress was the new religion, gray flannel was the style, and the smell of prosperity was riding on the air.

The city needed revitalization. There was a chronic shortage of decent housing, decay in many neighborhoods, and the city's overall financial picture was so dim that it was hard to attract new business or float municipal bonds with confidence. But the new technological religion harbored no understanding that communities are not replaceable, interchangeable units, like Leggo blocks; that a community is made of cords of blood and sinew as well as slabs of concrete and stone.

The saga of Boston's West End illustrates the triumph of the technocrats' vision, small and cramped and cold as ice cubes, its biological rhythms not the sounds and smells of the streets but the staccato of jackhammers and the rustle of money. The massacre of the West End left wounds in this city that have not healed. A community was excised, like an appendix, and the organism that is the city did not forget. Say "urban renewal" in many of the neighborhoods of Boston, and eyes turn hard, heads shake. They remember.

The West End was an immigrant district, a polyglot community with the sort of vitality possessed only by city neighborhoods where a great many people have come and gone. It was a microcosm of immigrant America, the melting pot in miniature. One West Ender told a reporter in 1942: "We West Enders have a lot of spirit. All the other districts in the city have facilities to honor their boys. We haven't got facilities. We've got spirit, though. We've got the largest cosmopolitan section anywhere in the U.S.—Jewish, Irish, Polish, Russians. Ah, we've got everything down here. . . . "

To the technocrats of the 1950s, to the bankers and realtors, to the editorial writers and the architects, the West End was a slum: decrepit housing, roadways hardly wide enough to let the fire engines through, overcrowding.

The community tried to fight, in the shadow of the bulldozer. The West End Development Plan, whose supporters included a former leader of the New Boston Committee, would replace their homes with luxury, high-rise apartment buildings and shopping areas. At one tumultuous meeting of the Boston Housing Authority, 500 West Enders jammed the auditorium in the State House. One of their spokesmen, Joseph Lee, a member of the school committee and a lifelong resident of the West End, drew cheers from the crowd: "You are trying to uproot a community and drive it into exile! . . . We deplore your efforts to kick people out of their homes and to replace them with another group of people. The United States has not got room for a mass deportation of American citizens. No group of people under American law can be so degraded. The many are not to be exploited for the profit of the few! It is not proper to take from the poor and give to the rich!"

The cries of pain and outrage went unheeded. The West End Development Plan ground its way through the channels of government. In the spring of 1958, there was a mass rally on Staniford Street sponsored by the Save the West End Committee. The federal housing inspectors were due within the week to start the process of relocation. There were defiant cries from the crowd: "Don't let them in!" "They'll get in over our dead bodies!"

The screams trailed off into the air and fell away to silence. The press called the residents "a few malcontents who tried to block the development with reckless charges." By August, the wreckers were at work. An old woman locked herself in a room and refused to budge; a group of elderly Jews could find no place to live within walking distance of a synagogue. The families of the West End, resigned, or dazed, or bitter, packed up like the villagers of Anatevka in *Fiddler on the Roof* and went off to exile. The West End died.

It was because of the West End that the planners met opposition in the neighborhoods, even when their efforts were geared to desperately needed new housing for low- and moderate-income families. But downtown, the New Boston was materializing as the 1950s ended and a new decade began. Boston began sprouting a skyline: the new Prudential tower soared fifty-five stories into the air, part of a spiny fin of sky-scrapers that climbed the back of the Hub like the armor on a dinosaur.

John F. Collins, who became Mayor in 1960, was in many ways a new breed of Irish politician. He was formally edu-cated, urbane, sophisticated—and very much at home with the bankers and money men whom Curley, years before, had railed against. It was Collins who brought to Boston a man who would be known to his admirers as the architect of the New Boston, and to his enemies as "Ed the Bomber."

Edward J. Logue was one of the most controversial figures in the city in the 1960s. As head man in Boston's renewal agency, Logue displayed what one New York *Times* reporter called "an instinct for aggregating power." He displayed also a genius for guiding his myriad projects through the treach-erous waters of the federal bureaucracy.

In seven years, he oversaw a $2 billion expenditure on renewal projects that covered 11 percent of the city's land area, including the completion of the Prudential Center and a huge Government Center complex. He attracted national attention with his program and his forceful personal style.

The publicity generated by Boston's urban renewal competed for attention in the national media with the theft of tons of valuable Boston Common loam dug up for an underground garage and the televised documentary of local police patronizing a bookie joint. As the Collins regime ended in 1967, most of the boosterism and national publicity that had marked the New Boston would go with it. The legacy of Hynes, Collins, Logue and The Vault—that collection of businessmen with new and old money who quietly helped guide the city's future—that legacy was mixed.

To be sure, there was a new, healthy mood of confidence among money men. Boston's urban renewal program, the largest of any city its size, had eaten up money for fifteen years and spit back a multitude of projects. Ironically, the new breed of Irish mayor, the reform-type mayor, could probably hand out more contracts and create more work than his job and project-conscious predecessors. Architects and developers replaced road and paving contractors as the influential men of government, the donors of campaign money. Boston suddenly had a skyline, a new image, and a service-oriented industry to fill the void left by the loss of manufacturing, fishing and apparel industries.

But the heart of Boston was not in the new Government Center or the Prudential tower. The heart of Boston remained with the people in the neighborhoods, and it was showing signs of wear and tear. From 1950 to 1960, Boston lost more than 100,000 residents: before the 1960s were over, the city would lose another 56,000.

Washington had provided millions for the rebuilding of America's downtowns and a fair amount for the bulldozing of neighborhoods and construction of some new housing, but very little for rehabilitating and stabilizing old neighborhoods.

While the experts exulted in the new federal-city money pipeline, in the new bureaucracy with its new words, the people in the neighborhoods mourned the memory of Jim Curley and those like him. All around them were signs of disease and death, a hardening of the arteries that lead to the heart. They worried about street crime, police protection, blight, absentee landlords, vandalism, abandoned buildings, deteriorating recreation facilities, racial tension, real estate blockbusting, dirty streets, clogged catch basins, illegal parking, traffic congestion, illegal dumping of trash, and an insensitive bureaucratic school system that seemed to encourage both white and black children to set their sights low.

If enthusiasm describes what pervaded the business and construction and money communities, then despair, alienation and neglect described the mood of the real Boston, the neighborhoods. This was the irony, the set of contradictions, the potential for tragedy that faced those running for office in 1967. Some of them seized upon it and campaigned on the theme that government must now respond to the alienated.

One candidate who caught this theme captured a national audience for her outspoken stands. Her name was Louise Day Hicks, and while she was called the antibusing candidate, as the school committeewoman who resisted the state's Racial Imbalance Law, she was more than that. She was South Boston, born and bred, part of and responding to a white Catholic constituency whose reputation for political power far exceeded reality. She spoke to the alienation. Everybody, friends and enemies, called Mrs. Hicks "Louise."

There was another candidate being greeted by his first name. He waded into crowds of elderly, of kids, of guys hanging on corners with a disarming technique he would later use to help save the city during the days of urban rebellion and confrontations. A critic said of him, "There is probably nobody better in the country with a coat over the shoulder. He's a master at street style, better than Lindsay."

Kevin Hagan White, grandson of a good-government city council president and son of a powerful former council president and school committee chairman, was busy using every technique in the book, from scholarly position papers to neighborhood house parties to wheeling and dealing with the Democratic regulars.

White beat Hicks in November 1967 by 12,429 votes. He vowed that his administration would pay attention to the neighborhoods, that its focus would not be in the executive suites downtown. He has tried to please both constituencies, actually, with programs that include little city halls in every major neighborhood. He took office in what was to be an explosive year for America. Robert Kennedy would be shot to death in a hotel kitchen in California, barely three months after Martin Luther King was felled on a motel balcony in Memphis.

For countless American blacks, the murder of King seemed

41

also the murder of a dream; the one he had proclaimed on a hot summer day in Washington, D.C., under the marble eyes of Lincoln. "I have a dream!" he said, but now the dreamer was slain and white society had barred the doors to the Promised Land. The ghettos blazed across America, ignited from soured hopes, rage as combustible as kerosene, and the squalor of city streets. The black neighborhoods of Boston danced on the edge of chaos, and there were indeed eruptions, but in the end, they did not explode in full-blown riot.

Today, as the city of Boston looks ahead, with the twentieth century three quarters gone, there are no editorial writers proclaiming sunlit vistas. It is a time when the conventional wisdom says that cities do not work, perhaps cannot work—that they will become increasingly poorer, largely black, strangled by a noose of affluent white suburbs. Some have even suggested that the cities be abandoned and left to rot, while we all start over again someplace in the green countryside.

The idea of Boston is that it is a city that can work, does work. So many American dreams have rooted here, flourished here. The dream of Republic began here and also that vision of the equality of man that spurred on the Abolition movement. The immigrants wove their personal destinies into the fabric of the city. ("Once I thought to write a history of the immigrant in America," says Oscar Handlin. "Then I discovered that the immigrants *were* American history.") Martin Luther King studied at Boston University. It was here that William Trotter and George Forbes started the *Guardian,* a black publication that sounded the clarion for equal rights eight years before the NAACP was founded. Through the late 1960s and early 1970s, Boston Common rang with shouts of opposition to the Vietnam War.

The vision of Boston is the "golden mean" of Aristotle, some geographical plot of sanity between extremes on either side. In scale, it is a livable city; small enough so that walking is not a lost art, large enough to provide the diversity that makes urban life interesting. Its ethnic stew lends variety and charm, in an era when so much of America seems to be bland, plastic, homogenized. The city is torn by all the tensions that strain at urban America—battles over *de facto* segregation, housing shortages, street crime, changing neighborhoods—and yet there is the sense that somehow, with enough luck and common sense and money, Boston can muddle through. There is not,

42

in most of the city's neighborhoods, the sense of bombed-out territory, of battlefields abandoned, which one senses in some other cities.

Boston's promise is precarious, however. Nothing is sure in urban America. A city is a fragile and complex organism; like the human body, it contains so many hormones, secretions, substances that must be in balance or it will not survive. The city needs middle-and upper-middle-income residents for a healthy economy, and yet it must not drive out the people whose roots help sustain the neighborhoods. A suburbanite who moves to the South End to remodel a handsome town house may force out the four families who live there and who will not be able to pay the rent in the renovated flats. A zoning exception allowing a high rise or fast food franchise means new tax revenues, but it destroys the character of a block and may cause those who live nearby to flee.

There is a crying need to upgrade the schools, provide services for the elderly, house people with low and middle incomes; but the flow of federal money to the cities is questionable in the foreseeable future. Inflation could wipe out the best-laid plans for keeping the city vital. If mortgage money is not available in the city, the prospective city homeowner will drift to the suburbs. If the banks "redline" a neighborhood, refuse to give mortgages for that area even if money is available, the neighborhood will decline. The city could float across some invisible point of no return, where, in the words of Yeats: "Things fall apart; the center cannot hold."

But now, at 1776 plus 200, the center is yet holding. The dream that is Boston, built like a coral reef on the histories of so many disparate lives, endures. That may be important for all of us. It was best said by one of the city's most eloquent voices, Ms. Elma Lewis of Roxbury, once described as black America's Barnum, Hurok and Guthrie: "We're big enough to be a city but small enough to handle our problems. If we can't do it here, it's over for America."

43

GETTING SETTLED IN BOSTON

GETTING IN AND OUT OF BOSTON

LOGAN INTERNATIONAL AIRPORT

By public transportation you can get to Logan by taking the Blue line to Airport station and from there catching the MBTA shuttle bus (fare 20¢) that stops at all the major airline terminals.

If you're driving, take the Callahan Tunnel which begins in Dock Square and is also accessible from the Fitzgerald Expressway. The toll is 25¢ and the route to the airport is well marked on the East Boston side.

You can also catch an airport shuttle bus (run by Airways Transportation Co.) at most of the major hotels in downtown Boston and at the Park Street MBTA station. The bus runs every 15 minutes from 7am to 1am daily, and costs $2.25. Call 267-4907, ext. 21 for more information.

RAILWAYS AND TERMINALS

Amtrak (800-523-5720) leaves from South Station and Back Bay Station, T-Copley or Prudential. National service.

Boston & Maine (227-5070) leaves from North Station, T-North Station. Service for areas within 35 miles north of Boston.

BUS LINES AND TERMINALS

Greyhound, 10 St. James Ave. (423-5810); near T-Arlington. National service.

Continental Trailways, 10 Park Sq. (482-6620); near T-Arlington or Boylston. National service.

Almeida Bus Lines, 10 Park Sq. (482-6620); near T-Arlington or Boylston. Service to southern Massachusetts and Cape Cod, with connections to Martha's Vineyard and Nantucket.

Filene's

A LOOK
AROUND BOSTON

At Filene's, fine clothing
and accessories are a
tradition for the entire
family. You'll find every
appealing and exciting
new idea in Filene's
upstairs and fantastic
Automatic Bargain
Basement, known
the world over.
Take a tour, walk
the Freedom Trail —
the better you
look, the more you'll
see in Boston.

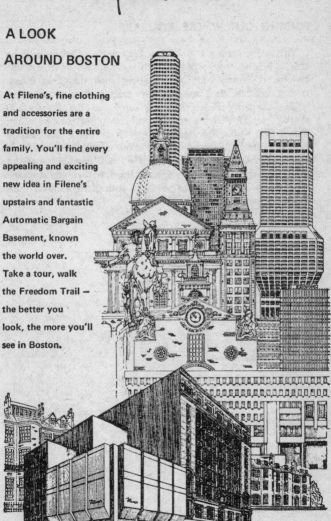

Peter Pan, 10 Park Sq. (482-6620); near T-Arlington and Boylston. Service to western Massachusetts and Springfield.

FINDING OUT WHERE YOU ARE

The major **Boston 200 Visitor Information Centers** will be able to help visitors to Boston with any problem or emergency. Inquire at Boston 200 Centers about such things as Bicentennial exhibits and events, day care centers, boat rides, tickets to performances, medical care, and the Boston 200 shuttle bus. Don't let a trifling problem upset your vacation; Boston 200 Visitor Information Centers can make your stay in Boston perfect. Secondary Information Centers will not have specific problem-solving facilities. They will provide the visitor to Boston with event information, brochures about historical sites, and tour information. See hotel listings for secondary information centers in Boston hotels.

MAJOR BOSTON 200 VISITOR INFORMATION CENTERS

City Hall Visitor Hospitality Center
City Hall—Plaza Level
T—Government Center

John Hancock Tower
Copley Sq.
T—Copley

Visitor Information Center
Boston Common—Tremont St.
T—Park St.

Massport
Logan Airport Terminals
T—Airport

Coming Soon:
1775.

John Hancock's 60-story Observatory is going to be more than a skyscraper with a view and a gift shop. *It's historic Boston:* A 20-ft. circular topographical model that re-creates Revolutionary Boston and the events of the 1770's – the Battles of Bunker Hill, Dorchester Heights and the Boston Massacre. *It's exciting Boston:* A cinematic helicopter Cityflight featuring a thrilling swoop around Tobin Bridge, through Callahan Tunnel and a flight over historic sites. *It's modern Boston:* A Photorama of backlighted transparencies shows you modern Boston's points of interest. High-powered binoculars give you a close-up of the sites pictured. *Free Information:* The Boston 200 Visitor Information Center in our Tower Lobby tells you where to go, and how to get there. And for Tower information call Morgan H. Plummer, Manager, Tower Observatory at 421-2632.

John Hancock

Mutual
Life Insurance
Company

Boston 200– at your service.

Let us entertain you. America will be 200 years old only once and the entertainment services created by Boston 200 are of once-in-a-lifetime value to those who join us in celebration.

Take the Boston 200 PassPort, for example. Take it and you'll get much more than you bargained for. The book offers over $300 worth of local discounts on everything from shops and sports to theaters and transportation — for only $3.00.

Now hear ye and you'll learn the lessons of history with greater ease and enjoyment through the By-Word Audio Interpretive System. By-Word Listening Posts are located all along the various City-game Trails and will help bring history to life with dramatizations, narration and sound effects related to the events that took place at each location.
Look for this symbol.

If you're interested in The Boston Tea Party and all the historical

causes that led colonials to commit such an "outrage," an opportunity to relive the entire event lies at anchor near the Congress Street Bridge on Boston's waterfront. The Boston Tea Party Ship and Museum, including the Brig Beaver II — a full-size working replica of one of the original Tea Party ships, are open daily from 9-5 in winter and 9-8 in summer. Admission is $1.50 for adults and 75 cents for children 5 to 14 years old. For more information, call 338-1773.
Look for this symbol.

Another Boston 200 service that we believe is revolutionary in its own right is the Grey Line Shuttle Bus Tour. One full-day ticket

allows you to travel to any of the Bicentennial points of interest throughout the city, stopping anytime you choose. Unlike other bus tours, this method is an inexpensive way to see Boston without having to conform to the limits of a tour. You can visit what you want, for as long as you want and simply move on with the next shuttle. Look for this symbol.

Entertainment services that will go down in history. From Boston 200.

Boston 200™

SECONDARY INFORMATION CENTERS
(NON-PROFIT INSTITUTIONS)

State House
Lobby—Information Desk
T—Park St.

J. F. K. Federal Building
Lobby
T—Government Center

Christian Science Center
Lobby—New Administration
  Building
T—Prudential

Massachusetts General
  Hospital
Lobby—White Building
Fruit St.
T—Charles

Traveler's Aid
Greyhound Station,
Park Sq.
T—Arlington

Greater Boston Chamber of
  Commerce
125 High St.
Visitors' and Convention
  Bureau
T—South Station

Massachusetts Department of
  Commerce and
  Development
100 Cambridge St.
State Office Building,
Room 1309
T—Bowdoin

Harvard University
Information Center
Holyoke Center
Harvard Sq.
T—Harvard

Park Street Subway
  Information
Park St. MBTA Station

Logan Airport,
International Terminal
T—Airport

Boston Public Library
Copley Sq.
T—Copley

ADDITIONAL TRAVELER'S AID

The International Institute of Boston, 287 Commonwealth Ave., Boston (536-1081) is a non-sectarian agency working to help the foreign-born visitor and newly arrived immigrants of all nationalities solve special problems of adjustment to American life. Gives personal guidance and conducts individual classes in English.

The Travelers' Aid Society of Boston, 312 Stuart St., Boston (542-7286) provides information, personal counselling and referral for travelers. The Society assists inexperienced and handicapped persons in making and completing travel plans. It offers the facilities of a nation-wide chain of inter-city services to assist runaways, children traveling alone, aged or handicapped travelers, the mentally ill, migrants, newcomers, and travelers encountering unexpected difficulties.

The following banks handle currency exchange. They have several currencies on hand—British, Canadian, Danish, Dutch, French, Italian, Norwegian, Swedish, Swiss, West German— and all others can be obtained from New York City on demand or advance notice:

First National Bank of Boston
100 Federal St.
Boston
434-2200
9am to 4:30pm, Mon-Fri

Forex, Inc.
Logan International Airport
North Terminal Complex
Boston
569-2900
12:30pm to 8:30pm,
  Open seven days

Logan International Airport
National Shawmut Bank
742-4900
9am to 3:30pm, Mon-Wed
9am to 5pm, Thurs-Fri
International Foreign Exchange
noon to 10pm, Mon-Sat
2pm to 10pm, Sun

National Shawmut Bank
40 Water St.
Boston
742-4900
8:30am to 4pm, Mon-Wed
8:30am to 5:30pm, Thurs-Fri

New England Merchant's
  National Bank
28 State St.
Boston
742-4000
8am to 6pm, Mon-Fri

State Street Bank
225 Franklin St.
Boston
786-3000
9am to 3:30pm, Mon-Fri

Barclay's Bank International
110 Tremont St.
Boston
423-1775
9am to 3pm, Mon-Fri

Harvard Trust Co.
1414 Mass. Ave.
Cambridge
876-1700
8:30am to 5pm, Mon-Fri
And all branches

For babysitters or day care centers, ask at the Boston 200 Visitor Information Centers.

Major downtown public toilets are located at:

City Hall Visitor Center
J.F.K. Building (Government Center)
State House, facing Boston Common
Hancock Building
Prudential Center
bus stations (open seven days)
department stores

For too much luggage or leaving behind safely items which you do not wish to carry everywhere, storage lockers are located at Logan Airport, Greyhound Terminal, Trailways Terminal, and the subway stations at Government Center, Park St., Washington St., Essex St., Copley Sq., State St., Haymarket and Harvard Square.

FINDING OUT WHAT'S HAPPENING

For fast, complete information about the day's events call "When it all Begins", Boston 200's daily events phone numbers (338-1975 and 338-1976) for special Bicentennial events, exhibits, lecture series, concerts, and sports events. Also call Artsline (261-1660) for fast information about the day's events.

Boston's two leading daily newspapers are the Boston *Globe* and the Boston *Herald American*. The Friday edition of the *Globe* and Sunday edition of the *Herald* have listings of the coming week's events. Daily editions have daily calendars. The *Christian Science Monitor*, a nationally distributed daily, besides superior news analysis, contains a helpful entertainment section for Boston. For the most complete listing of Bicentennial events, as well as other entertainment listings, articles on Boston history and cartoons, check the **Boston 200** newspaper. Also helpful for events listings and news about the youth scene are *The Real Paper* and *The Phoenix-Boston After Dark*, both available for a quarter from newsstands or street vendors.

The ticket outlets listed below handle tickets for all theater, musical and sporting events, so you do not have to go to the box office itself before the event. Most outlets include circus and ice shows as well. There is a service charge on top of the ticket price if you purchase your tickets through an agency.

just the facts, ma'am...

Facts for today's woman
on health, employment,
education, legal rights,
family matters and reform.
Visit the new "Woman's
Kiosk" information center
in Boston's City Hall lobby
and find out about progress
made and to be made.

Sponsored by
The Stop & Shop Companies

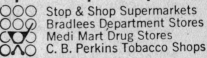 Stop & Shop Supermarkets
Bradlees Department Stores
Medi Mart Drug Stores
C. B. Perkins Tobacco Shops

Hub Ticket Agency
110 Stuart St.
Boston
426-8340

Tyson Ticket Agency
226 Tremont St.
Boston
426-2662

Out of Town Theatre Ticket
  Agency
Harvard Sq.
Cambridge
492-1900

Concourse Ticket Agency
South Station near track no. 1
Boston
542-3905

USEFUL PHONE NUMBERS

EMERGENCY NUMBERS

Fire	536-1500
Police Emergency	911
Police Non-emergency	338-1212
Ambulance	
Boston City Hospital	424-4073
Police Ambulance	338-1212
Rape Crisis Center	492-RAPE
Poison Center—Affiliated with four hospitals	232-2120
Dental Emergency	726-2000
24-hour Pharmacy—Phillips Drugs	
155 Charles St. (Does not deliver)	523-4372
Psychiatric—24 hours	
Mass. General Hospital	726-2994
Mass. Mental Health	734-1300
Boston City Hall (24 Hours)	
(Mayor's Office—city problems)	722-4100

MINOR EMERGENCIES

Lost and Found Phone Numbers
    Boston City Hall, Information Desk: 722-4100 ext. 253
    MBTA: 722-5716
    Boston Police Department: KE 6-6700

Complaint Phone Numbers
    Mayor's Office of Public Service (24 hour): 722-4100
    Boston Consumer Council: 722-4100 ext. 236
    Better Business Bureau, 150 Tremont St.: 482-9151, 482-9190
      (complaints)
    MBTA: 722-5700

DAILY DATA

Time Number: 637-1234 or NER-VOUS
Weather Number: 936-1234
Voice of Audubon (unusual birds seen lately): 259-8805
Satellite information: 491-1497
MBTA information: 722-5657 or 722-5700
Daily Events Phone Numbers: Call 338-1975 or 338-1976
(Boston 200) or 261-1660 (Artsline).

PROBLEMS AND HOW TO SOLVE THEM

EMERGENCY ROOMS AND OUTPATIENT CLINICS

The following emergency rooms and outpatient clinics will serve people from anywhere. Unless otherwise specified, a doctor, RN, and X-ray are available in the hospitals 24 hours a day. Languages spoken at the clinics are specified. In some cases fees may be slightly higher by the time of publication. The emergency services which the clinics provide will be designated as follows: G—General, P—Pediatric, E—Eye Care, D—Dental, O—Obstetrics, AM—Adult Medicine, MH—Mental Health, GY—Gynecological.

Boston Evening Clinic, 314 Commonwealth Ave., Boston (267-7171). Walk-ins welcome; Mon, Wed, and Thurs, 5:30pm to 7pm. Fee $10, lab and X-ray extra. GY O E AM MH.

Bridge Over Troubled Waters, One Walnut St., Boston, across from Park Street station, near State House (227-7114). Walk-ins welcome. Mon-Fri, 10am to 6pm. Free. Medical van Mon-Fri 2pm to midnight. GY P AM MH

Children's Hospital, 300 Longwood Ave., Boston (734-6000). Spanish. Fee $20 not including X-ray, lab, supplies. G P D GY

Massachusetts General Hospital, Fruit St., Boston (726-2000). Most languages. $25 minimum. G P D (oral surgery) O GY MH

Massachusetts Eye and Ear Infirmary, 243 Charles St., Boston (523-7900, ext. 601). Spanish and French. Other languages on call 24 hours. $17.50 minimum. G P

New England Medical Center Hospital, 171 Harrison Ave., Boston (482-2800). Spanish and Chinese. $26 base fee and sliding scale according to ability to pay. G P D GYN E AM MH

Peter Bent Brigham Hospital, 721 Huntington Ave., Boston (734-8000, ext. 2344, 2345, or 2346). Spanish. Fee $28 in main emergency room, $23 in general practice unit. G D E GY AM MH

Cambridge Hospital, 1493 Cambridge St., Cambridge (354-2020). Most languages. Fee $10 not including lab, supplies, X-ray. G P O D E GY MH

THE HANDICAPPED PERSON

The Visiting Nurse Association of Boston, 14 Somerset St., Boston (742-0900), maintains a staff of professional nurses who provide bedside nursing care in the home to individuals and families on an hourly or part-time basis. The nurses also instruct families in proper care of patients between the nurse's visits. If you are traveling with an invalid, the Association could be invaluable.

Wheeling Through Boston is a booklet designed to help Boston natives and visitors who are physically handicapped. The book contains staircase designations, door widths, elevator locations, bathroom accessibility and available ramps for Boston theaters, nightclubs, historic sites, and churches. The booklet also includes a map of Boston geared to the handicapped person. It is free in limited quantities from the Easter Seal Society, 14 Somerset St., Boston (227-9605).

For the Cambridge area, similarly, *Access to Cambridge: A Guide to Architectural Barriers* is available free from the M.I.T. information center (253-1000 ext 4795). The pamphlet contains information pertaining to grading, elevators, doors and doorways, entrances, ramps with gradients, and stairs for all places of business in the Cambridge area.

The Massachusetts Association for the Blind, 120 Boylston St., Room 446, Boston (542-3106) was organized to serve blind and visually handicapped people. It provides volunteer services, recreation and emergency financial assistance to the blind. This book is available in Braille and on tape cassettes, thanks to the National Braille Press, a non-profit service organization for the blind. Inquire at any Boston 200 Visitor Information Center.

DRUG-RELATED PROBLEMS

For emergency drug situations see the section on emergency rooms in the Boston area. Project Turnoff maintains a 24-hour hotline specifically for those with drug-related problems. The project is run out of Boston City Hospital's accident floor. Turnoff provides referrals to drug specialists or may arrange hospitalization (261-2600).

Project Place (Action Programs for Drug Abuse Prevention) is probably the best-equipped program for dealing with drug-

related problems of any sort. Project Place is located at 32 Rutland St., Boston, Mass. 02118 (267-9150), and maintains five programs to provide services which traditional social service organizations do not cover.

CRISIS INTERVENTION PHONE NUMBERS

Unless otherwise specified, the following numbers provide a large range of services including referrals for any medical, sexual, legal, or psychiatric problems. The people manning the crisis phones are either professional psychologists or volunteers backed up by a team of experts. The hotline teams are competent to deal with specific problems by referral and often clinical appointments, but they are also available for talking about any problem.

Cambridge Hot Line 876-7528
Seven days a week, 10am to 2pm. All manner of referrals. Not a rap line but provides solutions to specific problems. Non-professional counseling.

Cambridge Birth Control Information Service 338-6500
This number will be answered by an answering service who will give you the name of the person on duty for the day to provide information about VD, birth control, pregnancy counseling, sterilization, and individual help with birth control devices or prescription.

State Department of Public Health 727-2686
Referrals, counseling, doctors on hand. For VD and other communicable diseases. Mon-Fri, 9am-5pm.

Women's Center 354-8807
46 Pleasant St., Cambridge. Referrals for women. Sexual, pregnancy and emotional counseling.

Boston Legal Aid Society, 14 Somerset St., Boston (227-0200). The Legal Aid Society makes available legal advice and assistance in non-criminal matters, including court representation, to any resident unable to employ private counsel. The organization is partially funded by United Way. Walk-in services.

ACCOMMODATIONS

Greater Boston's tourist accommodations have been divided into three groups according to their relative proximity to downtown Boston and the availability of public transportation. Downtown accommodations are all located in Boston and are within easy walking distance of an MBTA station or streetcar stop. Near town encompasses suburbs adjacent to Boston which are adequately serviced by the MBTA and are no more than 20 minutes from downtown by bus or subway.

Many listings refer to the policy of a hotel or motel toward children. Where children under a particular age are accommodated free it is understood that they must be traveling with their parents.

The following is a list of abbreviations used in the listings:

s	single occupancy	H	health club with sauna
d	double occupancy	B	baby sitting available
R	restaurant	P	pets allowed
C	coffee shop	W	coin-op laundry
L	cocktail lounge	AE	American Express
S	swimming pool	BA	BankAmericard
K	kitchenettes	DC	Diners Club
AC	air-conditioning	CB	Carte Blanche
TV	television	MC	Mastercharge
V	valet service		

DOWNTOWN

1200 Beacon St. Hotel, 1200 Beacon St., Brookline (232-7979). T-Beacon St. line; free parking. 197 rooms, $18-s, $22-d, children under 12 free. R, L, AC, TV, V, B, P. Cards: AE, BA, CB, DC, MC.

Bradford Hotel, 275 Tremont St., Boston (426-1400). T-Boylston; free overnight parking. 350 rooms. $16-s, $21-d, children free. C, L, AC, TV, V, P. Cards: AE, DC, CB, BA.

Children's Inn, 342 Longwood Ave., Boston (431-4700). T-Longwood on Riverside Line, or bus lines; free parking. 82 rooms. $24-s, $26-d, children under 12 free. R, L, S, AC, TV, V. Cards: AE, DC, CB, BA.

Colonnade Hotel, 120 Huntington Ave., Boston (261-2800). T-Prudential; free parking. 300 rooms, $30-s, $38-d, children under 12 free. R, L, S, AC, TV, V, H, B. Cards: AE, DC, CB, BA, MC. Boston 200 Information Center.

Copley Plaza Hotel, 138 St. James Ave., Boston (267-5300). T-Copley; free parking. 450 rooms. $23-s, $37-d, children under 18 free. R, L, AC, TV, V, B, P. French, German, Japanese spoken. Cards: AE, DC, CB, BA, MC. Boston 200 Information Center.

Copley Square Hotel, 47 Huntington Ave., Boston (536-9000). T-Huntington Ave. line; free overnight parking. 155 rooms. $18-s, $22-d, children under 14 free. R, L, AC, TV, V, B, P. Greek, Italian spoken. Cards. AE, CB, DC, BA, MC.

Diplomat Hotel, 26 Chandler St., Boston (482-3450). T-Arlington or Dover; no parking facilities. 55 rooms. $13-s, $13-d. L. No credit cards.

Eliot Hotel, 270 Commonwealth Ave., Boston (267-1607). T-Auditorium; parking garages nearby. 96 rooms. $16-s, $25-d. R, L, K, AC. Televisions available. Cards: AE, DC, MC.

Essex Hotel, 695 Atlantic Ave., Boston (482-9000). T-South Station; free overnight parking. 400 rooms. $13-s, $20-d. Children under 14 free. R, L, AC, TV, V. Spanish, French spoken. Cards: AE, DC, CB, BA.

Fenway Boylston Motor Hotel, 1271 Boylston St., Boston (267-8300). T-Kenmore; free parking. 94 rooms. $17-s, $25-d, children under 14 free. R, L, S, AC, TV, V, B, P. Spanish, Greek spoken. Cards: AE, DC, CB, BA, MC, Phillips 66. Boston 200 Information Center.

Fenway Commonwealth Motor Hotel, 575 Commonwealth Ave., Boston (267-3100). T-Kenmore; free parking. 178 rooms. $19-s, $26-d, children under 14 free. R, L, S, AC, TV, V, H, B, P. Spanish spoken. Cards: AE, BA, DC, CB, MC, Phillips 66. Boston 200 Information Center.

Hilton Inn, Logan International Airport, Boston (569-9300). T-Airport, then bus; free parking. 580 rooms. $25-s, $29-d, children under 12 free. R, L, S, AC, TV, V, H, B, P. French, Spanish, German, Italian, Greek, Turkish, Arabic spoken. AE, BA, CB, DC, MC. Boston 200 Information Center.

Our nation is having a birthday.
And you can celebrate it all over New England.
Thanks to Holiday Inn.

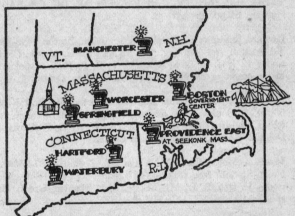

This year New England is more exciting than ever. And you can be part of that excitement. The Nation's 200th birthday will be kicked off the day Paul Revere took his famous ride. Your travel agent can help put your vacation in this historic setting with some great fly and drive packages featuring the Holiday Inns of New England.

Holiday Inn—Government Center, 5 Blossom St., Boston (742-7630). T-Government Center; free parking. 298 rooms. $25-s, $31-d, children under 12 free. R, C, L, S, AC, TV, V, W, B, P. Cards: AE, MC, BA, DC, Gulf. Boston 200 Information Center.

Hotel Avery, 24 Avery St., Boston (482-8000). T-Boylston or Essex; free parking. 150 rooms, $18-s, $23-d, children under 14 free. L, AC, TV, V, P. French, Spanish spoken. Cards: CB, DC, AE, BA.

Howard Johnson's Motor Lodge, Howard Johnson Plaza at exit 16 of Southeast Expressway, Dorchester (288-3030). T-Andrew Station; free parking. 100 rooms. $19-s, $23-d, children under 12 free. R, L, AC, TV, V, B, P. Cards: AE, DC, CB, BA, MC, Humble, Standard.

Howard Johnson's 57 Hotel, 200 Stuart St., Boston (482-1800). T-Boylston; free parking. 350 rooms. $29-s, $35-d. Children under 12 free. R, L, S, AC, TV, V, B, P. French spoken. All major credit cards. Boston 200 Information Center.

Lenox Hotel and Motor Inn, 710 Boylston St., Boston (536-5300). T-Copley; free overnight parking. 225 rooms. $20-s, $26-d, children free. R, L, AC, TV, V, H, B, P. Cards: AE, DC, CB. Boston 200 Information Center.

Madison Motor Inn, 25 Nashua St., Boston (227-2600). T-North Station; free parking. 467 rooms. $15-s, $18-d, children under 12 free. R, L, AC, TV, V, B, P. Spanish, Greek, Italian spoken. Cards: AE, DC, MC, BA, CB.

Midtown Motor Inn, 220 Huntington Ave., Boston (262-1000). T-Symphony or Prudential; free parking. 161 rooms. $20-s, $34-d, children under 12 free. R, S, AC, TV, V, H, B, P. French, Arabic spoken. Cards: AE, CB, DC, MC, BA.

Northeast Hall, 204 Bay State Rd., Boston (267-3042). T-Commonwealth Ave. line; parking $1/day. 6 rooms, $8 to $10-s, $10 to $14-d. TV.

Parker House, 60 School St., Boston (227-8600). T-Park or Government Center; free overnight parking. 483 rooms. $26.75-s, $34.75-d, children under 12 free. R, L, AC, TV, V, B, P. Spanish, French, German spoken. All major credit cards. Boston 200 Information Center.

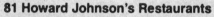

Ritz-Carlton Hotel, 15 Arlington St., Boston (536-5700). T-Arlington; parking $5 overnight. 260 rooms. From $40-s, $46-d. R, C, L, AC, TV, V, B, P. Several foreign languages spoken. No credit cards.

Sheraton Boston Hotel, Prudential Center, Boston (236-2000). T-Copley or Auditorium; free parking. 1434 rooms. $23-s, $40-d, children under 17 free. R, C, L, S, H, AC, TV, V, B, P. Cards: MC, BA, DC, CB, Sheraton, Pan Am. **Boston 200 Information Center.**

Statler Hilton Hotel, Park Square at Arlington St., Boston (426-2000). T-Arlington; parking garages nearby. 1024 rooms. $24-s, $34-d, children free. R, L, AC, TV, V, B, P, W. Many foreign languages spoken. Cards: AE, BA, CB, DC, MC, Air Canada, Hilton Hotels.

Terrace Motel, 1650 Commonwealth Ave., Boston (566-6260). T-Commonwealth Ave. line; free parking. 75 rooms. $16-s, $19-d, children under 12 free. AC, TV, V, K, B. Cards: MC, BA, AE, DC, CB.

Armed Services YMCA, 32 City Square, Charlestown (242-2660). T-City Square; free parking. 166 rooms. $6-s, $6-d. R, AC, K, TV, S, H, W, B. Spanish spoken.

Greater Boston YMCA, 316 Huntington Ave., Boston (536-7800). T-Huntington Ave. line; free parking. 150 rooms. $7.50-s without bath, $11-s with private bath. R, S, AC, V, H, W. Cards: BA, MC. Reserve if possible.

NEAR TOWN

Amber Motor Inn, 215 Concord Turnpike (Route 2), Cambridge (491-1130). T-Harvard Square; free parking. 82 rooms. $17-s, $22-d, children under 12 free. R, C, L, AC, TV, V, B. Italian spoken. Cards: AE, MC.

Brookline Motor Hotel, 1223 Beacon St., Brookline (232-7500). T-Beacon St. Line; free parking. 60 rooms. $16-s, $19-d, children under 12 free. C, L, AC, TV, K, V, B, P, W. Cards: AE, CB, MC, DC, BA.

After 200 years, isn't it time you called home?

Touring through two hundred years of our nation's past is far too fascinating to keep to yourself.

Why not call the folks back home tonight and share the fun of America's history, while you catch up on the local news.

Incidentally, if you'll need reservations on the road back, long distance is the best way to make sure you'll have a comfortable reception everywhere you go.

After all, you and America have traveled a long way. We'd like to make the rest of the journey as pleasant as possible.

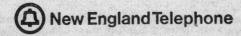 New England Telephone

Carlton House, 29 Hancock St., Quincy (328-1500). T-North Quincy; free parking. 100 rooms. $18-s, $23-d, children under 12 free. R, L, AC, TV, V. German, Polish spoken. Cards: AE, BA, MC, DC.

Chalet Susse Motor Lodge, 800 Wm. T. Morrissey Blvd., Dorchester (287-9100). T-Ashmont; free parking. 144 rooms. $10-s, $11-d. R, S, AC, TV, B. Spanish, Italian spoken. Cards: BA, MC, AE.

Charles River Motel, 1800 Soldiers Field Rd., Boston (254-0200). T-Watertown-Central Sq. bus line; free parking. 55 rooms. $16-s, $21-d, discounts to children. C, L, AC, TV, V, B, P. Major credit cards accepted.

Chestnut Hill Motor Hotel, 160 Boylston St., Newton (527-9000). T-Riverside line to Chestnut Hill; free parking. 150 rooms. R, L, S, AC, TV, V, B, P. Spanish spoken. Cards: AE, DC, MC.

Fenway Cambridge Motor Hotel, 777 Memorial Drive, Cambridge (492-7777). T-Central or Harvard; free parking. 205 rooms; $22-s, $29-d, children under 14 free. R, C, L, S, AC, TV, V, B, P. Spanish spoken. Cards: AE, CB, BA, MC, DC. **Boston 200 Information Center.**

Holiday Inn of Boston-Newton, 399 Grove St., Newton (969-5300). T-Riverside; free parking. 197 rooms. $20-s, $25-d, children under 12 free. R, L, S, AC, TV, V, B, P. Spanish, Hungarian, German French, Yiddish spoken. Cards: AE, MC, DC, BA, Gulf.

Holiday Inn of Boston-Somerville, 30 Washington St., Somerville (628-1000). T-Sullivan Square; free parking. 189 rooms. $24-s, $30-d, children under 12 free. R, L, S, AC, TV, H, W, V, B, P. Italian, Spanish spoken. Cards: MC, AE, BA, DC.

Holiday Inn of Cambridge, 1651 Massachusetts Ave., Cambridge (491-1000). T-Harvard; free parking. 135 rooms. $22-s, $28-d, children under 12 free. R, L, S, AC, TV, V, B, P. Cards: AE, DC, CB, BA, Gulf.

Homestead Motor Inn, 220 Alewife Brook Parkway (Route 3), Cambridge (491-1890). T-Harvard, then Arlmont or Belmont bus; free parking. 46 rooms, $18-s, $22-d. Children under 12 free. L, S, AC, TV, B, P. Cards: AE, CB, DC, MC.

Hotel Stanley, 15 Congress St., Chelsea (884-9080). T-Boston-Revere bus line; no parking facilities. 42 rooms. $12-s, $14-d. Children free. R, L, AC, TV, B, P. Italian, Spanish spoken. No credit cards.

Hotel Sonesta, 5 Cambridge Parkway, Cambridge (491-3600). T-Lechmere; free parking. 197 rooms. $26-s, $30-d, children under 16 free. R, C, L, S, AC, TV, V, B, P. German, Portuguese spoken. **Cards: AE, DC, MC, BA. Boston 200 Information Center.**

Howard Johnson's Motor Lodge, 320 Washington St., Newton (969-3010). T-Mass. Pike bus line; free parking. 272 rooms. $23-s, $32-d, children under 12 free. R, L, S, AC, TV, V, H, B, P. Cards: BA, AE, MC, DC, CB, Exxon, Chevron.

Kirkland Inn, 67 Kirkland St., Cambridge (547-4600). T-Harvard; free parking. 75 rooms, $10-s, $14-d. Apartments also available. TV, K.

Longwood Inn, 123 Longwood Ave., Brookline (566-8615). T-Beacon St. or Riverside line; free parking. 17 rooms. $7.50 to $10.50-s, $11 to $16-d. Some without private bath. TV in living room, W.

The Market Place, 200 Beacham St., Chelsea (884-8600). T-Sullivan Square; free parking. 20 rooms. $13-s, $18-d. Children under 5 free. R, C, L, AC, TV, V. Italian spoken.

President's City Motel, 845 Hancock St., Quincy (479-6500). T-Wollaston; free parking. 26 rooms. $18-s, $18-d. Children under 6 free. R, C, L, AC, TV, V, B, P. Cards: AE, DC.

Ramada Inn, 1234 Soldiers Field Road, Boston (254-1234). T-Watertown-Central Sq. bus line; free parking. 115 rooms. $20-s, $26-d. Children under 18 free. R, L, S, AC, TV, V, B, W. Cards: AE, DC, CB, MC, BA, Humble, Chevron. **Boston 200 Information Center.**

Ramada Inn, 225 McClellan Highway, East Boston (569-5250). T-Orient Heights; free parking and airport limousine. 250 rooms. $26-s, $32-d. Children under 18 free. R, L, S, AC, TV, V, H, B, P. Italian spoken. Cards: AE, DC, CB, MC, BA, Exxon, Arco.

Sheraton Commander, 16 Garden St., Cambridge (547-4800). T-Harvard; free parking. 107 rooms. $18-s, $24-d, children under 16 free. R, L, AC, TV, V, B, P. Italian, Japanese spoken. Cards: AE, DC, CB, BA, MC, Sheraton.

Town House Motor Inn, 100 N. Beacon St., Watertown (926-2200). T-Watertown bus; free parking. 40 rooms. $15-s, $21-d. R, L, AC, TV. Cards: AE, MC.

Treadway Motor House, 110 Mt. Auburn St., Cambridge (864-5200). T-Harvard; free parking. 72 rooms. $24-s, $30-d, children free. AC, TV, V, W, B, P. Cards: AE, MC, CB, BA, DC. **Boston 200 Information Center.**

Woodbridge Inn, 27 College Ave., Somerville (666-1300). T-Harvard, then bus; free parking. 40 rooms. $14 to $16-s, $18 to $20-d. No children. R, L, AC, TV. Cards: AE, BA, DC, MC, CB.

Cambridge YMCA, 820 Mass. Ave., Cambridge (876-3860). T-Central; no parking available. 125 rooms. $8-s, $10-d. R, S, H. No credit cards.

Cambridge YWCA, 7 Temple St., Cambridge (491-6050). T-Central; street parking. 110 rooms. $6.50-s. R, S, H, W. Spanish, French spoken. No credit cards.

BOSTON 200 INFORMATION CENTERS
OUTSIDE BOSTON

Holiday Inn, Rt 2, Fitchburg, Mass.
Holiday Inn, Rts 1 and 128 South, Dedham, Mass.
Holiday Inn, Rts 495 and 20, Marlboro, Mass.
Holiday Inn, Rt 495, Tewksbury, Mass.
Jug End Resort, South Egremont, Mass.
The Sheraton Tara, 1657 Worcester Rd., Framingham, Mass.
The Sheraton Tara Hotel, 37 Forbes Rd., Braintree, Mass.
The Colonial Hilton Inn, Rt 7, Pittsfield, Mass.
Dedham Inn, 235 Elm St., Dedham, Mass.
Fenway North Motor Hotel, 407 Squire Rd., Revere, Mass.
Marriott Motor Hotel, Commonwealth Ave. at Rt 128 and Mass.
  Pike, Newton, Mass.

YOUTH HOTELS

American Youth Hostels has two hostels in the area open from June 1 to September 1. The **Brookline hostel** is at 45 Strathmore Road (232-2451) and can be reached by the MBTA Beacon Street line. Rates are $2 per night with a three-day maximum. The **Dorchester hostel,** 1620 Dorchester Avenue (436-0893) also has a three-day maximum and is $1.50 per night. MBTA stop is Fields Corner. The **Charlestown YMCA,** 32 City Square, Charlestown (242-2660) also functions as a youth hostel. Check-in time at all hostels is 4-5pm and check-out is at 9:30am. A 10pm curfew is enforced.

CAMPING

Wompatuk State Reservation on Route 228 in Hingham is located near South Shore beaches and has 450 campsites. Hingham is 40 minutes south of Boston.

Harold Parker State Forest is 50 minutes north of Boston on Route 125, North Reading. 125 campsites are available and a lake within the park is used for swimming, boating and fishing.

Public campgrounds in Massachusetts are open between the last Saturday in June and the Saturday before Labor Day. Campsites are allotted on a first come, first serve basis and have a two-week maximum. The two parks listed have improved sanitary facilities. The daily fee is $3. (For more information, see Tours and Daytrips.)

A welcome to Boston from a 191-year-old resident.

Here's where our bank's history started — on Tremont Street (then called Long Acre) near Hamilton Place. The Governor of Massachusetts was one of our directors then and had an account with us. You'd probably recognize his signature: John Hancock. He put it on our first charter back in 1784.

All of us at The First wish you happiness in the midst of Boston's history. Have a nice stay.

The First

THE FIRST NATIONAL BANK OF BOSTON

RELIGIOUS SERVICES

APOSTOLIC

Church of the Lord, 640 Tremont St., Boston (262-8866).
Services: Sun, 11:30am.

BAPTIST

Concord Baptist Church, 190 Warren Ave., Boston (267-4225).
Services: Sun, 10:45am.

First Baptist Church of Boston, 110 Commonwealth Ave., Boston (247-9119). Services: Sun, 11am.

Tremont Temple, 88 Tremont St., Boston (523-7320). Services: Sun, 11am and 6:45pm.

CATHOLIC

Our Lady of Lourdes Chapel, 698 Beacon St., Boston (536-
2761). Services: Sat, 4pm and 5:10pm.

St. Anthony Shrine, 100 Arch St., Boston (542-6440). Services:
Sun, 5:30am, 6:15am, 7am, every half hour from 7:30am to
12:45pm, 3:45pm, 4pm, every half hour until 6:30pm.

St. Francis Prudential Chapel, Prudential Center, Boston (542-
6448). Services: Sun, 9am, 10am, 11am, noon, 4pm, 5pm,
6pm.

St. Paul's, 34 Mt. Auburn St., Cambridge (491-8400). Services: Sun, 7:30am, 9:30am, 11am, 12:30pm, 5pm.

CHRISTIAN SCIENTIST

The Mother Church, Christian Science Center, 105 Falmouth
St., Boston (262-2300). Services: Sun, 10:45am.

CONGREGATIONAL

Church of the Covenant, 67 Newbury St., Boston (266-7480).
Services: Sun, 11am.

Old South Church, 645 Boylston St., Boston (536-1970).
Services: Sun, 11am.

Park Street Church, 1 Park St., Boston (523-3383). Services: Sun, 10:30am, 7:30pm.

EASTERN ORTHODOX

Russian Orthodox Cathedral, 165 Park Drive, Boston (262-9490). Services: Sun, 10am.

St. John the Baptist Greek Orthodox Church, 15 Union Park, Boston (536-5692). Services: Sun, 9am-11am.

EPISCOPAL

Christ Church, 0 Garden St., Cambridge (876-0200). Services: Sun, 8am, 10am.

Old North Church, 193 Salem St., Boston (523-6676). Services: Sun, 9:30am (Holy Eucharist), 11am (Prayer and Sermon).

St. Paul's Cathedral, 136 Tremont St., Boston (542-8674). Services: Sun 9:30am (Holy Communion), 11am (Holy Communion and Sermon).

Trinity Church, Copley Square, Boston (536-0944). Services: Sun, 8am (Holy Communion), 11am (Prayer and Sermon).

FRIENDS

Beacon Hill Friends House, 6 Chestnut St., Boston (227-9118). Services: Sun, 11am.

JEHOVAH'S WITNESSES

Jehovah's Witnesses, Kingdom Hall, 136 St. Botolph St., Boston (267-1108). Services: Sun, 10am.

JEWISH

Charles River Park Synagogue, 55 Martha Road, Boston (523-9857). Services: Fri evening; Sat, 9am. *Modern Orthodox.*

Young Israel, 62 Green St., Brookline (734-0276). Services: Fri, 7pm; Sat, 7am, 8:30am. *Orthodox.*

Congregation Kehillath Israel, 384 Harvard St., Brookline (277-9155). Services: Fri, 7:30pm; Sat, 6:30am, 8:45am. *Conservative.*

One hundred years after the "Cradle of Liberty" was rocked,

Commercial Union first opened for business in the United States in Boston.
We've come a long way since then.
Boston, a great metropolis... Commercial Union, one of the largest international insurance groups in the world.
Commercial Union is pleased to remember our 200th birthday by hosting "Boston 200" headquarters at our own U.S. headquarters at ONE BEACON STREET right in the heart of Boston, where it all began.

Temple B'Nai Moshe, 1845 Commonwealth Ave., Brighton (254-3620). Services: Fri, 7pm; Sat, 9am. *Conservative.*

Temple Ohabeishalom, 1187 Beacon St., Brookline (277-6610). Services: Fri, 6pm; Sat, 10:15am, 6pm. *Reform.*

Temple Sinai, Charles St. and Sewall Ave., Brookline (277-5888). Services: Fri, 8:15pm; Sat, 10:45am. *Reform.*

LUTHERAN

First Church, 299 Berkeley St., Boston (536-8851). Services: Sun, 10am.

METHODIST

Church of All Nations, 333 Tremont St., Boston (357-5777). Services: Sun, 10am.

Harvard-Epworth Methodist Church, 1555 Mass. Ave., Cambridge (354-0837). Services: Sun, 10am.

Old West Church, 131 Cambridge St., Boston (227-5088). Services: Sun, 11am.

PRESBYTERIAN

Church of the Covenant, 67 Newbury St., Boston (266-7480). Services: Sun, 11am.

UNITARIAN

Arlington Street Church, 355 Boylston St., Boston (536-7050). Services: Sun, 11am.

Charles Street Meeting House, 70 Charles St., Boston (523-0368). Services: Sun, 11am.

First and Second Church in Boston, 64 Marlborough St., Boston (267-6730). Services: Sun, 11am.

First Parish, 3 Church St., Cambridge (876-7772). Services: Sun, 11am.

King's Chapel, 58 Tremont St., Boston (523-1749). Services: Sun, 11am.

SUGGESTIONS FOR A SHORT STAY

Three-Day Stay: Plan to arrive in the morning, and stop by a Boston 200 Visitor Information Center to check on special events, the time-saving Shuttle Bus and other hints. You may want to begin by riding the Shuttle Bus on its entire circuit (1 to 1½ hours) to get an overall view of the city without having to drive. Then get off the bus at Prudential Center to see Boston 200's exhibit Where's Boston: Visions of the City, the best introduction to 20th-century Boston. Finish with dinner at a restaurant in the surrounding Back Bay area.

The next day, see Boston's Revolutionary landmarks. Start with The Revolution: Where It All Began, Boston 200's exhibit at Quincy Market. When you have seen the exhibit, you can move directly into either the Freedom Trail: Downtown or the Freedom Trail: North End (both start here). The Freedom Trail: Downtown contains most of the famous sites associated with the Revolution, including Faneuil Hall, Old South Meeting House, the Boston Tea Party Ship and Museum and Granary Burying Ground. The Freedom Trail: North End includes Old North Church, Paul Revere's House and Copp's Hill Burying Ground, and also introduces you to a fascinating Italian community. After either trail, have an Italian lunch in the North End. In the afternoon you can easily visit either the U.S.S. *Constitution* ("Old Ironsides") in nearby Charlestown (and walk the Charlestown Discovery Trail from there) or go to the New England Aquarium and walk the Waterfront Discovery Trail. Then enjoy a seafood dinner at a restaurant near the harbor.

On your third day, explore Boston's 19th-century heritage. In the morning, visit Boston 200's Grand Exposition of Progress and Invention at Stuart St. Armory, an exhibit on the city's development in the 19th century. Then take a break in the adjacent Public Garden, and perhaps a Swanboat ride. After lunch, walk the Beacon Hill or Back Bay Discovery Trail for a look at the city's beautiful 19th-century houses. Alternatively, you may want to visit one of Boston 200's special exhibits— Boston Women, Literary Boston, Medicine in Boston and others are described in the section "Themes in Boston History"—or see one of the city's superb museums.

THE GRAND EXPOSITION

RELIVE AMERICA'S REMARKABLE 19TH CENTURY

Go back into one of the most explosively inventive periods in our history. With film, sound, motion, and panoramas, relive the development of the railroads, telephone, sewing machine, the start of modern entertainment and much, much more.

Trace the changes and progress contributed by Boston to our country's dynamic growth as a political, social and industrial leader.

It is all happening at the Gillette exhibit at the 1st Corps of Cadets Armory (Stuart Street Armory), easy to get to, and filled with excitement from this remarkable period in our history.

Address — Corner of Stuart and Arlington Sts.

Admission — $1.50 For Adults, $.75 For Children Under 12
Hours — 10 AM-8 PM Daily

By the Governor

Approved June 25 1792

John Hancock

True Copy

Attest

John Avery jun Secretary

Our declaration of independence.

With his usual flourish, John Hancock signed it on June 3, 1792. This document brought our predecessor, Union Bank, into existence.

Since then, our charter has stood as a declaration of banking ingenuity. It's also represented financial independence for a great many people.

STATE STREET BANK

We do our homework.

Boston, Mass. 02101

TRANSPORTATION

Boston is at its best when you walk. The downtown area is smaller than in most American cities, and is laced with winding one-way streets—the descendants of colonial wagon tracks —which are a delight for walkers but a headache for drivers. The city's finest features—its blend of old and new buildings, its beautifully integrated Common and Public Garden, its residents themselves—belong to the pedestrian rather than to the driver. Most Bostonians try to use the MBTA and their feet for travel within the city, thereby avoiding both the perennial parking dilemma (Boston police *do* tow) and the haphazard driving of their fellow citizens.

If you do plan to drive into town, think in advance about logistics. Equip yourself with a map that includes street directions, and check our list of large public parking facilities. (You may want to consider a cab—not outrageous in this city—as an alternative to taking your own car and having to park.) Keep in mind that the best times to drive in Boston are weekends and holidays—Sundays are especially quiet. Rush hours (8am to 10am and 4pm to 6:30pm) are of course worst, especially on Friday evenings. But downtown, particularly on Washington St., cars move at a snail's pace during the entire business day.

Traveling between the airport and the center of Boston can take anywhere from 15 to 40 minutes by cab, depending on the time of day. The average fare is about $3.00. The Callahan and Sumner Tunnels, which connect the North End to East Boston and the airport, cause bottlenecks at rush hours and on Friday and Sunday nights. At these times the fastest route to Logan is always the subway.

If you're coming to and from Boston by train or bus, remember that weekends, holidays and school vacations can be extremely busy. If you're not fettered by a schedule, take advantage of your freedom to travel in the middle of the week.

RIDING THE MBTA

In Boston some streetcars run in the subways and some subway trains run on elevated tracks over the streets. Don't let this bother you. To master the public transportation system, familiarize yourself with the four major MBTA lines (called the Blue, Orange, Green and Red lines) and remember that they all radiate from downtown Boston, so that each line passes through at least one of the downtown Boston stations—Park Street, Washington, State or Government Center. (Refer to the MBTA map at the front of the book.) MBTA stations are indicated by signs with a large circled letter T.

Most of the MBTA stations are named for the landmarks they are near (such as Aquarium or Symphony) or for the streets on which they are located (such as Essex or Washington). For the downtown shopping district, you can get off at Park Street or Washington; for the downtown theater district, Boylston station; and for the Back Bay shopping district, Arlington, Copley or Auditorium.

If you can't get to a place by subway you can almost certainly get there by bus (sometimes both). Pick up a map of surface bus lines at the information booth in Park Street station, the information kiosk on the Boston Common, or just about any hotel. Two lines which may be helpful to you are the Harvard/Dudley bus, which runs from Harvard Square down Massachusetts Ave. (past M.I.T.) to Washington St. and Dudley station in Roxbury, and the Harvard/Lechmere bus, which runs from Harvard Square along Cambridge St. to Lechmere station near the Museum of Science.

The MBTA runs from about 5:20am to 1am. If at all possible avoid the rush hour and ride the MBTA between 9:30am and 4pm and after 6:30pm. Not only will you keep your ribs intact but you may even save some money. From 10am to 2pm weekdays and all day Sunday, otherwise known as Dime Time, it costs only 10¢ to ride the subways; normally fares are 25¢ for the subway and 20¢ for surface lines. Have EXACT CHANGE for surface lines. If you get on or off a surface line one stop outside the subway, you don't pay an additional 20¢ surface fare. Call the MBTA at 722-5700 for more information and directions.

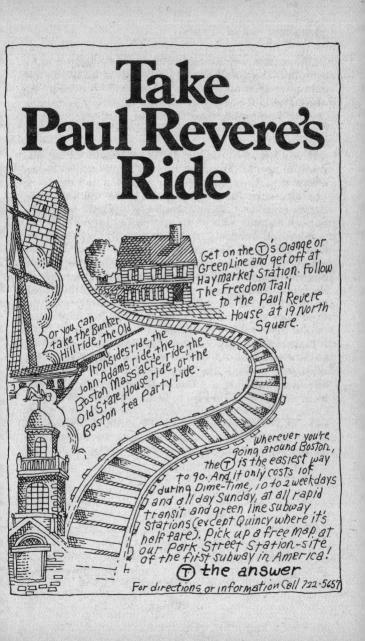

Take Paul Revere's Ride

Get on the Ⓣ's Orange or Green Line and get off at Haymarket Station. Follow The Freedom Trail to the Paul Revere House at 19 North Square.

Or you can take the Bunker Hill ride, the Old Ironsides ride, the John Adams ride, the Boston Massacre ride, the Old State House ride, or the Boston Tea Party ride.

Wherever you're going around Boston, the Ⓣ is the easiest way to go. And it only costs 10¢ during Dime-Time, 10 to 2 weekdays and all day Sunday, at all rapid transit and green line subway stations (except Quincy where it's half fare). Pick up a free map at our Park Street Station-site of the first subway in America!

Ⓣ the answer

For directions or information Call 722-5657

DRIVING

Driving in Boston can be as difficult for the resident as for the visitor. Therefore disregard any feelings of inadequacy and make every effort to be alert and imaginative when behind the wheel. Due to the age of the city and the lack of planning in its early development, many areas have no rational scheme of thoroughfares, one-way streets abound, and rush hour traffic is fierce.

If at all possible take the MBTA and avoid driving into downtown Boston. You'll get lost, you'll have trouble finding a place to park, you'll get stuck in traffic jams, and the people who were smart enough to take the MBTA will walk along the streets and laugh at you. However, if you *must* drive, make as much use as possible of the expressways that run along the periphery of downtown Boston. Storrow Dr., which follows the Charles River along the Back Bay and Beacon Hill, has exits at Clarendon, Arlington, and Charles Sts. On the Harbor side, the elevated Fitzgerald Expressway (Central Artery) has Haymarket Square, Dock Square (Callahan Tunnel), Congress St., South Station, and Mass Pike exits. Storrow Dr. and the Expressway are linked in the vicinity of North Station. Use these routes instead of attempting to drive crosstown.

Leaving the city poses less of a problem, since major routes are relatively accessible. Going west, the Mass. Pike (I-90), a toll road, begins at the Fitzgerald Expressway and can be entered at Arlington St., Copley Square, Newbury St. and Mass. Ave. Storrow Dr. leads to Rt 2, which goes to Lexington, Concord, and western Massachusetts. The Southeast Expressway (Rt 3) is an extension of the Fitzgerald Expressway and is the major road going south. To the north, Rts I-93 and I-95 are reached by the Mystic River (Tobin) Bridge.

PARKING

If you're headed downtown with your car, expect to find parking facilities scarce and expect to pay for them. Here are some conveniently located public parking facilities.

DOWNTOWN

Government Center Garage (Eastern Parking Co.), 50 New Sudbury St., 1,865 cars, $2 daily. $1 all night.

Tufts N.E. Medical Center, 274 Tremont St., 937 cars. $2.50 for 24 hrs. Near Chinatown.

Woolworth Garage, 350 Washington St., 900 cars. $3.75 daily. (See Shopping section.)

BACK BAY

Boston Common Parking Garage, Charles St. and Boston Common, 1,500 cars, $2 daily.

Prudential Center, 800 Boylston St., 948 cars; 81-115 Huntington Ave., 225 cars; Boylston, Exeter & Huntington, 894 cars; $3.00 daily.

Hancock Building Garage, 100 Clarendon St., 1800 cars, $2.50 daily.

GETTING TOWED AND BREAKING DOWN

If you have been towed, call the Boston Police at 911 for the garage where your car has been stored. You'll have to go to the garage, pick up your car and pay a fine—$12 to $17 for the tow and $3 per day for storage.

AAA, 1280 Boylston St., Chestnut Hill (738-6900). Route maps and emergency services. Branch office at 6 St. James Ave., Park Sq.

ALA, 888 Worcester St., Wellesley (237-5200). Route maps and emergency services.

TAXIS, RENT-A-CAR, BOSTON 200 SHUTTLES

Some major taxi stands in Boston are located at: Logan International Airport; Bowdoin MBTA station at Bowdoin and Cambridge Sts.; the State Street Bank on Franklin St.; the Parker House on School St.; Park Square; Copley Plaza Hotel in Copley Square; and Kenmore Square. Rates are about 50¢ initial fare and 10¢ for each one-fifth mile or one waiting minute thereafter. If you're sharing a cab with another party, the taxi driver is required by law to restart the meter at each stop. Call the Hackney Division of the Boston Police with complaints about service or overcharging.

Checker Cab (536-7000), Town Taxi (536-5000), Yellow Cab (522-3000) and Boston Cab (536-5010) all service the Boston area. Look in the Yellow Pages for other companies.

To rent a car you can call Hertz (482-9100), Avis (262-3300) or National (426-6830), which all have offices in Logan Airport and Park Square. Refer to the Yellow Pages for other listings.

Boston 200 is setting up additional transportation services for the Bicentennial. Ask at the Boston 200 Visitor Information Centers for routes and schedules of water taxis and shuttle buses.

For listings of bicycle rentals, refer to Outdoor Activities, p. 261.

TOURS AND DAYTRIPS

If you've had enough of walking around Boston, relax and do some sightseeing from a boat. Three companies which give cruise tours of Boston harbor and its islands are: **Boston Harbor Cruises**, Long Wharf (227-4320); **Baystate-Spray and Provincetown Steamship Co.**, Long Wharf (723-7800); and **Massachusetts Bay Line**, Rowe's Wharf (542-8000). All are located near the New England Aquarium and give harbor tours several times a day. Baystate-Spray also runs a boat to Provincetown and Mass. Bay Line a ferry to Nantasket Beach.

Another short excursion from Boston is a visit to **Quincy** by MBTA Red line to Quincy Center (and from there another bus). See the saltbox cottages where Presidents John Adams and John Quincy Adams were born; the **Adams National Historic Site**, including the "Old House," which served as the Adams' family home for four generations; the **Quincy Homestead**, once the home of Dorothy Quincy (wife of John Hancock); the **Colonel Josiah Quincy Homestead**, the home of a prominent merchant and patriot which has been restored by the Society for the Preservation of N.E. Antiquities; and the **United First Parish Church**, where the two Presidents Adams are buried. For more information on sights in the area, contact the **Chamber of Commerce**, 36 Miller Stile (479-1111).

Those with more time or ambition may want to take a daytrip from Boston. This book describes five of the most popular places to see outside Boston, but you may also consider going to the colonial ironworks in **Saugus**, the salty fishing port of **Gloucester**, the historic shipbuilding town of **Newburyport** and the adjacent wildlife refuge on **Plum Island**, the wealthy resort town of **Newport**, and the 19th-century whaling port of **New Bedford**. For more information on other places worth a visit, pick up a copy of *The Commemorative Guide to the Massachusetts Bicentennial* (Official Publication of the Commonwealth of Massachusetts) at State Information Centers and Turnpike rest stops. The Guide is also available through local Bicentennial Commissions. By mail write to: Massachusetts Bicentennial Guide Book, P.O. Box 5134, Boston, Mass. 02107 (send check or money order for $2.95). You can also pick up a booklet of historic houses belonging to the Society for the Preservation of New England Antiquities at the **Harrison Gray Otis house**, 141 Cambridge St. (227-

3956) and a brochure listing wildlife sanctuaries and nature centers at the Massachusetts Audubon Society, Great South Rd. in Lincoln (259-9500). Farther afield, you may want to visit the Berkshires in western Massachusetts for hiking, swimming, fishing and (in the summer) symphony concerts at Tanglewood. Check with the Berkshire Hills Conference, 107 South St., Pittsfield (413-443-9186) or write to the Mohawk Trail Association, Charlemont, Mass.

Most of these places are serviced by the bus lines of Greyhound, Continental Trailways, Peter Pan or Almeida, and by the Boston & Maine Railroad.

For those of you who want to take an organized bus tour, Hub Bus Lines offers tours of Boston, Cambridge, Lexington, Concord and Roxbury. Copley Motor Tours and The Gray Line both have tours of Boston, Cambridge, Lexington and Concord, Salem and Marblehead, the North Shore and Cape Ann, Quincy and Plymouth, and the South Shore and Cape Cod. The Gray Line also offers trips to Martha's Vineyard and a "coastline tour" to Maine. You can catch Hub Bus Lines

at the Boston Public Library in Copley Square; Copley Motor Tours at the Copley Plaza Hotel; and The Gray Line at the Copley Plaza Hotel, the Sheraton-Boston and the Statler-Hilton. Call them for schedules and prices (The Gray Line, 427-8650; Hub Bus Lines, 445-3770; Copley Motor Tours, 266-3500).

Be sure to do some advance planning on your daytrip, especially during tourist season. If you want to camp out, keep in mind that it's difficult to camp within quick driving distance of most places. You can write to **Mass. Dept. of Commerce & Development**, Div. of Tourism, 100 Cambridge St., Boston 02202 for a brochure on camping. **Boston 200 Visitor Information Centers** can also help you with camping as well as give you information about places and the best ways to reach them. Ask about special transportation services set up for the Bicentennial—it may be possible to park your car outside a town and then ride in on a shuttle bus.

LEXINGTON AND CONCORD

Make a visit to **Lexington**, Paul Revere's destination on his famous ride, and then (unlike Revere, who was stopped by the British) continue to **Concord**, to the site of the first battle of the Revolution. You can finish up your day with a visit to Longfellow's Wayside Inn in nearby Sudbury.

Your first stop in Lexington should be the **information center** at Massachusetts Ave. and Meriam St., across from the Minute Man statue. (Ask for a combination ticket to some of the historic houses while you're here.) Then, armed with pamphlets, brochures and maps, make your way to **Lexington Green**, where the first group of Minute Men tried to stop the British march on Concord. ("Stand your ground, don't fire unless fired upon, but if they mean to have a war let it begin here," ordered Minute Man Capt. Parker.) You may also want to visit **Buckman Tavern**, the rendezvous point for the Minute Men on the morning of the battle; the **Hancock-Clarke House**, the place where Samuel Adams and John Hancock were hiding out on that famous day and year; and the **Munroe Tavern**, the headquarters for Earl Percy when he came with relief troops for the British retreating from Concord.

From Lexington head for **Concord** on Rt 2A. At the 750-acre **Minute Man National Historic Park** in Concord you can

visit the site of the first battle of the Revolution and relive in your imagination "How the British Regulars fired and fled/ How the farmers gave them ball for ball/From behind each fence and farm-yard wall." In the park are the Old North Bridge, where the Minute Men made their stand; the graves of some British soldiers ("they came 3000 miles and died/To keep the past upon its throne"); and Wayside Inn (not to be confused with Longfellow's), the home of the Concord Muster Master on the day of the battle. For information on other historic Revolutionary sites in the area, stop at the town information booth at Hayward St. and Rt 2A. You should also visit the part of the park which commemorates some of Concord's famous 19th-century authors: Orchard House, Bronson Alcott's School of Philosophy and the place where Louisa May Alcott wrote *Little Women;* Emerson House, the home of Ralph Waldo Emerson from 1835 to 1882; Antiquarian House, a museum with period furniture, a "Thoreau" room, and an herb garden; and the Thoreau Lyceum, a museum of Thoreau memorabilia. Nearby is the Sleepy Hollow Cemetery, where you can climb the "Authors' Ridge" to see the graves of the Alcotts, Emerson, Thoreau and Hawthorne.

Rest up from your touring at Walden Pond, now a state beach a mile and a half south of Concord on Walden St. (Rt 126), with picnic areas and a footpath to Thoreau's cabin; or visit the Great Meadows National Wildlife Refuge, 950 acres of ponds and freshwater marshes on the Concord River northeast of the North Bridge information station. The entrance to the Refuge is located on Monsen Rd. off Rt 62.

SALEM

Salem, founded in 1626, is famous for its witch trials of the 1690s, and more happily, for its prominence as a Yankee clipper ship port of the 1850s. Today you can visit Salem and follow a well-marked trail that includes most of the historic sites in the city. The trail is long, so expect to spend the entire day in Salem. Start at the information booth at 18 Washington Sq. (open 8:30am to 4pm daily; 744-0004) and pick up pamphlets and maps. If you're interested in the Salem witch trials, you can visit the Witch Museum across the street, a multimedia presentation of the 17th-century witch hysteria. Otherwise head for the Essex Institute at 132 Essex St., a

The can that opened America.

It first appeared in the late 1830's in Boston. In a small waterfront building, William Underwood, a pioneer in the preservation of food, started packing his products in tin cans instead of glass. An innovation that opened up a whole new menu for a country raised basically on fresh meats and vegetables. Suddenly America could buy food now, and eat it later. Fresh food packed safely in tins. Everything from a unique spiced deviled ham to fish, turkey, fruits and vegetables.

The word spread quickly. When young men went West they usually laid in a good supply of Underwood provisions. Few clipper ships left port without cases of Underwood cans stocked below. In both world wars Underwood products were served in both C and K-rations.

Today Underwood markets a whole line of canned foods. It's not only the nation's oldest canner, but one of the most versatile. Everything from canned meat spreads and beans to sardines and Ac'cent....all high quality products.

This is the William Underwood Company in the 1970's. Yankee ingenuity with a quality heritage that spans over a century and encircles the globe. An ingenuity in products—traditional and new—that are found in homes all across America. Where each year more and more Americans are opening the can that opened America

UNDER WOOD

historical museum with collections of books, manuscripts, dolls, toys, costumes and uniforms.

Slightly farther down the street, at 161 Essex, is the Peabody Museum (open weekdays 9am to 5pm, Sunday 1pm to 5pm), the oldest continuing operating museum in the country—it was founded in 1799—and the only one begun by a Marine Society. The museum contains ship models, marine paintings, nautical instruments, shipbuilder's tools, figureheads, porcelain from the China Trade, art and artifacts from the South Pacific, and the full-size cabin of the yacht *Cleopatra's Barge*. If you like, you can learn more about Salem's marine history by touring the old wharves, now known as the Salem Maritime National Historic Site. You can visit three historic houses here: Derby House, a restored Georgian house built for a prosperous merchant family in the Far East trade; the Customs House, where Nathaniel Hawthorne worked as a hard-hearted customs inspector and scribbled the manuscript of *The Scarlet Letter* in his spare time; and the House of Seven Gables, where the tour takes you through Hepzibah's Penny Shop, up the secret staircase to Clifford's room and then downstairs to the parlor where the old Judge was found dead.

Before leaving the city take a walk down Chestnut St., lined with the stately homes of Salem's old merchant aristocracy. In this area you can visit the Witch House, the site of the preliminary hearings of the witch trials, as well as the Ropes Mansion, the Peirce-Nichols House and the Assembly House. Then head to the other side of town to Pioneer Village, a reconstruction of the early Salem settlement with bark-covered wigwams, pine cottages with thatch roofs, herb gardens, a forge, a brick kiln, and a pit for sawing logs. The Village is located by the ocean and is open June to Labor Day, 9:30am to 6:30pm daily, and Labor Day through November, 10am to 5pm daily.

PLYMOUTH

If you've heard of Pilgrims, you've heard of Plymouth. Most visitors come here to see Plimoth Plantation, the early Pilgrim village rebuilt according to old records, eyewitness accounts, the writings of Pilgrims William Bradford and Edward Winslow, and a little modern archaeological digging. You're free to wander around the Plantation and watch members of the community demonstrate various farm tasks like thatching a roof or making a barrel. The Plantation staff has been hired to live here as the Pilgrims did: they inhabit the houses, grow their own vegetables and cook their meals in big pots over the fireplaces. Near the village is the reconstruction of an early 17th-century Indian settlement—researched, directed and staffed by Native Americans—where you can watch the making of clay pottery, the harvesting of reeds from a dug-out canoe, and the preservation of fish by smoking. To visit the third part of the Plantation, the Mayflower II, you'll have to leave the village and the Indian camp and take a three-mile trip towards the center of town. The Mayflower II is a full-size facsimile of the original ship and it made its own Atlantic crossing in 1957 (the trip took 53 days). You can go on board.

Before you leave Plymouth be sure to see **Plymouth Rock**, according to legend the place where the Pilgrims first set foot on the New World. (Legend happily ignores that their ship stopped at Provincetown before coming to Plymouth.) Across the street from the Rock are Brewster Gardens, a park on the site of the colony's first gardens, and Cole's Hill Burying Ground, the mass grave for the Pilgrims who died during the first winter. If you have time to spend in the town, try to see Pilgrim Hall (the Pilgrim museum), 75 Court St. (open 10am to 4:30pm daily), which displays relics of the colony such as Governor Bradford's Bible and the cradle of Peregrine White, the baby born on the Mayflower.

OLD STURBRIDGE VILLAGE

About 56 miles west of Boston is **Old Sturbridge Village,** a re-creation of a typical New England village of the early 1800s. Old Sturbridge Village and its outlying farm cover about 200 acres and include forty buildings—homes, shops, a meeting house, and a schoolhouse among them—all restored and furnished to the style of that period. You can watch demonstrations of tinsmithing, broommaking, potting, and candlemaking by appropriately costumed artisans, and taste fresh gingerbread at the farmhouse. At special times of the year you can also see maple-sugaring and sheep-shearing (call or write ahead to Old Sturbridge Village, Sturbridge, Mass. 01566, 347-3362).

The Village is open all year except Christmas and New Year's; admission costs $4 for adults and $1.25 for children. To get there you can go by car on the Mass. Turnpike to Exit 9, or you can take Peter Pan Bus Lines from the Trailways station in Park Square. A bus leaves Boston daily at 10:30am, stops at the gate of the Village, and returns to Boston from Sturbridge around 7pm. Round-trip bus fare costs about $11 for adults and about $5 for children, with the cost of admission to the Village included in the fare.

A Restful
Step Backward
to Sturbridge

Historic Sturbridge is a small town where modern visitors relax in the New England countryside, eat memorable meals in authentic settings, sleep well in excellent accommodations, and visit the many and varied lovely shops in the area. Daily life in rural New England during the half-century following the American Revolution is portrayed at Old Sturbridge Village. A visit to Sturbridge is a restful step backward, and only 50 minutes by auto from Boston.

For information write the Greater Sturbridge Area Tourist Association, Sturbridge, Massachusetts 01566, or the Central Massachusetts Tourist Council, 100 Front Street, Mechanics Tower, Worcester, Massachusetts 01608.

The Boston Tea Party Ship & Museum. An adventure in history.

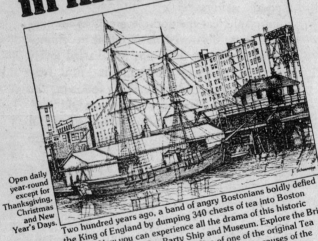

CITYGAME—THE CITY IS THE EXHIBIT

Because of its prominent position in American history, Boston plays a special role in the Bicentennial of the United States. Not only was it a well-established community before the American Revolution, but it also became directly involved in the events which led to the establishment of our country. Moreover, the roots of American government, cultural life, industry and technology may be found in Boston. Each of the periods of political, economic, social, and intellectual change in American history has, in some way, left its mark on the Boston landscape. Thus Boston is an urban environment that encompasses a rich variety of individuals, resources, and institutions which have grown to form the fabric of the city.

The focus for Boston's Bicentennial is the city itself. Through Citygame, Boston's cultural and educational institutions, its fascinating ethnic neighborhoods, its historic areas, and its citizens themselves become the basis for celebration.

The three major exhibitions reveal the world of Boston in the 18th, 19th and 20th centuries. The Revolution: Where It All Began, located on the Freedom Trail, is an extensive series of displays which invites the visitor to confront the choices available to Patriots and Tories. The Grand Exposition of Progress and Invention at the Stuart Street Armory depicts the sensational technological innovations which changed the face of Boston in the late 19th century. And a multi-screened slide presentation called Where's Boston: Visions of the City, located at the Prudential Center, celebrates Boston today: its people at work and at play, its architecture, and its uniqueness as a city in which the old and new exist side by side.

New walking trails highlight Boston's heritage and present-day activity. These trails challenge the Citygame participants to see Boston in new and imaginative ways and to recreate its past even as they experience the present-day city. Color-coded markers guide visitors along each trail, and maps can be found at all information centers and in MBTA stations.

The Revolution: Where It All Began

THE REVOLUTION: WHERE IT ALL BEGAN

The year is 1773, and the issue is the right of the lawful government to tax. Three ships bearing taxable tea wait in Boston Harbor to unload. The Crown and its Governor claim the Tea Act of 1773 is fair and just. Many Bostonians denounce the Act as tyrannical. Both sides say that basic principles are at stake. There are public meetings, rallies. Tensions mount. Then, on the night of December 16, a number of men secretly board the ships and toss the tea chests overboard: the Boston Tea Party. Were they right to destroy the tea? Should they have obeyed the law and accepted the tax?

As John Adams observed, the Revolution consisted not of battles, but of the changes in the hearts and minds of people in the years leading up to 1776. This exhibit, appropriately situated near Faneuil Hall on the Freedom Trail, will recreate the process as it developed through the Non-Importation Boycotts, the Boston Massacre, the Boston Tea Party, the "Intolerable Acts," and finally the battles of Lexington and Concord. Like Bostonians of 200 years ago, you will witness both sides of controversial events, and like them, you will have to form your own conclusions.

The Revolution: Where It All Began makes everyone a participant in American history. The exhibit, located in Quincy Market behind Faneuil Hall, is open daily. Call 338-1975 for information.

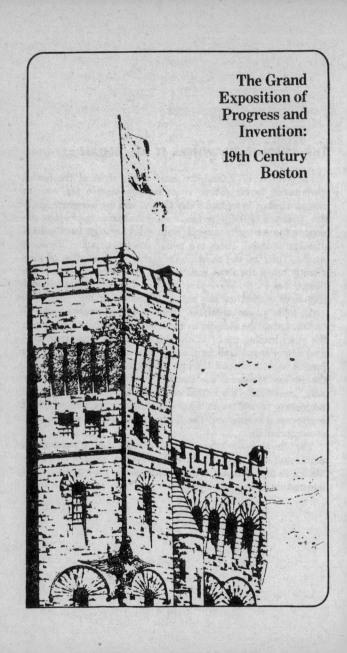

The Grand Exposition of Progress and Invention:

19th Century Boston

THE GRAND EXPOSITION OF PROGRESS AND INVENTION: NINETEENTH-CENTURY BOSTON

What do the safety-razor, the telephone, and the sewing machine have in common? They were all technological innovations that contributed to the great economic growth and social ferment that marked the last third of the 19th century in Boston. Boston 200's 19th-century exhibit dramatizes a time period in Boston's history that was uniquely exciting and productive, a period from which Boston emerged as a mature industrial metropolis.

As a visitor to the exhibit, which is located at the First Corps of Cadets Armory at Arlington St. and Columbus Ave. and is sponsored by Gillette, you will encounter a variety of 19th-century themes. You will be able to trace the change from a home-oriented, handcraft technology to a factory-oriented, machine-made technology, and you'll have the chance to try out 19th-century gadgets and inventions that were utilized in both public and domestic life. A section on transportation will use film clips to convey the sounds and motions of early motorized vehicles. Urban planning and topographical growth will be described by large-scale panoramic views detailing land reclamation and the introduction of Olmsted's Emerald Necklace park system. Most important, you will meet the people who actually shaped the 19th-century city: Boston's politicians, inventors, industrialists, labor leaders, architects, urban planners, reformers, educators, writers, artists, immigrant factory workers and merchants.

Come see The Grand Exposition of Progress and Invention. More than a history lesson, it is a basis for understanding the physical and personal makeup of the city today. The exhibit is open daily, 10am to 8pm. Admission is $1.50 for adults, 75¢ for children.

WHERE'S BOSTON?

WHERE'S BOSTON: VISIONS OF THE CITY

Did you know that Haymarket, Boston's open air fruit and vegetable market, has been operating for 200 years at Dock Square? Have you noticed the 200,000 students who attend over 100 colleges and universities in the Boston area, providing a continuing flow of new ideas and vitality to one of America's oldest cities? Did you know that today Beacon Hill is a neighborhood where young Bostonians continue the tradition of city living established by Harrison Gray Otis, Daniel Webster, Louisa May Alcott, and many others in the 19th century? Have you taken a ride on the Swan Boats which have delighted children and adults alike since 1877?

A visit to the Where's Boston exhibit sponsored by the Prudential Life Insurance Co. will introduce you to the people, architecture, neighborhoods, parks and parades that make Boston in the 20th century an exciting and vital city in which the old and new go hand in hand.

As you enter the red, white and blue Prudential Pavilion on the Huntington Ave. side of the Prudential Center, huge photomurals will introduce you to the faces of Boston. Once inside you will become a part of the city, a player in the Citygame. Clues to the character which is uniquely Boston will surround you as you wend your way through the maze of activities and neighborhood exhibits.

In the Pavilion theater 2560 images of Boston will be projected on an eight-faceted screen. Quadraphonic speakers will supplement the visual display with sounds of the city and the voices of Bostonians sharing their feelings about living in one of America's most livable cities. Through Where's Boston you will glimpse several Boston communities today and will look back at the city's past to see what strands of continuity link it to the founding fathers. You will see how the city is meeting current challenges and will finally become a part of an exuberant celebration of city life.

Use the Prudential Pavilion to organize your visit to Boston; select aspects of the city that intrigue you, then walk the streets and explore.

The exhibit is open daily, 10am to 10pm. Admission is charged.

THEMES IN BOSTON HISTORY

BOSTON'S UNIVERSITIES

In 1636, to guarantee an everlasting supply of educated ministers of God, the General Court of Massachusetts voted 400 pounds to found a "schoale or colledg" in Cambridge. Two years later, a young minister bequeathed his library of 320 books to the school, which was afterward named Harvard in his honor. For over fifty years, no other college existed in North America.

Today 179,000 students live and study within fifteen miles of the center of Boston. Boston University, Boston College, the Massachusetts Institute of Technology, Wellesley College, Tufts University, Northeastern University and many other schools have joined Harvard here, and together their faculties, libraries, laboratories and museums make Boston one of the most vibrant intellectual centers in the world. Meanwhile the students themselves, besides contributing life and color by their very presence, have nourished a growth of bookstores, cafes, boutiques and night spots that will intrigue visitors of all ages.

The following information centers can acquaint you with coming events on their campuses, and offer regularly scheduled tours.

Boston University Bicentennial Information Center, George Sherman Union Center, Commonwealth Avenue, Boston (353-2921). For tours, call the President's Hosts at 353-2934.

Harvard University Information Center, Holyoke Center, 1353 Massachusetts Ave., Cambridge (495-1000). Summer tours weekdays at 10, 11:15, 2 and 3:15. Call for academic year schedule.

Massachusetts Institute of Technology Information Center, Room 7-111, 77 Massachusetts Ave., Cambridge (253-4795). Tours weekdays at 10 and 2.

Northeastern University, Huntington Avenue, Boston. Tours from Admissions Office, Richards Hall 150, weekdays at 11 and 3. For tours call 437-2211; for events, call Student Activities, 437-2632.

The 400 year old cranberry

Cranberries were already 200 years old when John Hancock was signing the Declaration of Independence. They are definitely a part of our country's heritage, for they alone have the distinction of being the only berry native to North America. The American Indian made use of the cranberry not only as a fruit, but also for dyeing their blankets and rugs. Cranberries were originally called "Crane-berries" because the Pilgrims thought their blossoms resembled the head of a crane. The idea of serving cranberries with the Thanksgiving dinner is not a new one, the Pilgrims themselves enjoyed cranberries at that very first festive occasion. Today when you enjoy one of the many Ocean Spray products made from the little red berry, be it fresh cranberries, cranberry sauce, cranberry juice cocktail or a delicious cranberry blended drink, remember, you are sharing in a small piece of our country's heritage.

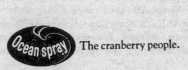

Ocean spray The cranberry people.

BOSTON ARCHITECTURE

The city of Boston is both a vital urban center and a splendid exhibit for people interested in architecture and urban design over the past three and one-half centuries. From the early 19th century onwards, Boston city planners undertook leveling and land-filling operations which were unique in their era. As a result of these operations, Beacon Hill and Back Bay were each developed as residential areas over a short, continuous period of time, and today are architectural museums —Beacon Hill commemorating the Federal and Greek revival styles of the late 18th to mid-19th centuries, and Back Bay reflecting the building fashions of the late 19th century. Boston's waterfront district represents a similar series of land fills, this time undertaken for business purposes. The buildings of the area offer a chronological history of commercial design from 1825 to the present.

Boston contains buildings by some of the world's foremost architects. Charles Bulfinch designed the Massachusetts State House, the Ether Dome at Massachusetts General Hospital, St. Stephen's Church in the North End, University and Stoughton Halls at Harvard, and many Beacon Hill houses. Alexander Parris designed Quincy Market, several Navy Yard buildings, and the Appleton-Parker Houses on Beacon St. H.H. Richardson's masterpieces include Trinity Church in Copley Sq. and Sever and Austin Halls at Harvard, while the Boston Public Library was done by the firm of McKim, Mead and White. Contemporary Boston architecture includes the many buildings of I.M. Pei (the Christian Science Center, the Hancock Tower, Harbor Towers, the Green Building at M.I.T. and the overall design for Government Center); buildings by José Sert (Mugar Memorial Library at Boston University and Holyoke Center, Peabody Terrace and the Science Center at Harvard) and work by the firm of Kallman and McKinnell (Boston City Hall, Government Center Garage and the Boston Five Cent Savings Bank). Boston—or rather, Cambridge—can also lay claim to the only building in America by Le Corbusier: Carpenter Center for the Visual Arts at Harvard. Other contemporary buildings include M.I.T.'s chapel and Kresge Auditorium, both by Eero Saarinen, Minoru Yanasaki's William James Hall at Harvard, Paul Rudolph's Hurley Building and Linde-

Things we wish we'd built.

Faneuil Hall, the handsome brick structure given to Boston in 1742 by Peter Faneuil for use as a market and public meeting-place, still serves its donor's original purposes more than 230 years later. Architect: John Smibert. Enlarged by Charles Bulfinch in 1805. We wish we'd built it, but we weren't around then. We're all around now, though. Almost any place you look there's a Vappi building.

Everything we do is constructive

VAPPI

Vappi & Company is a subsidiary of Tech/Ops Inc., Boston

mann Center, Alvar Aalto's M.I.T. dormitory, and Philip Johnson's new wing of the Boston Public Library.

Boston's modern skyscrapers are laid out in a "high spine" that extends from the Harbor Towers to Prudential Center, flanked on each side by older and lower sections of the city. The design has allowed innovative new buildings to complement the city's more traditional architecture without destroying the visual impact of historic areas. Quincy Market, Old City Hall, the Warren Tavern in Charlestown, and the Institute of Contemporary Art building are outstanding examples of the adaptation of attractive old buildings to new uses.

You will discover these and hundreds of other important buildings on the Neighborhood Discovery Trails. In addition, a brochure on Boston architecture is available at Boston 200 Visitor Information Centers. Guided tours of Boston's architecture by professional architects can be arranged in advance for special interest groups at a nominal charge. Telephone the Boston Society of Architects, 267-5175.

LITERATURE IN BOSTON

As you follow the Discovery Trails through Boston's neighborhoods, you will find a number of buildings, statues and markers related to Boston's rich literary past. Christ Church, immortalized as Old North in Longfellow's poem "The Midnight Ride of Paul Revere," and King's Chapel Burying Ground, which contains the grave of Nathaniel Hawthorne's model for Hester Prynne of *The Scarlet Letter*, are only two of the many Boston sites with literary associations. For more examples, take the literary history trail described in the brochure "Literary Boston," available at the Boston Public Library and at Boston 200 Visitor Information Centers. The library is also presenting a major exhibit on literature in Boston, featuring films, artifacts, lectures and poetry readings.

Boston Public Library, Copley Sq. Open weekdays 9am to 9pm; Saturdays, 9am to 6pm; Sundays (except June-September) 2pm to 6pm. See Back Bay trail, p. 195.

Boston Athenaeum, 10½ Beacon St. Founded in 1807 by a group of literati who later started the *Boston Review*, the Athenaeum became an exclusive literary club. The libraries of the original members were pooled to form the nucleus of the present library, open to members and researchers only. Visitors may tour the art gallery on the second floor. Open daily 9am to 5:30pm; in summer, weekdays only.

RELIGION IN BOSTON

Protestantism: Boston's early history is inseparable from religion, since Puritanism was the motivating force of the town's early settlers. A congregational church was founded in the colony in 1630, and although it had no official connection with government, it was a powerful political and social force. Boston's First Church (1630), Second Church (1650) and Old South Church (1669) all trace their origins to this period. Eight more congregational churches joined them by the time of the Revolution, but Puritan intolerance kept out most other sects, and only five non-congregational churches existed by 1776: a Baptist one (1665), a Quaker meeting house (1697) and three Anglican churches. Anglicanism had been introduced by Governor Andros, much against the Puritans' will, with the construction of King's Chapel in Tremont Street in 1688.

The century following the Revolution brought a flowering of Protestantism, evident in the building of 120 new churches. Many of these were the homes of newly established sects like the Unitarians, while others were built by dissenters who split off from an existing congregation. Some of the most beautiful of these Protestant churches were built during the city's expansion into the Back Bay, and await you on that Discovery Trail. There you will also find The Mother Church of Christian Science, founded in Boston by Mary Baker Eddy (see page 196). Other churches are scattered along the Freedom Trail.

Catholicism: Priests first visited Boston in 1647, but Puritan rule kept Catholicism from becoming active before the Revolution. In the decade after independence was won, Father (later Bishop) Jean de Cheverus gained the support of many influential Bostonians, including John Hancock, Samuel Adams and the architect Charles Bulfinch. All three men contributed toward building the city's first Catholic Cathedral, and the first Mass was publicly celebrated in Boston in 1788.

In the 19th century waves of Catholic immigrants—first Irish, then Italians and Slavs—arrived in Boston, and the Church grew to absorb them. Neighborhood parishes provided these newcomers with a source of continuity from the Old

World to the New, preserving their language and social customs as well as serving their religious needs. Other institutions were born as a response to this growth as well: *The Pilot*, America's oldest Catholic news weekly, began publication in 1829, and **Boston College**, New England's largest Catholic college, was founded in 1863. The vitality of Catholicism in Boston is evidenced by the continuing political power of Catholic voters and by the enormous growth of Catholic institutions in the 20th century, especially under the leadership of Richard Cardinal Cushing. The archdiocese of Boston, which celebrates its own bicentennial in 1975, contains the largest school system in New England, with six Catholic colleges and literally hundreds of grammar and high schools.

Catholic churches of particular interest to visitors include **St. Joseph's Church** at 66 Chambers St., **St. Stephen's Church** in the North End, **Our Lady of Perpetual Help Basilica** in Roxbury, and **The Paulist Center** at 7 Park St. The Paulist Center offers a variety of exhibits during the Bicentennial.

Judaism: Boston's first Jewish resident, Solomon Franco, arrived in 1649, and Isaac Lopez was elected town constable in 1720. But a true Jewish community was not established until 1842, with the founding of **Temple Ohabei Shalom** at 1187 Beacon St. in Brookline. Boston, therefore, was the last city in the Northeast to become a major Jewish population center. As late as 1890 the Jewish population of Boston did not exceed 5000, and was composed primarily of German immigrants.

Within the following decade the Jewish population burgeoned as a result of the massive immigration of East European Jewry, predominantly Russian and Orthodox.

The first Jewish charitable organization was founded in 1864, and by 1895 the network of charities was sufficient to warrant the formation of the Federation of Jewish Charities, the first such federated body in the United States. Mt. Sinai Hospital opened in 1902 as an outpatient clinic in the West End, but was replaced in 1915 by Beth Israel Hospital at 300 Brookline Avenue. 1921 marked the establishment of the Hebrew Teachers College, now Hebrew College at 43 Hawes St., Brookline.

Brandeis University, founded in Waltham in 1948, stands as a major manifestation of Jewish dedication to learning, as do Harvard's chairs of Jewish philosophy and literature and its renowned Hebraica and Judaica collection in Widener Library.

The American Jewish Historical Society will be glad to furnish information on Bicentennial events pertaining to the Jewish community in Boston. Call 891-8110.

BOSTON WOMEN

The essential role of women in United States history has too often been overlooked—not so in Boston in 1975 and 1976. Boston has traditionally been a city of strong women. Elizabeth Glendower Evans, a social reformer who helped make Massachusetts a leader in progressive penal techniques, also led the Massachusetts campaign which resulted in the first minimum wage act for women in the United States. Pauline Agassiz Shaw, daughter of naturalist Louis Agassiz, organized a chain of day nurseries in 1877 and in 1881 founded the North Bennet Street Industrial School, where public school children learned cooking, printing, and metal and wood working. Abigail Adams kept her husband John informed by letter of military and political developments in Boston while he served as a delegate to the Continental Congress in Philadelphia. "And, by the way," she added in March, 1776, "in the new code of laws which I suppose it will be necessary to make, I desire you would remember the ladies and be more generous and favorable to them than your ancestors. Do not put such unlimited power into the hands of the husbands. Remember all men would be tyrants if they could. If particular care and attention is not paid to the ladies, we are determined to foment a rebellion, and will not hold ourselves bound by any laws in which we have no voice or representation."

These are only three of the many outstanding women—novelists, teachers, abolitionists, welfare workers, scientists, missionaries, doctors, poets, theosophists and many more—who have lived and worked in Boston. You are invited to visit the exhibit Boston Women, which celebrates the contributions women have made to the city during the last 300 years. The exhibit will travel to a variety of locations throughout the city during 1975 and 1976, sponsored by women's groups who will combine the exhibition with events of special interest to women. The schedule of locations is in the Boston 200 Newspaper.

MEDICINE AND HEALTH IN BOSTON

Boston got off to a healthy start, since its location on a hill saved it from the malaria and typhoid epidemics that decimated most colonial towns. From that beginning the city grew to become a world-famous health care center, whose hospitals, teaching facilities and research institutions have been responsible for dozens of medical "firsts". Boston clinics saw the first use of ether, the first smallpox vaccination, the first development of gamma globulin, and the first artificial kidney unit. Massachusetts was the first state to pass pure food legislation, and Boston the first city to establish a municipal water supply. And Boston institutions graduated the first trained nurse and the first black nurse.

Visitors to Boston can view a special exhibit on Boston medicine at the Museum of Science (see p. 234 for location and hours). The exhibit will trace changes in our understanding of the human body over the past 300 years, including special sections on the heart, the brain, the cells and cancer. In addition, the following places offer tours and exhibits concerning medical history. For more suggestions, pick up a Boston 200 medical brochure.

Massachusetts General Hospital, Fruit St. at Charles St. T-Charles. The Ether Dome, designed by Bulfinch, contains an exhibit on the first use of ether anaesthesia. Call 726-2000 for schedule of Ether Dome tours and slide shows on hospital history.

Massachusetts Eye and Ear Infirmary, 243 Charles St. T-Charles. An exhibit of 300 years of eyeglasses and other aids to vision is on display Mon-Fri, 9am to 5pm. Tours given one day a week, by appointment: call 523-7900, ext. 603.

Harvard Medical School, Longwood Ave. T-Longwood on Arborway line. Founded in 1782, the school had six locations before these monumental white marble buildings were built in 1906. Countway Medical Library has changing exhibits on the history of medicine (open Mon-Thurs, 8am to 11:30pm; Fri, 8am to 5pm; Sun, 2pm to 11:30pm). For tours of the school, call 734-3300, ext. 438.

BANKING AND FINANCE IN BOSTON

Boston commerce began with the sea. The town's career as the merchant center of New England started with an active 17th-century trade in fish, lumber and other commodities, which later expanded to include rum, tea and manufactured products. The fortunes of some of Boston's proudest families—the Hancocks, the Otises, the Forbeses, the Parkers—were made in trade with the West Indies, Europe and later China. And already by the time of the Revolution banking operations were keeping pace with business: in 1784 a group of merchants formed the Massachusetts Bank, the first independent joint-stock bank in the country.

In the century that followed, Boston grew into a vital banking center for the new nation, providing capital which financed the railroads, opened the mines of the West and transformed rural New England into one of the most highly developed industrial areas in the country. A number of the city's museums and exhibits unfold this exciting history.

Boston Stock Exchange, 53 State St. Adult visitors can view the active trading floor. Mon-Fri, 10am to 2pm, by appointment. Call 723-9500 ext. 71.

The State Street Bank's banking office, 53 State St. The architecture and accouterments of this business office echo the maritime and banking history of Boston. It contains ship models, nautical materials, and a 17th-century banking office. Open Mon-Fri, 9am to 5pm.

The Federal Reserve Bank of Boston, 30 Pearl St. Guided tours are available weekdays by appointment. Call 426-7100, extension 511. The new Federal Reserve Bank building at Federal Reserve Plaza is scheduled for opening in the spring of 1976, and will offer guided tours, a "Money Museum" and economics exhibits. Call the Federal Reserve Bank of Boston for further details.

Boston Five Cents Savings Bank, 10-30 School St. Facing Old South Meeting House, this dramatic building has a small park where you can rest as you walk the Freedom Trail. From 8:30am to 4pm weekdays, you can view an exhibit in the main lobby of rare coins and unique mechanical coin banks from the Victorian era.

NEIGHBORHOOD DISCOVERY TRAILS

Explore Boston on the Neighborhood Discovery Trails. Because Boston is above all a city to walk in, Boston 200 has designed these neighborhood walking trails to help you discover the city on your own. Each trail begins near an MBTA station, and sites of interest are explained by interpretative markers sponsored by the Liberty Mutual Insurance Companies. The trails are designed to take about 1½ hours each (longer if you spend time in exhibits and museums) and to include places to eat and rest along the way. To follow each trail, look for the color-coded trailblazer signs. Public restrooms are marked on the trail maps. Remember that this section is not intended as a textbook on Boston. It contains stories and accounts which we hope will give some pleasure and a flavor of the way some Bostonians have viewed their past.

You will learn as you walk the trails that every section of Boston is unique. You can explore a different part of the city's life on each trail, and find very little repetition. The Freedom Trail, of course, covers the sites where the Revolution began, but its Downtown landmarks rub shoulders with high-rise banks and the dramatic Government Center buildings, while its North End portion will introduce you to a colorful Italian community in the shadow of Old North Church. The Charlestown Trail contains "Old Ironsides," a historic burying ground and a number of magnificent homes dating from just after the Revolution, set in a community that has done much to preserve its distinctive nineteenth-century architecture. The Waterfront Trail traces Boston's history as a port, from the days of smuggling and privateers through the clipper ship era to the coming of the railroads and the decline of sea trade.

The Beacon Hill and Back Bay Trails are the city's tribute to the nineteenth century. On Beacon Hill you'll find not only the elegant homes of Boston's oldest elite, but also the meeting houses where the Abolitionist movement began, and even a tunnel that was part of the Underground Railroad. And in Back

Bay you'll see a nineteenth-century land fill that became the pet project of Boston's First Families, who built museums, churches, private clubs and palatial homes on land that had once been under water.

The South End Trail is for city-watchers: it shows you the changing fortunes of a section that has gone from mansions to tenements and is now being rediscovered by people with varying backgrounds and incomes. And the Cambridge Trail gives you a glimpse of Boston's neighbor across the Charles, and particularly of Harvard University, the institution with which Cambridge's fate has been linked since 1636.

Unless you plan a long stay, you won't have time to walk all eight trails. But we urge you to take more than one in order to get a sense of the contrasts that exist in the city. Read through the trail descriptions before you go, to find the trails that especially appeal to you. Then put on your walking shoes, board the MBTA, and discover your own particular Boston.

FREEDOM TRAIL: DOWNTOWN

(*Map, pp. 130–131*)

Begin your tour of the oldest part of Boston with the new Government Center complex. After emerging from the subway (appropriately called Government Center) find a suitable spot on the eight-acre expanse of City Hall plaza and pick out the prominent buildings of the area. If you stand facing City Hall, to your left will be the twin towers and low-lying rectangular building of the John F. Kennedy Federal Office Building, and farther in the same direction, the piered tower and surrounding bulwark of the State Service Center, designed by the well-known architect Paul Rudolph. You should be able to see the white spire of Old North Church in the distance. To your right and behind you is a study in architectural reflection, the 19th-century Sears Crescent reflected in its distinctive curving shape and red-brick texture by the modern Center Plaza office building. The architectural theme of red brick is further carried out in the City Hall plaza, as an extension not only of Sears Crescent, the meeting place of writers, artists and poets in the last century (Emerson and Hawthorne included), but also of other historic Boston landmarks such as Faneuil Hall.

The overall concept for Government Center was the work of architect I. M. Pei, who stipulated the size, height and style relationships for the buildings. It was built on the site of old Scollay Square, a colorful but dilapidated section of Boston where the famous Old Howard burlesque theater once stood. "They're hanging crepe on Scollay Square," lamented poet-songwriter Francis W. Hatch. "Some coward/ Closed the Old Howard/ We don't have burley anymore!" Today cheesecake has given way to businessmen and bureaucrats.

The heart of Government Center is the City Hall, whose design by the architectural firm of Kallmann, McKinnell and Knowles won Boston's four-year national competition for a new City Hall. Both the structure and its surrounding funneling plaza represent the ideals of openness and accessibility in city government: the city is particularly proud of the plaza, which continues from outside into the building in "a gesture of welcome," and of the interior stairways designed so that visitors can walk through City Hall without ever opening a door. In good weather the plaza serves as a stage for political rallies, plays, and concerts. If you want to learn more about City Hall and the Government Center area, visit the information booth in the ground-floor lobby for tours of the building that are given every weekday 10am to 4pm every half-hour. You also may want to see the public art galleries on your own (see p. 230).

Start the Freedom Trail by picking up brochures of times and admission fees of Freedom Trail sites at the special Boston 200 Visitor Information Center in City Hall (open 10am to 6pm daily; follow the signs in City Hall plaza). Then proceed to the first official site, Faneuil Hall, a historic marketplace and the political forum for Revolutionary leaders. The markets are in the lower floors and the meeting hall is on the second floor. Francis W. Hatch once wrote: "Here orators/In ages past/Have mounted their attack/Undaunted by proximity/Of sausage on the rack." Merchant Peter Faneuil built the Hall and gave it to the city in 1742, as replacement for an earlier structure. That first market building was made of wood and dismantled by a mob who were unconvinced that a fixed market was better than house-to-house peddling. You may notice that Faneuil Hall, Boston's second attempt at a fixed market, is made of brick.

In front of the Hall is a statue of "the man of the town

meeting," patriot Samuel Adams. Beginning with the Sugar Act in 1764, Adams led the town meetings at Faneuil Hall in thwarting British attempts at taxation. With a short bow to this patriot leader, proceed around the building to the entrance of the Hall (it faces away from City Hall) and climb the stairs to the second-floor chamber. This hall is still used for public meetings, thus continuing a tradition over 200 years old.

As you leave Faneuil Hall, you may give a glance to its world-renowned grasshopper weathervane. Then continue straight ahead to the restored buildings of Quincy Market (built 1824), to the Boston 200 exhibit on the American Revolution. There you can put yourself in the places of Patriot and Tory with a variety of films, broadsides, pictures and puppet shows, and decide on the major issues and events that led to the Revolution.

The Market itself is named for Josiah Quincy, the Boston mayor who conceived of and executed the plan for these buildings. Years later he wrote with justifiable pride, "All this was accomplished in the centre of a populous city, not only without any tax, debt or burden upon its pecuniary resources, but with large permanent additions to its real and productive property."

As you come out of Quincy Market into Dock Square (the site of 18th-century Town Dock), follow the trail to the next official Freedom Trail site, the Old State House. On your way, pause at 53 State St., where a plaque marks the site of the Bunch of Grapes Tavern, a patriot meeting place. Continue until you come to the area in front of the Old State House. You may notice the traffic whizzing by in five different directions—this is still a crossroads in Boston.

As early as 1634 the Puritans used this place to set up their pillory and stocks. Offenders were locked up in these devices, shouted at, and pelted with rotten vegetables. Later the square became a common place for political protest before the Revolution. When effigies of British officials were hanged on the Liberty Tree to protest the Stamp Act, patriots dressed as pallbearers cut them down, carried them respectfully down present-day Washington St., and held the "funeral" in front of the Old State House. But the best-known event connected with this place is the Boston Massacre. The Massacre occurred on March 5, 1770, about a year after British soldiers began occupying Boston to help enforce British taxation laws. Of course relations between the soldiers and the townspeople were never very good: the soldiers would prick people with their bayonets to move them out of their way, and the townspeople would haul the soldiers into court on the smallest pretext. Other differences of opinion were resolved by tavern brawls or fistfights in back alleys. The Boston Massacre came about when a mob led by former slave Crispus Attucks began to assault soldiers on guard at the Royal Customs House (now the intersection of Congress and State Sts.) The soldiers fired into the crowd and Attucks and four others were killed. Patriot spokesmen used the incident to have the soldiers withdrawn from the city (but not for long—the soldiers were back in two years), and later they propagandized the Massacre as the first military action of the Revolution. In front of the Old State House is a circle of cobblestones, an official Freedom Trail site which commemorates the Massacre. You are urged to skirt this marker in reaching the Old State House. And watch the traffic.

Before you go in, give a glance to the balcony, where the Declaration of Independence was first read to the people of Boston on July 18, 1776 (it's still read from there every July 4th). The lion and unicorn statues higher up are symbols of the British crown. These are copies—the patriots burned the originals. You may also notice the arcades on the ground floor. When the Old State House was built in 1713, the architects retained the medieval characteristic of open arcades "for the country people that come with theire provisions . . . to sitt dry in and warme both in colde raine and durty weather." Today the portico, as a subway station, still shelters people from "durty" Boston weather.

Once inside the Old State House, follow the spiral staircase up to the second-floor Council Chamber, where patriot James Otis argued in 1761 against the Writs of Assistance, general search warrants used by the British to track down smuggled goods. The normally phlegmatic John Adams was present when Otis made his case against the Writs, and years later he wrote:

Every man of a crowded audience appeared to me to go away, as I did, ready to take arms against writs of assistance. Then and there was the first scene of the first act of opposition to the arbitrary claims of Great Britain. Then and there the child Independence was born.

121

Now resume the trail by going down Devonshire Street, formerly known as "Pudding Lane," "Crooked Lane," and "Wilson's Lane." "Wilson's Lane" is probably the oldest name, "Wilson" being the Reverend John Wilson, the first pastor of the Puritans' church. According to the secretary of the colony, he "came hither to avoid persecution and to have freedom to think and speak as he chose. He left his wife in England." Another former resident of the street was Elizabeth Vergoose, or Mother Goose, who came to live here with her daughter and son-in-law after her husband died. Her son-in-law, Thomas Fleet, was the first one to gather and publish the songs she sang to her grandchildren.

On your way down Devonshire you can explore two old lanes that run off the street: Quaker Lane, the branching path through a Quaker cemetery that was once here, and Spring Lane, the place where the Puritans drew water from the so-called "Great Spring."

Now proceed to the intersection of Milk and Devonshire where a plaque on the Post Office marks the stopping point of the fire of 1872. The fire began at the intersection of Summer and Kingston Sts. and burned out 65 acres in the heart of the city. In recognition of its magnitude Bostonians dubbed it the "Great Fire of 1872"—thus giving it equal honors with the "Great Fires" of 1711, 1747, 1761, 1787, and 1794. The tradition of fires in this section of the city began with the Puritans. Their first houses burned down because they built their chimneys out of wood.

Now take a right on Milk St. and quicken your pace to the end of the street. High up on the building at 17 Milk you'll see a bust of Franklin and the words "Birthplace of Franklin" carved in relief. Turn right on Washington St. to the next official Freedom Trail site, the Old South Meeting House. Inside the Meeting House are exhibits about colonial and Revolutionary Boston, including a copy of George Washington's will.

On December 16, 1773, 5000 citizens of Boston met in the Old South Meeting House to decide what they would do with the three tea ships at Griffin's Wharf. Although the British government had repealed all import taxes except the one on tea, the patriots felt that this single remaining tax supported the principle of British power to tax the colonies. They were determined that the tea would not be unloaded from the ships, but their problem was time. Since the ships had docked, the patriots had managed to "persuade" the shipowners not to unload the tea; but, according to law, after twenty days Customs officials could confiscate unloaded cargoes and land it themselves. The twenty-day limit was to expire at midnight that night, and the next day the British Customs officials would certainly land the tea. At first the meeting sent a message to the Royal Governor and demanded he give the ships special permission to leave Boston harbor and return to England. When the Governor refused to do this, Samuel Adams stood up and said in a tone of defeat, "This meeting can do nothing more to save the country." Rather than admitting defeat, however, Adams was signalling certain men in the hall to slip away and put a pre-planned operation into effect. Soon afterwards the audience noticed at the doorway a small group of men with blackened faces, blankets, and tomahawks. The "Indians" gave a few whoops and then ran down Milk St. to Griffin's Wharf. With cries of "Boston harbor a teapot tonight!" the people in the Meeting House raced after them.

At Griffin's Wharf about 100 "Indians" had gathered and were methodically cracking open chests of tea and spilling them into the harbor. When they were finished, they lined up at the dock and shook out their clothes and shoes to show they had stolen no tea. Then, with commendable military precision, the "Indians" arranged themselves in rank and file, shouldered their tomahawks, and marched up the wharf to the music of a fife. ("Depend on it," John Adams said later, "they were no ordinary Mohawks.") At the end of the wharf was a house where the British admiral was staying. As the procession passed by, he raised a window and called, "Well, boys, you've had a fine pleasant evening for your Indian caper, haven't you? But mind you have got to pay the fiddler yet!" Their replies will not be recorded here. But afterwards they did pay the fiddler when the British retaliated by closing the port of Boston—an act which further united the colonies and brought them one step closer to war.

You can take the **Tea Party Path** from Old South yourself (the walk takes 10 to 15 minutes). Turn left onto Milk St., continue to Post Office Square, and then turn right down Congress St. From Congress St. you should be able to see the Boston Tea Party Ship, a full-size working facsimile of one of the original tea ships. The **Boston Tea Party Ship and Mu-**

seum have documents and exhibits about the Tea Party, including one of the 340 chests purportedly thrown overboard that night. (See p. 224 for hours and admission.) On your way back to pick up the trail at Old South, you can stop off at 185 Franklin St., where New England Telephone has restored the room in which Alexander Graham Bell heard the first telephone sound.

If you like you can take another side-trip from Old South down Washington St., the heart of Boston's shopping district, and learn a little about Boston topography at the same time. You can follow the loop on the map and rest your feet along the way at the new Lincoln Filene Park on Franklin St. next to Filene's. (If you want information on Washington St. stores, see p. 245). In the 17th and 18th centuries Boston was still a peninsula and Washington St. was the road that began near Dock Square, ran the length of the peninsula and crossed Boston Neck to the mainland. Starting near the Old State House, you'll see the street takes its first curve near Spring Lane to avoid the Great Spring and Governor Winthrop's estate, makes another bend around Franklin St. to skirt a swamp, and then takes another curve near Bedford St. to round a pond. From Essex St. it follows the path over the Boston Neck, a strip of land that connected the peninsula to the mainland. You'll understand just how narrow that strip was if you realize that Bay Village, about two blocks west of Washington St., and Chinatown, about one block east, were both shore communities on opposite sides of the Neck. (For more on Chinatown, see p. 224.)

Back at Old South Meeting House, cross the street to the next Freedom Trail site, the Old Corner Bookstore at School and Washington Sts. The Bookstore is located on the site of the home of Anne Hutchinson, the woman banished from Boston in 1638 because her beliefs conflicted with Puritan orthodoxy. According to John Winthrop, "she was a woman of haughty and fierce carriage, a nimble wit and active spirit, a very voluble tongue, more bold than a man, though in understanding and judgment inferior to many women." (In 1915 Boston changed its mind about Anne Hutchinson and placed a statue of her on the State House lawn. The city waited until 1945, however, before it revoked the edict of banishment against her.)

The building you see now was constructed in 1711 as the home of apothecary Thomas Crease and converted from private residence to bookstore in 1828. In mid-19th century the Old Corner became famous as a gathering place for Longfellow, Emerson, Hawthorne, Holmes, Whittier, Julia Ward Howe, and Harriet Beecher Stowe. If you walk into the Old Corner, you can see some first editions of their books and Oliver Wendell Holmes's desk.

From here continue up School St. (with a backward glance to Old South) and proceed to the Old City Hall, a famous Victorian building which has been "recycled" to house some private offices and a chic French restaurant. The two statues in front of Old City Hall are Benjamin Franklin and Josiah Quincy. The artist who sculpted the Franklin statue said that if you look at Franklin's left profile he wears the appropriately serious expression of a statesman, and if you look at his right profile he wears the whimsical expression of the writer of *Poor Richard's Almanac*. You'll have to judge for yourself.

Both Franklin and Quincy went to the Boston Latin School, whose original site near here makes this spot part of the official Freedom Trail. In 1634 the town decided that "Philemon Pormont be intreated to become a schoolmaster for the teaching and nourtering of the children with us," "children" referring exclusively to boys. The Latin School was the first public school in the United States and in colonial days its alumni included John Hancock, Robert Treat Paine and Samuel Adams.

Proceed to the end of School St., past the famous Parker House at 60 School, where Parker House rolls originated. Both Ho Chi Minh and Malcolm X worked here as waiters (though not at the same time!) Then turn left on Tremont. At this point you're about halfway through the trail, and if you like you can continue all the way down Tremont to the Common and take a break before you finish the rest of the trail. Otherwise stop off at the next Freedom Trail site, the Granary Burying Ground on Tremont.

The Granary takes its name from a barn-like structure which used to stand near here and which was supposed to store grain for poor people in times of shortages. In the words of the old records, however, "the weevils have taken the wheet, and mice annoy the corn much, being very numerous." The mice annoyed the corn so much that town officials gave up their idealistic project and tore down the granary at the beginning of the 19th century. Its name, nevertheless, lingers on with the cemetery.

If you read the plaques on the outside gates you'll see that the Granary, dating back to 1660, is the burying ground for patriots. Take a right after entering the cemetery until you come to the grave of the Boston Massacre victims, and next to it, the grave of Samuel Adams. Not far from here Samuel Adams was strolling one day with his cousin John (later the second U.S. President) when he pointed to John Hancock's house overlooking the Common and said, "I have done a very good thing for our cause, in the course of the past week, by enlisting the master of that house into it. He is well-disposed, and has great riches, and we can give him consequence to enjoy them." (You can see Hancock's marker from Adams's grave. It's the white pillar near the church wall.)

Adams and Hancock rose together as political leaders in the Revolution; people used to say that Hancock paid the postage while Adams did the writing. They both signed the Declaration of Independence and they shared the distinction (at least in Adams's eyes) of being the only patriots outlawed by King George III. After the war Hancock served as first governor of Massachusetts, and when he died before completing the last of several terms, Adams, the lieutenant governor, succeeded him and then served a couple of terms of his own as governor. Despite his high position, Samuel Adams never lost his distrust of a strong government: in the words of a contemporary, "he will have no capitulation with abuses; he fears as much the despotism of virtue and talents as the despotism of vice."

Now if you follow the brick wall from Adams's grave you'll come to the tomb of Robert Treat Paine, the third signer of the Declaration of Independence buried in the Granary. From here continue on the path to the memorial for Franklin's parents, the pyramid near the center of the graveyard. After reading the epitaph (he "a pious and prudent man", she "a discreet and virtuous woman"), continue left along the path and look three rows inside for the gravestone of Elisha Brown. When the British occupied Boston in 1769, Brown refused to quarter soldiers in his house, barred all the doors and windows, and proceeded to survive on several months' food he had stored there. The soldiers laid siege all around the house, but after seventeen days they gave up and occupied Faneuil Hall instead. Thus the stone states that Brown "bravely and successfully opposed a whole British regt. in their violent attempt to FORCE him from his *legal Habitation*." Once you've deciphered the whole epitaph for yourself, take a right on the path to the marker for John Hancock's tomb.

Farther up the path from Hancock's tomb are two stones with epitaphs you ought to read. Start with the stone of Captain John DeCoster, which begins compellingly, "Stop here my Friend," and then move on to the more introverted epitaph for Edward Carter which says, "Farewell Vain World I have Enough of the(e)."

From here walk up the path (past the stone of James Bowdoin, another Massachusetts governor and life-long friend of Benjamin Franklin) to the tombs of the three Faneuils. People used to snicker that the Faneuils were much closer in death than they ever were in life. Andrew Faneuil, the one who first accumulated the family fortune, disinherited his elder nephew Benjamin for marrying without his consent, and except for the "five shillings and no more" which he gave Benjamin, he left all his money to his younger and more dutiful nephew, Peter. Peter was the one who built Faneuil Hall and gave it to the city. Only eight years after his inheritance, however, Peter died and willed his money to his brother; so Benjamin enjoyed his uncle's fortune after all.

Now return to the main path and follow it to the grave of that midnight rider, Paul Revere. The fancy white monument was erected by the city; Revere's original and unpretentious stone is in front of it. When not on a horse Revere worked in metals, edited a newspaper, pulled teeth, and manufactured gunpowder. He also engraved the plates for and printed the first U.S. paper currency.

From here turn down the center path and keep an eye on the left side, until you come to the place where the Fleets are buried. (It's near the Franklin monument, underneath a tree.) Next to Thomas Fleet's stone is a marker for "Mary Goose." Unfortunately this is not Mother Goose, but her husband's first wife, Mary. If you find a stone around here for Elizabeth Foster Goose (or Vergoose), then you've found the real Mother Goose.

Once back at the front gate, take a right to the grave of James Otis. Eight years after his brilliant case against the Writs of Assistance, Otis was "assaulted" in a tavern by a British official (so the story goes) and he became slowly insane from the head injury he suffered. He ceased to be an active figure in the Revolution long before the outbreak of war. In 1783, while watching a storm from the doorway of a friend's house, Otis was struck by lightning and killed instantaneously: his friends said it was the way he would have wanted to die.

From the Granary continue on Tremont and turn up Park St. (Farther down Tremont is the Visitor Information Center bordering the Common.) For years Park Street was the dividing line between business and residential Boston, or, as the saying went, "No gentleman takes a drink before three o'clock or east of Park Street." Here you can visit the next official site on the Freedom Trail, the Park Street Church, where William Lloyd Garrison gave his first public anti-slavery speech in 1829. The site of the church was once called Brimstone Corner, because brimstone for gunpowder was stored in a cellar here during the War of 1812.

After you've seen the church, proceed up Park St. You can now visit another important Freedom Trail site, the Massachusetts State House, whose Archives Museum has on display documents dating back to the Pilgrims. (See Beacon Hill trail, p. 163). Otherwise take a right on Beacon St. and make a loop back to the next official site, King's Chapel and its adjacent burying grounds. First mention of the burying grounds occurred in 1631, when Puritan Isaac Johnson died and was buried in a corner of his garden as he wished. As the years passed other members of the colony asked to be buried next to him (Johnson had been a likable fellow) and the plot began to fill up. Eventually the town decided to set aside the area as a burial ground; as the records noted, "Brother Johnson's garden is getting to be a poor place for vegetables."

Now go into King's Chapel, the seat of the Church of England and of royalism before the Revolution. In 1688 Governor Andros appropriated part of the cemetery to build an Anglican chapel, because no Puritan would sell him land for that purpose. (It was "a bare-faced *squat*," in the words of historian N. I. Bowditch.) This wooden chapel stood until 1753, when the present stone chapel was built to enclose it so that construction would not interrupt services. Once the new structure was completed, workmen took apart the old wooden chapel and threw the pieces out the doors and windows. Inside the Chapel are high enclosed pews, so designed to keep their occupants warm during lengthy services in the winter. It was once the custom for families to rent or buy their own pews: numbers 31 and 32 belonged to the Governor, number 102 to Oliver Wendell Holmes. To the right of the main entrance is a special pew where condemned prisoners heard their last sermon before being hanged on the Common.

Now walk outside to the adjacent burying ground, the first cemetery of the Puritans. If you go down the leftward path, you'll come to the tomb of John Winthrop, the first Puritan governor. (It's a brown slab on curved posts.) Behind Winthrop's tomb is a stone for four early Puritan pastors, John Cotton, John Davenport, John Oxenbridge, and Thomas Bridge.

You can also take the path which runs to the center of the graveyard. Here you'll find the tomb of Mary Chilton, by legend the first Pilgrim to step on Plymouth Rock; she's buried with her husband, John Winslow. Almost opposite from the Winslows is the tomb of William Dawes, who made a midnight ride like Paul Revere but whose name was less euphonious to Longfellow's ears.

Continue to follow the paths and look for the tomb of Hezekiah Usher, the first bookseller in New England. During the witch scare of the late 1600s, one of Usher's neighbors accused him of being a witch (she said he stuck pins in her), but Hezekiah's brother was a town official and refused to prosecute him. Less fortunate was John Alden, the son of Pilgrims John and Priscilla (he's buried here—look for his stone). When he was accused of being a witch, Alden had to take refuge in the houses of friends for two years, until the witch scare died down. As you come up to the end of the path on the chapel side you might pause by the stone of Elizabeth Pain, a young Puritan woman branded with an "A" for adultery because she bore a child by her minister. Two hundred years later Nathaniel Hawthorne retold her story in *The Scarlet Letter*.

You won't find a stone for him, but Captain Kidd is supposed to be buried in this cemetery. In the 1690s Kidd was sent by the Royal Governor at Boston to capture pirates off the coast, but rather than capture pirates Kidd reportedly became one. When he himself was finally taken, he was sent to

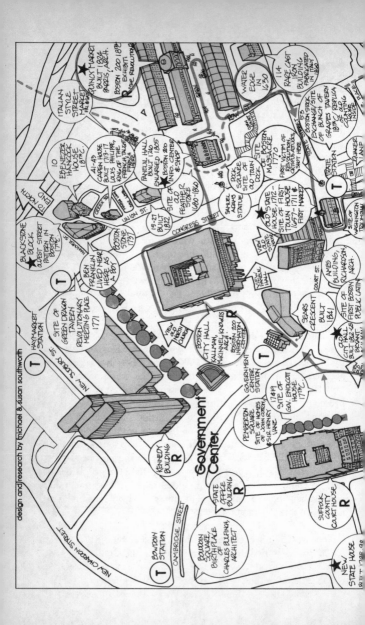

design and research by michael & susan southworth

QUINCY MARKET BUILT 1824. PARRIS, ARCH. BOSTON 200 187?

ITALIAN STYLE STREET MARKET HAYMKT

10 EBENEZER HANCOCK HOUSE 18THC.

41-43 CAPEN HOUSE BUILT 1713-17 WAS PHIL'S. UNION OYSTER HOUSE. FRENCH TAUGHT FRENCH HERE

FANEUIL HALL BUILT 1740 ENLARGED 1805 BOSTON 200 INFO. CENTER & E-SHOP

WATER EDGE IN 1630

114 RARE CAST IRON BUILDING PREFABRICATED IN ITALY IN 1860

BOSTON STOCK EXCHANGE OF BUNCH OF GRAPES TAVERN 18THC REPLICA OF OLD COUNTING HOUSE INSIDE

BLACKSTONE BLOCK OLDEST STREET PATTERN IN BOSTON

15-21 BUILT 1832

BOSTON STONE 1737

SITE OF OLD FEATHER STORE 1680-1860

DOCK SQUARE SITE OF TOWN DOCK

SAMUEL ADAMS STATUE

OLD STATE HOUSE, 1712-SITE OF FIRST TOWN HOUSE 1711 FIRST MKT

SITE OF BOSTON MASSACRE 1770 FIRST VICTIM OF REVOLUTION CRISPUS ATTUCKS SHOT HERE

STATE T

QUINCY VANE

SITE OF GREEN DRAGON TAVERN REVOLUTIONARY MEETING PLACE 1771

HAYMARKET STATION T

BEN FRANKLIN LIVED NEAR HERE AS A BOY

NEW FANEUIL HALL

NEW OLD STATE

SEARS CRESCENT ST 1841

AMES BUILDING

SITE OF RICHARDSON ARCH.

SITE OF WASHINGTON TOWN HOUSE

VIEW OLD NORTH CHURCH

BOSTON CITY HALL KALLMAN, MCKINNEL KNOWLES ARCH. BOSTON 200 MACHINE HEAT INTERPRETIVE

OLD CITY HALL BUILT 1862-65 FIRST BOSTON BRYANT, GILMAN, PUBLIC LATIN SCH.

GOVERNMENT CENTER STATION T

KENNEDY BUILDING R

STATE OFFICE BUILDING R

PEMBERTON SQUARE SITE OF HOMES OF JOHN GORTON & SIR HENRY VANE

1749 SITE OF GOV. ENDICOTT HOUSE 1770

Government Center

BOWDOIN STATION T

CAMBRIDGE STREET

BOWDOIN SQUARE BIRTHPLACE OF CHARLES BULFINCH ARCHITECT

SUFFOLK COUNTY COURT HOUSE R

NEW STATE HOUSE BUILT 1795-98

NEW SUDBURY ST

NEW CHARDON STREET

CONGRESS STREET

COURT ST

UNION ST

MARSHALL ST

CREEK SQ

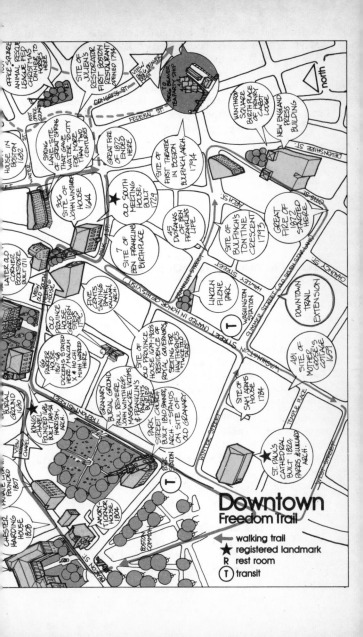

Downtown
Freedom Trail

→ walking trail
★ registered landmark
R rest room
T transit

north

England and there tried, convicted, and sentenced to death. "My Lord, it is a very hard sentence," Kidd said to his judges. "For my part, I am the most innocent person of them all, only I have been sworn against by perjured persons." His accusers were unimpressed; they led him outside, bound him in chains, and hanged him. According to legend, if you knock on the stones of King's Chapel three times and whisper, "Captain Kidd, for what were you hanged?", Captain Kidd will answer . . . nothing.

Return to the front gate and turn right on Tremont St. This will take you back to Government Center, your starting point on the trail.

FREEDOM TRAIL: THE NORTH END

(*Map, pp. 134–135*)

The North End is Boston's tribute to Europe. Its historic architecture and foreign flavor make it unique in the city. As one of the oldest parts of the original Shawmut peninsula settlement, its history goes back to the Puritans and spirals down through Cotton Mather, Paul Revere, Eben Jordan of Jordan Marsh, the Fitzgeralds and the Kennedys, and Sacco and Vanzetti. The North End Loop of the Freedom Trail encompasses all of these and begins at Faneuil Hall. To get there take the Green line of the MBTA to the Haymarket station and walk up Congress St., or exit at Government Center and use the slightly longer route across the brick plaza to Dock Square.

From the statue of Samuel Adams in front of Faneuil Hall follow the map to Union St. The section from Union St. to the Expressway is the **Blackstone Block,** Boston's oldest commercial area and the only district of the city that retains the original 17th-century street patterns and alleyways. The streets twist and wind—not because of wayward cows, but because the earliest settlers established their shops wherever they wanted them to be.

The brick buildings along Union St. date mainly from the early 19th century and were constructed as combination shops and residences. At 41 Union St. is the **Capen House,** which was built between 1713 and 1717 and served as a dress shop for Hopestill Capen. Louis Philippe, who was later to become king of the French, taught French here to Boston merchants when he was hard-pressed for money and was awaiting relief from Europe. Since 1826, the building has served as the **Union Oyster House,** generally considered the oldest restaurant in Boston.

A block away from here at Union St. and Hanover, where the Bell 'N Hand Restaurant is now, is the site of the boyhood home of Benjamin Franklin. His father owned a candleworks here in which the younger Franklin worked as a boy. Franklin's primary responsibility was to dump the factory rubbish into nearby Mill Pond, an inlet of the Charles River.

Bear right at the Capen House and follow the red brick path to Creek Square, the heart of the district. At 10 Marshall St. is the **Ebenezer Hancock House,** which dates from 1760. John Hancock owned it from 1764 to 1785, during which time it was occupied by his brother Ebenezer, paymaster of the Continental Army.

Across from the Hancock House, the building housing the gift shop has embedded in its side the **Boston Stone,** which is the official centerpoint of the city. All distances to and from Boston are measured from this point.

Around the corner is Blackstone St., which has been the home of three centuries of Boston butchers. Originally this street was a creek connecting Mill Pond and Town Creek, and was the only place in the town where butchers could dispose of animal entrails legally. The trail leads from this point across Blackstone St. and through the pedestrian tunnel under the Expressway. A detour up Blackstone St. will lead you to **Haymarket,** Boston's open-air market. Here on Fridays and Saturdays you can find fresh produce among the carts and stands of street vendors.

You are now entering the North End proper. Don't look for serenity. This part of Boston is old, crowded and in many places not as clean as it could be. It has great vitality and charm, however, and reputedly the safest streets in the city, thanks to neighborhood cohesiveness. The North End has been

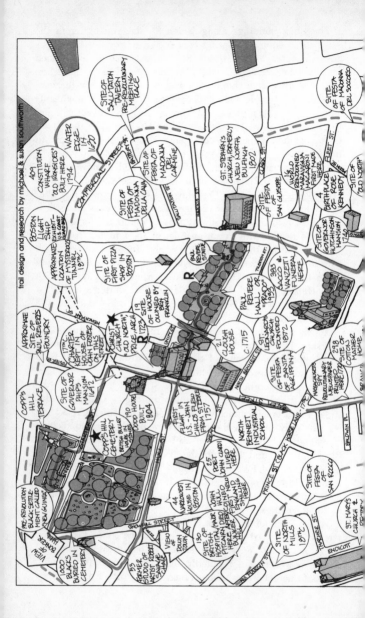

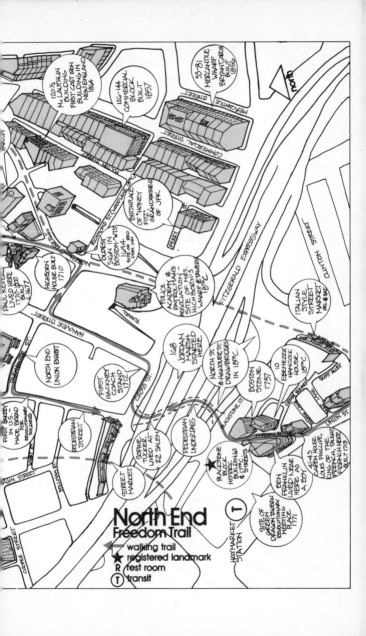

North End
Freedom Trail

- walking trail
- ★ registered landmark
- R rest room
- T transit

North

120½ McLAUTHLIN BUILDING FIRST CAST IRON BUILDING IN NEW ENGLAND 1864

126-144 COMMERCIAL BLOCK BUILT 1857

55-81 MERCANTILE WHARF BRYANT/GILMAN BUILT 1850

BIRTHPLACE OF "HONEY FITZ" GRANDFATHER OF JFK

OLDEST SIGN IN BOSTON "WT5" SITE OF RED LYON INN 1654

PAUL REVERE LIVED HERE 1770-1800 BUILT c.1677

HICHBORN HOUSE BUILT 1710

NORTH END UNION EXHIBIT

FIRST HACKNEY COACH STAND BUILT 1712

POLICE ACADEMY & PATRIOTS PARK LOCATION - SITE OF MRS. HICHBORN'S WHARF & TAVERN 1871

ITALIAN STYLE STREET MARKET FRI. & SAT.

168 JORDAN MARSH STARTED HERE

NORTH ST. & HANOVER ST. DRAWBRIDGES IN 18TH C.

BOSTON STONE 1737

10 EBENEZER HANCOCK HOUSE 18TH C.

FIRST BAKERY IN U.S.- MADE BREAD FOR REVOLUTIONARY SOLDIERS

SOPHIE TUCKER LIVED AT 22 SALEM

PEDESTRIAN UNDERPASS

PEDESTRIAN STREET

STREET MARKET

BLACKSTONE BLOCK OLDEST BUILDINGS & 17TH C.

41-43 MARSHALL HOUSE LOUIS PHILLIPE KING OF THE FRENCH, TAUGHT FRENCH HERE BUILT 1713

BEN FRANKLIN LIVED NEAR HERE AS A BOY

SITE OF GREEN DRAGON TAVERN REVOLUTIONARY MEETING PLACE 1773

HAYMARKET STATION

FITZGERALD EXPRESSWAY

CLINTON STREET

COMMERCIAL STREET

MERCANTILE STREET

HANOVER STREET

CROSS ST.

UNION ST.

SCOTT ALLEY

MARSHALL ST.

SALEM STREET

CREEK SQUARE

COOPER STREET

SULLIVAN STREET

MORGAN STREET

BLACKSTONE ST.

TUNNEL

the port of entry for every major ethnic group that has ever lived in Boston. The Yankees and the blacks lived there first in the original Puritan settlements. With the expansion of the city through landfill, these groups moved to new quarters in Beacon Hill and later Back Bay. Next it was the Irish who dominated the neighborhood. The Dearos , an organization founded by "Honey Fitz" Fitzgerald, is dedicated to remembering the "Dear Old" North End. Eastern European Jews migrated to this section of town and called it their own for a time, and now the area is a very close-knit Italian-American community.

As you emerge from the pedestrian tunnel, turn right on Cross St. and walk one block over to **Hanover St.** The drawbridge to the rest of the Shawmut peninsula made this, with North St., one of the two main streets of the old North End. Before the Revolution, the street was lined with the mansions of Boston's aristocrats. With the defeat of the British, those who had been Loyalists fled to Canada, and their houses were appropriated by merchants who converted them into shops. One of these new shopkeepers was Eben Jordan, who started a dry goods store at 168 Hanover St. It later merged with Mr. Marsh's business and moved downtown to become Jordan Marsh.

A right turn onto Richmond St. away from Hanover will bring you to North St. and in sight of the oldest sign in Boston (1694). The Red Lyon Inn once stood at the corner of North and Richmond Sts. and was owned by Nicholas Upsall, who was persecuted and imprisoned for aiding Quakers. The sign is on the upper side of the building that now occupies the site, and bears the initials of Upsall's granddaughter and her husband, "T.W." and "S.W."

In colonial Boston, North St. was named Ann St. and was the site of several taverns where revolutionaries brewed their political plans. By the early 19th century it had degenerated into a rough waterfront area of brothels, saloons and gambling houses. The "nymphs of Ann Street" were notorious until 1854 when the area was cleaned up and the name changed to the present one. The neighborhood is now primarily a Sicilian-American community. A left turn onto North St. will bring you to the junction of Sun Court, Moon St. and Garden Court which forms **North Square. Rachel Revere Park,** the enclosed area on your right, was once the site of a colonial marketplace and is now a community play area and meeting place.

At 29 North Square is the **Moses Pierce-Hichborn House.** Nathaniel Hichborn was Paul Revere's cousin and a shipbuilder. His three-story home is one of the two 18th-century buildings still standing in this section of Boston. It has been completely restored and gives a clear sense of early 19th-century town life. Notice that the huge wooden beams are held together by giant pegs rather than nails.

Next door is the **Paul Revere House,** the oldest wood building in Boston proper and an official Freedom Trail site. The first home on this land was that of a Captain Kemble who was condemned by the Puritans to suffer for two hours in the stocks for "lewd and viscious behaviour." In returning from a three-year absence at sea, he had kissed his wife on the front steps of their home on a Sunday. Ownership of the house then passed to the Mathers, Old Boston's most famous family. It was a convenient location for them, as both Increase and Cotton served as ministers of the Church at North Square. The Mather home was destroyed by fire in 1676, and the land was bought by a John Jeff who constructed the present house.

Paul Revere purchased the building in 1770 and moved in with his wife, mother, and five children. Two more daughters were born before the first Mrs. Revere died in 1773. Paul's second wife, whom he married that same year, bore seven more children between 1774 and 1785. The unusual size of the Revere family made this house the only one in North Square that did not have to quarter British soldiers during the Revolution.

On March 5, 1771, the first anniversary of the Boston Massacre, at the urging of Samuel Adams and the Sons of Liberty, Revere staged a re-enactment of the event on oiled paper stretched across his North Square windows. The shadow-figure drama depicted the whole bloody sequence, from the line-up of British soldiers on King St. to the appearance of the ghosts of the victims of the Massacre, complete with a warning: "Sneider's pale Ghost fresh bleeding stands/And vengeance for his Death demands."

At 11 North Square is the **Mariner's Home** (1838), an all-purpose lodging house and refuge for seamen and a reminder of the area's maritime importance. A short walk up Garden Court to Prince St. will bring you to the site where Thomas Hutchinson built his mansion in 1710. His son, Governor "Stingy Tommy" Hutchinson, lived there, and after the Stamp Act of 1765 the house was sacked by an angry mob.

Nearby was the Clark mansion, built in 1711. In 1756 it became the property of Sir Charles Henry Frankland, who scandalized Boston society when he brought his Marblehead mistress Agnes Surriage to his home in order to "supervise her education." He was tutoring her in Lisbon during that city's massive 18th-century earthquake. She saved his life and became Lady Frankland in return. The Clark/Frankland home was razed in 1833.

Across the street from the site of the Hutchinson home, at **4 Garden Court,** is the brick tenement building in which Rose Fitzgerald Kennedy was born in 1890. With the flight of the wealthy after the Revolution, cramped tenement buildings like this began to fill in the old gardens and open spaces of the North End. The successive waves of famine, especially the potato-crop failures of 1824 and 1847, brought thousands of Irish immigrants who filled the crowded new buildings and inherited the old mansions usually on the scale of one family per room. John "Honey Fitz" Fitzgerald, Rose's father and a mayor of Boston, was the son of one such family, and was born in the vicinity of North Square.

Leave the North Square area by way of Prince St. and walk over one block left to Hanover. A walk up Hanover St. quickly imparts the Mediterranean character of the neighborhood. From the store front signs to the street-corner philosophers, the language is most likely to be Italian. Espresso cafes and pastry shops seem to be on every corner—try a taste of some traditional Italian sweets. Hanover St. is also home to a number of restaurants which serve only home-cooked meals.

In the summertime, Hanover St. and the neighboring side streets open up with the traditional European religious *festas*. These are lively block festivals commemorating various saints' days and are carried on by local civic groups almost every summer weekend. For a list, see the Festival American Calendar.

On your right at the corner of Hanover and Clark is the very beautiful brick **St. Stephen's Roman Catholic Church.**

It was originally the "New North Meeting House" and included Paul Revere among its members. Charles Bulfinch designed the building in 1804. Ten years later it was taken over by the Unitarians. Soon after, however, all of the old Yankee families moved out to the South End or Back Bay and considered attending services in the then-Irish North End "ungenteel." In 1862 the church became Roman Catholic and was renamed. It has served successive Irish, Portuguese, and Italian communities. In 1965 it was renovated and restored by Richard Cardinal Cushing.

The **Paul Revere Mall** or Prado connects St. Stephen's Church with Christ Church. It was constructed by the city in 1933 and "dedicated to the memory of those men and women who helped make Boston the pride of later generations." Like its European counterparts and every other sizeable open space in the North End, the Prado is a natural gathering place, a neighborhood park used by residents all year round.

The side walls of the Prado are laid with bronze plaques that are worth reading for an over-view of Boston's history. One is dedicated to the Salutation Tavern which stood on the far side of St. Stephen's at the foot of Salutation St. In 18th-century Boston it was the site of many of the meetings of local patriots. As the North End was the maritime center of Boston, a large number of these men were ship's caulkers, those who filled in the seams of the ship to make it seaworthy. To summon them to meetings messengers would run through the narrow streets of the North End crying "Caulkers! Caulkers!" With repeated use this soon degenerated into "Caucus! Caucus!", thereby adding a new political term to the American lexicon.

As you exit from the rear of the Mall you will cross Unity St. Around the corner on Unity Court, where there is most likely to be a street hockey game going on, lived John Fitzgerald, Rose Kennedy's father. At 21 Unity St. is the **Clough House**, the second of the North End's two remaining eighteenth-century homes. Erected in 1715, it was one of a row of six identical houses, including one owned by Benjamin Franklin and inhabited by his sister. That house was razed at the time of the construction of the Mall. The Clough House was formerly the home of Ebenezer Clough, a member of the Sons of Liberty and one of the warpainted participants in the

Boston Tea Party. The building, which is not open to the public, has been restored and is used by Christ Church.

A short walk past the Clough House, through the tiny courtyard and up the stairs will bring you to the front of **Christ Church,** popularly known as **"Old North."** The name "Old North" is one that has been applied to several of the city's churches, but thanks to Paul Revere and Longfellow, Christ Church is by far the most famous. As the oldest church building in Boston, it is an official Freedom Trail site. It was built in 1723 as the second Anglican parish in the city. The pews are all numbered and labeled with the names of the original owners. Don't forget to notice the wine glass-shaped pulpit or the cherubim around the organ in the rear balcony. The latter were the gifts of Captain Thomas Gruchy, whose notoriety you will read about later.

"Old North" achieved its fame on the 18th of April in 1775 when its sexton Robert Newman hung two lanterns in its steeple as a signal that the British were advancing by sea toward Concord to seize arms stored there. Meanwhile, Paul Revere made his way with muffled oars under British gunboats across the Charles and began his famous ride. The lantern-hanging is re-enacted every year on the eve of Patriots Day.

Christ Church is surrounded by several little gardens that are quiet resting places. The Washington Memorial Garden is the best of these. The most curious of its many plaques is the one to the left of the entrance gate which commemorates the flight of John Childs from the steeple of the Church. It took place in 1757 in a bird-like contraption, and was authentic enough that the Colonial Dames donated the plaque at the time of the first transatlantic airplane crossing.

Leave the Old North Church area by way of Hull St., which begins at the front entrance of the Church. At **44 Hull St.** is a building reported to be the narrowest house in Boston. It's two hundred years old and has been the victim of several street widenings. Across the street is the entrance to the **Copp's Hill Burying Ground,** Boston's second oldest cemetery and an official Freedom Trail site. It was appropriated in 1660 when King's Chapel Burying Ground became too crowded. The Mathers, Robert Newman, Thomas Hutchinson, Sr., and others are all buried here. Stop and wander among the gravestones and pick out other notables.

The Snowhill St. side of the cemetery was originally reserved for slaves and freedmen, of whom over 1,000 are buried here. Prince Hall, founder of the African (Masonic) Grand Lodge of Massachusetts, is one of these and has a marker to the right of the Snowhill St. side pathway. The Mathers—Cotton, Increase, and Samuel—occupy a huge tomb near the Charter St. side and are surrounded by an iron railing. Cotton and Increase were the foremost ministers in the town, while Samuel was the man who negotiated the first provincial charter. One of Cotton Mather's most famous sermons at the Old North Church concerned "divine delights" and was delivered in 1686, two weeks after he had married Abigail Phillips. His most "divine delight", the young bridegroom confessed, was reading the Bible. In later years, Cotton Mather was to achieve his greatest prominence in the Massachusetts Bay Colony as its most persistent witch-hunter. He did, however, encourage inoculation against smallpox, even though he believed that "sickness is the whip of God for the sins of man."

Copp's Hill is best for epitaph-reading. One of the better ones is that of Peter Gilman:

Stop here my friend, and in a mirroir see,
What you though e'er so healthy soon must be
Beauty with all her rosebuds paints each face;
Approaching death will soon strip you of each grace.

There are numerous others equally as cheerful.

Leave the Burying Ground through the Hull St. gate. At the corner of Hull and Snowhill Streets, if you glance downtown, you can see Government Center, the Hancock, and the Prudential Center. Follow the trail around the tiny side street and back to Snowhill. At 53 Snowhill Street are the former studios of Robert Chase, designer of the Prado plaques.

A right turn at the top of the hill will bring you to Charter Street. It was here that the original charter for the Massachusetts Bay Colony was hidden after the British attempted to revoke it because it gave the settlement virtual autonomy. As you walk along Charter Street you are at the summit of Copp's Hill, the North End's highest point. During the Battle of Bunker Hill, the homes along Charter Street served as an excellent vantage point for spectators. Afterwards, the street was converted into a makeshift hospital for the wounded of both sides.

The Charter St. Playground on Copp's Hill Terrace on your left is a good place to rest before continuing your walk past the Burying Ground. Across the harbor from left to right you can see Charlestown, Chelsea, and East Boston. The gray obelisk off to the far left is the Bunker Hill monument. You are at the point where the British stationed their batteries and fired on Charlestown. At the foot of the hill, over to the left, is the site of Boston's first black settlement, "New Guinea."

A short walk up Charter Street to the corner of Salem will bring you to the site of the colonial mansion of William Phips, the first provincial governor of the Massachusetts Bay Colony. In 1745 Thomas Gruchy arrived in Boston from the Isle of Jersey and purchased the old Phips home. In its basement he constructed a 14-foot wide tunnel leading under Charter and Henchman Streets to the waterfront. At night mysterious ships would anchor in the harbor and there would be a bustle at the mouth of Gruchy's tunnel. In the morning, the ships would disappear. Captain Gruchy was a church deacon and a smuggler, using his secret tunnel to bring in plunder from Spanish galleons, thereby avoiding taxation. When it appeared that he might be caught, he threw a lavish party for all his friends. In the course of the evening Gruchy made a short speech and excused himself. Boston never saw him again.

Take a right turn onto Salem Street. At number 190 is the **Dodd House**, which was built in 1805 on a part of the old governor's estate. The Dodds were the last of the North End's old families and were deeply entrenched in the past, so much so that theirs was the last home in Boston to continue using its fireplace for cooking—well after stoves had come into common use.

Salem Street used to be the center of the clothing and millinery industries. In the 19th century it was an area of Jewish merchants and street peddlers, mostly Eastern European immigrants who first arrived in the 1850s. With each new set of arrivals, Salem Street was lined with wagons crammed with immigrants identifiable to their American relatives only by their name tags. For the next fifty years, the North End was the social and religious center of Greater Boston's Jewish community. The influx continued until the 1920s when the colony began to filter out to the suburbs. By 1950 the Jewish population of the area was negligible.

Salem St. today is distinctly Italo-American. This walk down from Copp's Hill is the final stretch of the North End Trail and should be taken leisurely. It is along here that you can get a sense of the area as a living community. In addition, the aroma of freshly-baked bread and pastry make a walk down Salem Street irresistible. At North Bennet St. is the Industrial School, while further up that street is the area where the first Italians—Genoese—settled in 1860. The butcher shops along Salem St. display their products in the open air. At Easter time whole lambs and goats hang in the windows. If you would like to get more of a feel for the area you might take a right on to Cooper St. and wander along the narrow side streets.

Continuing along Salem St., around the corner of Parmenter St. is the **North End Branch Library.** It was designed after a Roman villa with an open-air atrium, and houses a model of the Ducal Palace of Venice. In the summertime there are Italian-style puppet shows there. Behind the library is the home of DeFerrari, the street peddler who invested in the stock market and became a millionaire. He left a million dollars to the Boston Public Library and helped finance the addition to it. Across from the library is the North End Union where you can rest awhile and see an exhibit about the history of the North End.

At 99 Salem St. is the site of the oldest bakery in America, where bread was baked for the Continental Army. The foot of Salem St. today is a shoppers' mall and an open-air market similar to Haymarket. It's an appropriate place to conclude a walking tour of the North End. The mall will lead you to the pedestrian tunnel and back to Faneuil Hall.

CHARLESTOWN TRAIL

(*Map, pp. 144–145*)

Charlestown is older than Boston. It was founded in 1629 by a handful of settlers sent by the Massachusetts Bay Company to inhabit the company's holdings in New England. The group consisted of ten men, their families and their servants; they were joined one year later by John Winthrop, the first governor of the colony, and his shipload of Puritans. Their

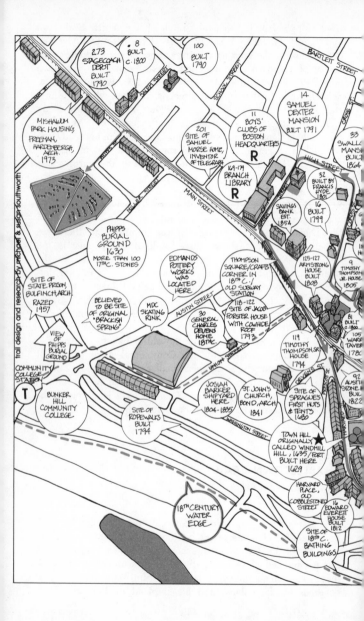

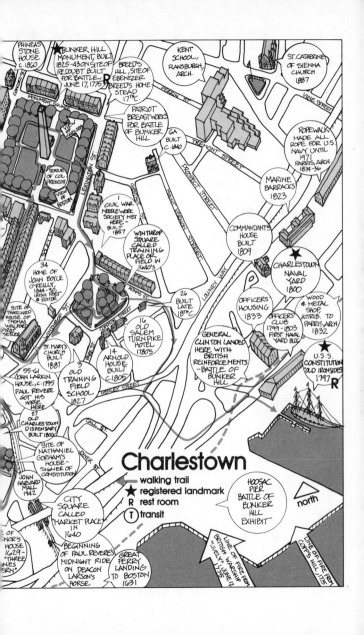

PHINEAS STONE HOUSE c. 1860

BUNKER HILL MONUMENT, BUILT 1825-43 ON SITE OF REDOUBT BUILT FOR BATTLE, JUNE 17, 1775 R

BREED'S HILL, SITE OF EBENEZER BREED'S HOMESTEAD 17TH C.

KENT SCHOOL, FLANSBURGH, ARCH.

ST. CATHERINE OF SIENNA CHURCH 1887

PATRIOT BREASTWORKS FOR BATTLE OF BUNKER HILL

GA BUILT c. 1840

ROPEWALK MADE ALL ROPE FOR U.S. NAVY UNTIL 1971 PARRIS, ARCH. 1834-36

MONUMENT SQUARE

VIEW OF BOSTON

STATUE OF COL. PRESCOTT

MARINE BARRACKS 1823

VIEW OF BOSTON

CIVIL WAR NEEDLEWORK SOCIETY MET HERE—BUILT 1867

WINTHROP SQUARE CALLED TRAINING PLACE OR FIELD IN 1640'S

COMMANDANT'S HOUSE BUILT 1809

CHARLESTOWN NAVAL YARD 1800

34 HOME OF JOHN BOYLE O'REILLY, 1844-90, IRISH POET & EDITOR

26 BUILT LATE 18TH C.

OFFICERS HOUSING 1833

WOOD & METAL SHOP ATTRIB. TO PARRIS, ARCH. 1832

SITE OF THATCHED HOUSE OF THOMAS WALFORD FIRST SETTLER

16 OLD SALEM TURNPIKE HOTEL 1780'S

OFFICERS CLUB 1799-1803 FIRST NAVAL YARD BLDG.

ST. MARY'S CHURCH BUILT 1887

14 ARNOLD HOUSE BUILT c. 1805

GENERAL CLINTON LANDED HERE WITH BRITISH REINFORCEMENTS—BATTLE OF BUNKER HILL

U.S.S. CONSTITUTION OLD IRONSIDES 1797 R

55-61 JOHN LARKIN HOUSE, c. 1795 PAUL REVERE GOT HIS HORSE HERE

3 OLD TRAINING FIELD SCHOOL 1827

27 OLD CHARLESTOWN DISPENSARY BUILT 1800

SITE OF NATHANIEL GORHAM'S HOUSE—SIGNER OF CONSTITUTION

JOHN HARVARD MALL 1942

OF -NOR'S HOUSE 1629— "THREE NES ERN"

CITY SQUARE CALLED "MARKET PLACE" IN 1640

Charlestown

★ walking trail
★ registered landmark
R rest room
T transit

HOOSAC PIER BATTLE OF BUNKER HILL EXHIBIT

north

BEGINNING OF PAUL REVERE'S MIDNIGHT RIDE ON DEACON LARSON'S HORSE

GREAT FERRY LANDING TO BOSTON 1631

LINE OF FIRE FROM BRITISH WARSHIP "LIVELY," JUNE 17, 1775

LINE OF FIRE FROM COPP'S HILL, 1775

first years were dogged by epidemics, fear of Indians, and a water supply so foul that it drove Winthrop to pack up half the colony and move across the Charles to a purer spring. Thus it was Charlestown's bad water that brought on the founding of Boston.

But the others remained loyal to their original site, and Charlestown grew. By the end of the 17th century it had formed a democratic town meeting, founded a church, a school and a mill, and even hanged Massachusetts's first witch. As colonial resentment of British authority deepened, Charlestown's sentiments kept pace with Boston's, and when the Revolution finally came, Charlestown was the site of its first major battle. Its citizens paid for Bunker Hill by seeing their town burned to the ground.

Rebuilding began the moment the war ended, and most of the fine 18th-century buildings on the trail are the product of new-born national enthusiasm. In 1786 a bridge between Charlestown and Boston opened amid shouts of, "You Charlestown Pigs, Put on your wigs, And come over to Boston town." By 1830, rudimentary public transit made it possible to commute, and the resultant boom created most of the buildings on Main St. An influx of Irish immigrants doubled Charlestown's population in the 1850s, and caused the introduction of multi-family and row houses.

The Navy Yard was built early in the 19th century, and soon became the town's chief employer, building 35 warships between 1825 and 1868. Shipbuilding flagged after the Civil War, although the Yard continued to supply the Navy with rope and anchor chain. But during World War II the Yard and Charlestown experienced a renaissance: between Pearl Harbor and 1945, 141 ships were built and 5000 were serviced.

Except for the wartime boom, the first half of the 20th century was a dark period for Charlestown. The Depression struck hard: businesses failed, employment slacked off, shops and houses were left to decay. But since the sixties an enthusiastic population and an active urban renewal program have wrought drastic changes. Private citizens have restored most of the 18th-century houses for their own use. The town's biggest triumph was the "Second Battle of Bunker Hill" over the future of the U.S.S. *Constitution* and the Navy Yard. Thanks to citizen action and proposals by the Boston Redevelopment Authority, the National Park Service has now decided to maintain the most historic portions of the Navy Yard as a park dedicated to "Old Ironsides."

From the new Community College station on the MBTA Orange Line, follow the map up Washington and Union Sts. to Thompson Square where the trail begins. The elaborate Victorian style of the old elevated station at Thompson Square is mirrored by the 120-year-old **Charlestown Savings Bank** across the street. You are opposite the **Thompson Square Triangle**, a triangular slice of land between Warren and Main that was long known as Craft's Corner, because Elias Craft kept an apothecary shop here until 1869. In that year, the City Council ordered the enlargement of the public square area, and it was renamed Thompson Square in honor of a prominent Charlestown family which had lived for years in the neighborhood. James Thompson had arrived with Winthrop in 1630, and Timothy fought at Bunker Hill.

The first building of note you pass is 125-27 Main, the **Armstrong House.** Samuel T. Armstrong started a printing shop on the street floor here in 1810. Among his customers were the members of the Universalist Society (forerunners of the Unitarians) who met upstairs in Edmands Hall, while the rest of Charlestown looked on in horror at their sinful doings.

Across the street from you is 118-22 Main St., now a vacant lot on the corner of Union. Pause in memory of Jacob Forster, who in 1793 built a house here and thatched the roof with cowhides, thinking they would keep him as dry as they had kept the cows. Unfortunately, he forgot the action of the sun, and on the first warm day the smell of Jacob's roof forced him and his irate neighbors to leave the area.

The **Timothy Thompson House** at 119 Main St. was built in 1794 by the Bunker Hill Timothy, who set up his carpentry shop here when he came home from the Revolution. Next door on the corner of Main and Pleasant is the old **Warren Tavern.** Built soon after the burning of the town, it belonged in 1780 to Eliphalet Newell, the baker. Before long it became the General Warren Tavern (named in honor of the hero of Bunker Hill), and was headquarters for King Solomon's Lodge, founded by the general's brother John, with Paul Revere as a charter member. It has been restored to resemble a 1790s tavern and is a good spot for lunch or a beer. See p. 273 for hours and prices. Before you leave Main St., go around the corner and up Pleasant for a glance at another of Timothy's homes, the beige **Thompson-Sawyer House.**

Now retrace your steps to the intersection of Main, Devens, Prescott and Harvard Sts. In 1630, Devens St. contained a group of huts and tents erected by the three Sprague brothers and their fellow colonists. Called Crooked Lane at that time, it later became Bow St., and contained fashionable brick houses with gardens and bathing piers on the river. The odd little stone house at the corner of Harvard and Main (**92 Main**) was built in 1822 by General Nathaniel Austin, a sheriff of Middlesex County who carried out the execution of "Mike Martin alias Captain Lightfoot," the last of the highwaymen. Turn up Harvard St. to Harvard Place, a cobblestone courtyard dating from before the Revolution, that takes off to your right.

Just beyond Harvard Place is the **Edward Everett House,** 16 Harvard St. Unquestionably the finest of the Federal houses in Charlestown, it was built by the merchant Matthew Bridge for his daughter in 1812 and purchased by statesman Edward Everett in 1830. A famous orator during the Civil War, Everett is best known today for his bad luck: he gave the two-hour speech that preceded Lincoln's Gettysburg Address!

Harvard St. now brings you down into **City Square,** which was the heart of colonial Charlestown and is still the major crossroads for traffic and pigeons. It began as the Market Place, the open area in front of the governor's mansion, which stood where Harvard Mall is now. This entire area is still collectively known as Town Hill, and is the site of the first permanent Charlestown settlement.

Harvard Mall is one block to your left as you enter the square from Harvard St. This is the spot where the colonists built a fort in 1629 for protection against the Indians. Later, deciding that no protection was necessary, they replaced the fort with a frame house for Governor Winthrop. The governor, however, took the house away with him when he accepted Blackstone's invitation to move across the Charles and found Boston. Undaunted, the remaining settlers built another mansion, the Great House, which became the legal, administrative and religious center of the infant colony. It housed the Court of Assistants (established in 1630; you pass a commemorative plaque on the police station en route to the Mall), the First Church (1632) and William Witherell's first school (1636).

By 1775, City Square was a bustling commercial center. It was from here that Paul Revere began his ride on the night of April 18, 1775. His journal reads, "When I got into (Charlestown), I met Colonel Conant and several others; they said they had seen our signals. I told them what was acting and went to get me a horse; I got a horse of Deacon Larkin."

The land for Harvard Mall was the gift of a Harvard alumnus to commemorate John Harvard, an early Charlestown inhabitant. Harvard settled on Town Hill in 1637, and "was sometime minister of God's word" in Charlestown. He died of consumption only a year after his arrival, at the age of 27, but gained immortality by bequeathing his library (320 books) and half his estate to the struggling college in Cambridge.

Turn right when you reach the John Harvard memorial, and leave the Mall through the gap in the wall between the two plaques. Facing you is **27 Harvard Square,** another diminutive split-stone house which served for years as the town dispensary.

Continue down Henley St. and turn left on **Main St.,** one of the oldest streets in town. In the early part of the 19th century, Main St. residents were often awakened by the horns of fox hunters galloping past. Later the part of Main nearest the bridge became a leather district, selling morocco goods from nearby factories. Most of the buildings you are passing are 19th-century, built to house shops and offices on the street level and families on the floors above. 55-61 Main, the newly painted white house on your right, is the post-Revolutionary **Deacon Larkin House** (built 1795), home of the man who loaned Paul Revere a horse. (Revere was captured by the British during the ride, and although they let him go, they made him trade horses with a British officer whose mount was tired. So Larkin never got the animal back.) The **John Hurd House** next door at 65-71 Main is of the same period. Both houses have lost some 18th-century detail with restoration.

Now turn right up 19th-century **Monument Ave.,** and climb the hill where the patriots first met the British in a major battle. The **Battle of Bunker Hill** began on the morning of June 17, 1775, when the sailors on board the British man-of-war *Lively* awoke to see a group of colonials busily fortifying the nearer of the two hills above Charlestown. They were acting specifically to draw British fire, since the American generals had learned that the British planned to attack Dorchester Heights and the hills above Charlestown on the following day, with the help of guns on Castle Island and the Neck. The success of such a maneuver would trap the colonial forces in Cambridge and insure British control of Boston.

The colonial ploy worked. General Howe advanced up the hill in textbook style with a force of about 3000 redcoats. The colonials, whose ammunition was low, obeyed Colonel Prescott's famous order not to fire "until you see the whites of their eyes." The volley which met the redcoats when they finally reached that range, fired by farmers who took pride in their marksmanship, is said to have mown down one-third of the advancing men. A second attack by Howe met with the same fate.

Howe then sent instructions to General Burgoyne to set fire to Charlestown, whose citizens had been sniping at him during the attack. While the town burned, Howe assaulted the hill again—this time successfully, thanks to the Americans' lack of powder. The colonials sustained most of their losses, including that of General Joseph Warren, during the ensuing retreat.

Although technically a British victory, the battle had decimated the British troops and left the remaining force stalemated in Boston harbor. American losses had been small, and the experience destroyed the patriots' awe of Britain's world-famous army. "I wish," said General Nathanael Greene, "that I could sell them another hill at the same price."

The hill where Ebenezer Breed pastured tame antelope has thus become a symbol of American initiative. Plans for a permanent monument and a public square got under way in 1822, and the obelisk that now stands on the site of the fortification was designed by Solomon Willard. You can climb to the top for the view of Boston.

Leave Monument Square via Winthrop Street and go downhill to **Winthrop Square.** This lovely spot, where late 18th and late 19th-century houses coexist peacefully, was for a century the Training Field used to teach Charlestown boys the art of war. From here, soldiers went on to fight in the Revolution, the War of 1812 and the Civil War. As you go around the square you'll pass the old **Salem Turnpike Hotel** at 16 Common St. and the yellow **Arnold House** at 14 Common St., both attractive Federal buildings dating from the early 1800s. The **Old Training Field School** (1827) on the west border of the square has been beautifully restored as a private residence.

From Winthrop Square you can follow the trail to the **Navy Yard** and "Old Ironsides" (see p. 236). If you'd rather visit the Navy Yard separately, continue down Winthrop St. and turn right on Warren past the site of the thatched hut of Thomas Walford, the smith who was Charlestown's first settler. He and his wife lived here alone in harmony with the Indians, but the Puritans threw him out of town by a court order two years after they arrived. The Walfords moved north to Piscataqua (now Portsmouth), where the smith became a wealthy and respected citizen. **81 Warren St.** is a striking Federal house built in the 1790s. The house at the back of the court, **81 1/2 Warren,** was built 75 years later, and the ensemble of houses and court has been restored to look as it did in the last century. Turn right at Pleasant St. to get a glimpse behind the chain-link fence of **81B Warren,** a charming little brown-shingled Georgian house with a gambrel roof.

Then come back to Warren and continue to Cordis St. Laid out by Captain Joseph Cordis in 1799, it reflects the post-Revolutionary building fervor that raised Charlestown from the ashes. On your left you pass **16 Cordis,** a small, dark brown Federal house built about 1799—probably the oldest on the street. **21 Cordis,** a Federal house dating from 1802, is made particularly lovely by fine brickwork and an adjoining tulip tree.

Turn left on High St. The block was part of the estate of Samuel Dexter, Secretary of the Treasury and of War under John Adams. (The President said of Dexter, "He was the ablest friend I had on earth.") As you turn left down Green St. to go back down the hill to Main, you'll pass the once-elegant **Dexter Mansion** at 14 Green, now in need of restoration.

At the bottom of the hill proceed down Main, take a left at Miller St. and continue to the **Phipps Street Burying Ground.** One of the three oldest cemeteries in Boston, this fascinating knoll provides the best historical record of pre-Revolutionary Charlestown. The reason is its unique layout: families were buried in rectangular plots, and the plots were arranged to correspond to the location of each family's house on Town Hill. Since the colonial town was burned, the graveyard has provided historians with the only surviving house-by-house map of its layout.

The oldest remaining tombstone, dating from 1652, is to your left as you approach the monument. Over 100 other stones from the 17th century survive: look for their simple Puritan style, showing only the name and date of death. The early 18th-century stones feature death's heads and angels, while the Federalists were partial to classical urns and willow designs.

Phipps Street Burying Ground is the last site on the trail. From here you can retrace your steps along Main St. to Thompson Square and catch the MBTA back to Boston.

WATERFRONT TRAIL
(*Map, p. 153*)

Boston was a born port. From Captain John Smith on, early visitors to the Bay praised the fine depth of the harbor, the natural breakwater provided by islands, and the beauty and protection of the surrounding hills. It took only a few years for early settlers to develop the town's possibilities: John Josselyn, a visitor in 1663, reported Boston houses as "for the most part raised on the Sea-banks and wharfed out with great industry and cost. . . ." "Wharfing-out" has gone on without pause ever since, including four major land fills which turned sea into city each time the port's business outgrew its berths.

The waterfront area survived the mid-19th-century changeover from sail to steam, but decline of foreign markets, the rise of the railroads and the growth of New York seriously undercut Boston trade. By the early 1920s many of the great wharves were in use only as fish piers and dwellings for the Bohemian "Wharf Rats." Waterfront buildings decayed gradually until the fifties, when an urban renewal program and resident action began to reverse the trend.

Start the trail at **Quincy Market,** where you can visit Boston 200's Revolution exhibit before setting out. The Market was the product of the first of many harbor landfills. In the early 1820s Mayor Josiah Quincy filled the part of the cove between Long Wharf and the Town Dock (which had existed since Puritan days, and still gives its name to the surrounding Dock Square). By the time of Quincy's administration the Town Dock had become a squalid area littered with oyster shells

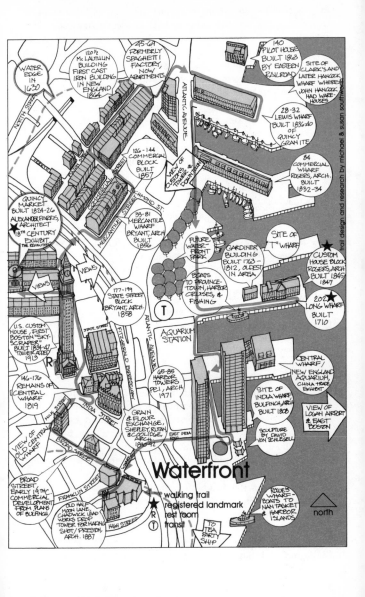

WATER EDGE IN 1620

McLAUGHLIN BUILDING FIRST CAST IRON BUILDING IN NEW ENGLAND 1864

120½

45-69 FORMERLY SPAGHETTI FACTORY, NOW APARTMENTS

140 PILOT HOUSE BUILT 1863 BY EASTERN RAILROAD

SITE OF CLARK'S AND LATER HANCOCK WHARF WHERE JOHN HANCOCK HAD WAREHOUSES

28-32 LEWIS WHARF BUILT 1836-40 OF QUINCY GRANITE

126-144 COMMERCIAL BLOCK BUILT 1857

84 COMMERCIAL WHARF ROGERS, ARCH. BUILT 1832-34

QUINCY MARKET BUILT 1824-26 ALEXANDER PARRIS, ARCHITECT 18TH CENTURY EXHIBIT THE REVOLUTION

33-81 MERCANTILE WHARF BRYANT, ARCH. 1856

SITE OF "T" WHARF

CUSTOM HOUSE BLOCK ROGERS, ARCH. BUILT 1845-1847

177-199 STATE STREET BLOCK BRYANT, ARCH. 1858

GARDINER BUILDING BUILT 1763-1812, OLDEST IN AREA

VIEWS

BOATS TO PROVINCETOWN, HARBOR CRUISES, & FISHING

202 LONG WHARF BUILT 1710

U.S. CUSTOM HOUSE, FIRST BOSTON "SKYSCRAPER" BUILT 1834-47 TOWER ADDED 1913

VIEWS

FUTURE WATERFRONT PARK

AQUARIUM STATION

CENTRAL WHARF / NEW ENGLAND AQUARIUM CHINA TRADE EXHIBIT

146-176 REMAINS OF CENTRAL WHARF 1819

65-85 HARBOR TOWERS PEI, ARCH. 1971

SITE OF INDIA WHARF BULFINCH, ARCH. BUILT 1808

VIEW OF LOGAN AIRPORT & EAST BOSTON

VIEW OF OLD CENTRAL WHARF

GRAIN & FLOUR EXCHANGE, SHEPLEY, RUTAN & COOLIDGE ARCH. 1890-92

SCULPTURE BY DAVID VON SCHLEGELL

BROAD STREET EARLY 19TH C COMMERCIAL DEVELOPMENT FROM PLANS OF BULFINCH

OLD HALF MOON LANE CHADWICK LEAD WORKS DROP TOWER FOR MAKING SHOT / PRESTI, ARCH. 1887

ROWES WHARF - BOATS TO NANTASKET & HARBOR ISLANDS

Waterfront

walking trail
★ registered landmark
R rest room
T transit

TO TEA PARTY SHIP

north

trail design and research by michael & susan southworth

and dead cats, so Quincy's project was an early attempt at urban renewal. On the new land Alexander Parris designed a majestic granite market building, flanked by granite warehouses. In honor of the Bicentennial the ensemble has been restored to much of its past elegance.

Follow the map from Quincy Market under the expressway and up Mercantile St. past the granite head of **Mercantile Wharf**. If Quincy Market represents the first of the granite wharf buildings, Mercantile Wharf is the last. Built in 1857, it shows you how business architecture had by then evolved a new style of commercial temple, more compatible with shopkeeping than the majestic market buildings. The design borrows from Renaissance palazzos, but at street level it uses heavy posts and lintels to create enlarged doorways where shopkeepers could display their wares. The original tenants of Mercantile Wharf were ships' chandlers, sail makers (who used the high roof and vast bays to stretch their sails) and riggers, who took advantage of the damp basement to store their ropes and thus increase their weight and price!

Turn left at Richmond St. and cross **Commercial St.** which parallels Mercantile St. Pause to look up and down Commercial, which in the 1830s and 40s ran along the very edge of Town Cove, and has been preserved intact as an outstanding example of early commercial architecture.

Continue to the end of Richmond and turn right on **Fulton St.** The oldest buildings on Fulton and Commercial are of brick, and combine earlier Federal upper stories with post-and-lintel shop fronts on the street floor. 120 Fulton is the **McLauthlin Building,** the earliest building in Boston with a complete cast-iron facade. This proto-skyscraper was built in 1863, during a period when iron first began to be used by builders who thought it was a fire-proof material. Other structures soon proved them wrong, but the McLauthlin Building never burned, and still houses the elevator company which originally owned it.

Turn right at the head of Fulton St. and pass the **Prince Building,** formerly the home of Prince Spaghetti and now a modern apartment house. Then head up Commercial toward the water, and cross busy **Atlantic Ave.,** which represents another drastic change in the Waterfront area. The avenue was built in the 1860s to provide a roadbed for a railroad line between North and South Stations. In the process, it sliced through many of the great wharf buildings, cutting off their heads from the sea. The railroad was a sign that the city was beginning to face inland, turning from the sea towards the rest of the country.

Now come out to the end of **Lewis Wharf** for your first full view of the harbor. This was the site of Thomas Clarke's wharf, one of the first wharves to be built and used for foreign trade during the British Civil War. Ships sailed from here to Africa with rum from the New England distilleries, exchanged it for slaves who were carried to West Indian plantations, then brought molasses north from the islands to be turned into more rum. Besides rum and slaves, Boston merchants traded other commodities with the islands, the southern colonies and Europe, usually in express defiance of English law, which sought to limit New England's export market to the mother country, or at least collect a share of the take from Boston's foreign trade. The colonials contested Britain's claims, declaring that "they were as much Englishmen as those in England, and had a right, therefore, to all the privileges which the people of England enjoyed." The battle began officially with the Navigation Acts in 1660, and continued unabated throughout the next 100 years.

Bostonians were brazen smugglers all during this period, but nobody was more brazen than John Hancock, who owned Clarke's Wharf by the 1760s. In June, 1768, one of Hancock's ships arrived from Madeira with a cargo of wine. When a customs officer came on board, Hancock's captain imprisoned him in the hold until the wine had been unloaded. The next morning the captain appeared at the Customs House with a few barrels, and vowed that it was his entire cargo. When officials tried to seize the ship, they were beaten almost senseless by a mob. As a result, a British regiment landed in Boston seven years before the battles of Lexington and Concord to restore order.

Lewis Wharf was built in the 1830s to match Commercial Wharf, and became a center of the clipper trade with China, Europe, Australia and Hawaii. Boston took up clipper building in 1850, when the outcry for rapid passage to California's gold fields, added to the quickening pace of the China tea trade, suddenly made it profitable to crew these complicated vessels.

Long, low and streamlined, clippers boasted a veritable forest of sails, which were manned by sailors who "worked like horses at sea and behaved like asses ashore." Boston's master-builder Donald McKay populated American ports with clippers for nearly thirty years, and every ship he built taught him lessons that made the next one better. "I am in love with the ship, a better sea boat or working ship or drier I never sailed in," wrote the master of McKay's first clipper, the *Staghound*. Even landlubbers agreed, and proved their devotion by placing huge wagers on the chances of McKay's ships beating all competitors in the runs to California, Liverpool or China. This they invariably did.

From Lewis Wharf you can look north to **Sargent's Wharf** with its massive **Quincy Cold Storage building**, a former refrigerator-warehouse whose fate is now in question. The attractive smaller brick building in the foreground is the **Pilot House**, built around 1863 and probably used as a land-sea transfer station for cargo traveling by rail. In 1972, renovators discovered a false floor in the building with storage space underneath, leading them to speculate that the building may also have been used by opium smugglers.

Commercial Wharf is the next wharf you come to as you continue down Atlantic Ave. Built in 1834, this was the first of the Greek revival wharf buildings. Isaiah Rogers designed the north side of "the best Charlestown brick" and the south side of Quincy granite. As Colonel Forbes remarks in *The Old Wharves of Boston,* "It was a hightoned wharf in those days and if a fishing smack or a lobster boat stuck its nose into the dock it would have been turned out instanter." However, by the 1870s the tone of the wharf had been lowered, and fishing vessels crowded the dock. Today the portion of the wharf that still fronts on the water contains offices and apartments.

As you walk from Commercial to Long Wharf look inland towards the granite Mercantile Wharf building and Commercial Block. The open area between these buildings and Atlantic Ave. closely approximates the line of the 19th-century Great Cove, and plans are under way for a waterfront park in this space. Between Commercial and Long Wharf was **T Wharf**, which extended parallel with the shore from Long Wharf with a crossbar running out into the harbor. T Wharf did a thriving business in fish and packet cargos until the early decades of this century. In 1909, old-timers claim, it was still

156

possible to walk from Long Wharf to T Wharf to Commercial Wharf on the decks of the vessels moored there.

Now walk out to the end of **Long Wharf,** which in colonial times was part of a road from the Old State House straight into the deepest part of the harbor. It was built in 1710 by Captain Oliver Noyes and lined with elegant brick warehouses in the same style as the Chart House Restaurant (the **Gardiner Building**), which is the only building that still survives from the late 18th century. At the head of the wharf was the Bunch of Grapes Tavern, once, in John Adams' words, a "breeding ground for bastards and legislators." To give you an idea of how long Long Wharf really was, the site of the tavern is now far inland on State Street (you saw it on the Freedom Trail).

John Hancock headed the Long Wharf Company in Revolutionary times, and may have had his office in the Gardiner Building. John Singleton Copley, the famous American portraitist, grew up on the wharf, where his mother kept a tobacco shop.

Long Wharf stayed busy throughout the 19th century, both as a merchant wharf and as the headquarters of the customs officials for Boston harbor. The granite **Customs House Block,** now used for shops and apartments, was built here in 1845 by Isaiah Rogers. Nathaniel Hawthorne served there as an inspector, and used to deal so mercilessly with sea captains that one of them, according to a contemporary account, "fled up the wharf . . . inquiring, with a sailor's emotions and a sailor's tongue, 'What, in God's name, have you sent on board my ship as an inspector?'" Hawthorne may have been impatient to get back to his writing—he was working on *Twice Told Tales* at the time.

Other milestones in Long Wharf history include the departure of the first missionaries to Hawaii in 1819 (described in James Michener's book), the arrival of the first bananas in New England in 1871, and the embarkation of Joshua Slocum in 1895 on a one-man voyage round the world in the *Spray.* The wharf also participated in the boom created in Boston by the California Gold Rush in the 1850s, when hundreds of cowboy-hatted New Englanders, drunk on whiskey and high hopes, departed for San Francisco. Donald McKay's *Flying Cloud,* the fastest ship ever built, was moored here briefly before being taken to New York by the company that owned it.

From the end of Long Wharf you can see the Greek temple

157

design at the end of Commercial Wharf. You can also take boats from here to Provincetown or the harbor islands, many of which have stories of their own. **George's Island** was used as a fort and a prison, and acquired a ghost during the Civil War. A woman was caught trying to help her Confederate husband escape from the prison, and he was executed. She was hanged soon after in widow's weeds, and her black-clad ghost is said to have haunted the island ever since. Another smaller harbor island is now known as **Nix's Mate** in honor of a pirate who was hanged there, and predicted that the island would disappear as proof of his innocence. Sure enough, it is now submerged at high tide.

Central Wharf, your next stop, now houses the excellent **New England Aquarium** (see p. 234). Stop to admire (but *not* feed) the seals and, if you like, visit the huge saltwater tank and the new mammal barge. During the Bicentennial the Aquarium will show a film called "Boston and the Sea," which was produced by the Museum of American China Trade—see it if you can. Central Wharf, which was completed in 1817, had its peak during the 19th-century cotton and fruit trade. It was part of an elaborate development financed by Uriah Cotting and designed by Charles Bulfinch, whose magnificent India Wharf building was destroyed in the 1960s to make way for the **Harbor Towers** (the two skyscrapers just south of you).

If you wish, you can continue along Atlantic Avenue to **Rowe's Wharf,** where boats leave for Nantasket Beach, George's Island, Hull and tours of the harbor. Following Atlantic Avenue further (see the map) will bring you to the **Boston Tea Party Ship and Museum** (see p. 224). Otherwise, follow the markers back under the expressway to **Broad St.** and the old financial district. Laid out to feed into **India Wharf,** the street has attractive early 19th-century brick buildings on the water side, and monumental granite ones on the land side. Turn left on Half Moon Lane to see a lead shot tower, once used by the Chadwick Lead works. Molten lead was dropped off the top of the tower, and on the way down it formed little balls of shot, which were hard by the time they reached the ground.

Continue up Broad to Milk St., and turn right to reach the **Grain Exchange,** a High Victorian fruitcake of a building by the firm of Shepley-Bulfinch. Across the street from it is the very old brick **Jenney Building,** once the head of Central

158

Wharf. Beyond is the **Boston Custom House,** the last granite shrine to commerce on your tour. Completed in 1847, it gained its tower in 1915 and became for a while the tallest building in Boston. If you arrive between 8am and 5pm on a weekday, take the elevator up to the observation floor for a last view of what Oliver Wendell Holmes called "the rebel bay."

BEACON HILL TRAIL
(*Map, pp. 160–161*)

Beacon Hill, the residential district for very proper Bostonians, was founded by a less than proper Anglican clergyman named William Blackstone. Blackstone came to Massachusetts in 1622, as pastor to a shipload of London ruffians under royal grant to colonize Shawmut peninsula. After a couple of years they returned to England, but Blackstone stayed, built a fine frame house for himself, planted an apple orchard, and led an uneventful existence until the Puritans arrived. "Shawmut's pioneer" liked strong drink and Indians, whereas the Puritans, who had settled on the opposite side of the river, liked neither. He further annoyed his strait-laced neighbors by riding his tame white bull up and down the beach at night. At the low point in their relationship, an outraged Puritan described Blackstone as a clergyman only in that he still had his clergyman's coat. The antipathy was mutual. But when the Puritans began to die from their foul water sources, Blackstone rode over to the Puritan colony and offered his spring and his territory. Governor Winthrop moved his colony to Blackstone's side of the river and Blackstone left Massachusetts for the more liberal atmosphere of Rhode Island.

The colony thrived. In 1634 the General Court ordered, "There shalbe forthwith a beacon sett on the sentry hill att Boston, to give notice to the country of any danger," and the area eventually took on the name of its principal landmark. The beacons of Beacon Hill have had a long if not entirely happy history. The Puritans' beacon, set up to warn

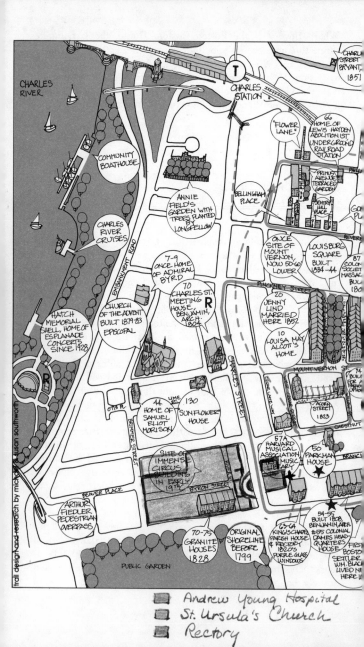

CHARLES STREET
BRYANT,
1851

CHARLES RIVER

T CHARLES STATION

"FLOWER LANE"

COMMUNITY BOATHOUSE

66 HOME OF LEWIS HAYDEN ABOLITIONIST UNDERGROUND RAILROAD STATION

PRIMUS AVENUE TERRACED GARDEN

PHILI

ANNIE FIELD'S GARDEN WITH TREES PLANTED BY LONGFELLOW

BELLINGHAM PLACE

SENTRY HILL PLACE

GO PLA

CHARLES RIVER CRUISES

ONCE SITE OF MOUNT VERNON, NOW 50-60 LOWER

REVER

7-9 ONCE HOME OF ADMIRAL BYRD

EMBANKMENT ROAD

LOUISBURG SQUARE BUILT 1834-44

87 COLO SOCIET MASSA BOU 180

70 CHARLES ST. MEETING HOUSE, BENJAMIN, ARCH. 1804

R

PINCKNEY STREET

20 JENNY LIND MARRIED HERE 1852

HATCH MEMORIAL SHELL, HOME OF ESPLANADE CONCERTS SINCE 1928

CHURCH OF THE ADVENT BUILT 1879-83 EPISCOPAL

10 LOUISA MAY ALCOTT'S HOME

R

MOUNT VERNON

74 BUILT FOR COPH

CHARLES STREET

WEST CEDAR STREET

ACORN STREET 1823

OTIS PL.

44 HOME OF SAMUEL ELIOT MORISON

LIME ST. 130 SUN FLOWER HOUSE

CHESTNUT

BRIMMER STREET

57A HARVARD MUSICAL ASSOCIATION, MUSIC LIBRARY

50 PARKMAN HOUSE

BRANC

SITE OF IMMENSE CIRCUS BUILDING IN EARLY 19TH

BYRON STREET

BEAVER PLACE

ARTHUR FIEDLER PEDESTRIAN OVERPASS

54-55 BUILT 1808 BENJAMIN, ARCH #55 COLONIAL DAMES HEAD-QUARTERS HOUSE

70-75 GRANITE HOUSES 1828

ORIGINAL SHORELINE BEFORE 1799

63-64 KING'SCHAPEL PARISH HOUSE & RECTORY 1820s PURPLE GLASS WINDOWS

FIRST BOSTON SETTLER WM. BLACK LIVED NI HERE 16

PUBLIC GARDEN

[trail design and research by michael & susan southworth]

Andrew Young Hospital

St. Ursula's Church

Rectory

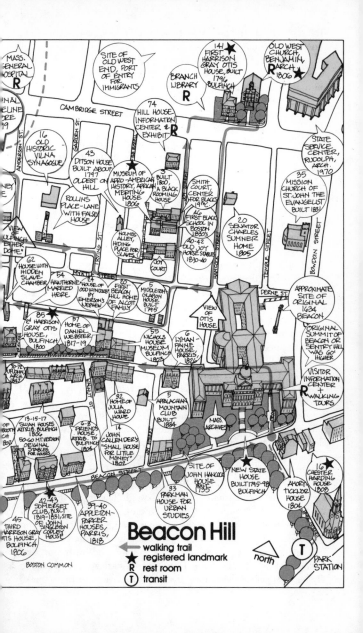

MASS. GENERAL HOSPITAL R

SITE OF OLD WEST END, PORT OF ENTRY FOR IMMIGRANTS

141 ★ FIRST HARRISON GRAY OTIS HOUSE, BUILT 1796 BULFINCH

OLD WEST CHURCH, BENJAMIN, ARCH 1806 ★

BRANCH LIBRARY R

...INE ...RE ...9

CAMBRIDGE STREET

16 OLD HISTORIC VILNA SYNAGOGUE

43 DITSON HOUSE BUILT ABOUT 1797 OLDEST ON HILL

74 HILL HOUSE INFORMATION CENTER & EXHIBIT R

STATE SERVICE CENTER, RUDOLPH, ARCH. 1970

...NEY

...E

ROLLINS PLACE-LANE WITH FALSE HOUSE

MUSEUM OF AFRO-AMERICAN HISTORY, AFRICAN MEETING HOUSE 1806

BUILT 1800, A BLACK ROOMING HOUSE

SMITH COURT, CENTER FOR BLACKS 1800's

35 MISSION CHURCH OF ST.JOHN THE EVANGELIST BUILT 1831

...VIEW ...ULFINCH ...THE "S ...DOME"

HOLMES ALLEY, HIDING PLACE FOR SLAVES

46 FIRST BLACK SCHOOL IN BOSTON 1830's

20 SENATOR CHARLES SUMNER HOME 1805

40-42 OLD JOY HORSE STABLES 1830-40

JOY COURT

62 HOUSE WITH HIDDEN SLAVE CHAMBER

54 HAWTHORNE MARRIED HERE

4 HOUSE OF ODD WINDOWS BY EMERSON'S NEPHEW

20 FIRST BEACON HILL HOME OF ALCOTT FAMILY

5 MIDDLETON GLAPION HOUSE BUILT 1795

MYRTLE STREET

APPROXIMATE SITE OF ORIGINAL 1634 BEACON

DERNE ST

VIEW OF OTIS HOUSE

85 ★ 2d HARRISON GRAY OTIS HOUSE, BULFINCH 1800

57 HOME OF DANIEL WEBSTER 1817-19

55 NICHOLS HOUSE MUSEUM BULFINCH 1803

6 LYMAN-PAINE HOUSE, PARRIS, 1824

ORIGINAL SUMMIT OF BEACON OR SENTRY HILL WAS 60' HIGHER

VISITOR INFORMATION CENTER + R WALKING TOURS

...URBAN ...ARCH ...1847

32 HOME OF JULIA WARD HOWE

5 APPALACHIAN MOUNTAIN CLUB BUILT 1884

MASS. ARCHIVES

...OF ...BOOTH ...CH 802

13-15-17 SWAN HOUSES ATTRIB. BULFINCH 1806

50-60 MT.VERNON ORIGINAL STABLES FOR HOUSES

6-8 FRIENDS HOUSE, ATTRIB. TO BULFINCH 1804

14 JOHN CALLENDER'S "SMALL HOUSE FOR LITTLE MONEY" 1802

SITE OF JOHN HANCOCK HOUSE BUILT 1725

NEW STATE HOUSE BUILT 1795-98 BULFINCH

16 ★ CHESTER HARDING HOUSE 1808

BEACON STREET

42-43 SOMERSET CLUB, BUILT 1819-1831, SITE OF JOHN SINGLETON COPLEY HOUSE

59-40 APPLETON-PARKER HOUSES, PARRIS, 1818

33 PARKMAN HOUSE FOR URBAN STUDIES

★ AMORY-TICKNOR HOUSE 1804

T PARK STATION

45 THIRD HARRISON GRAY OTIS HOUSE, BULFINCH 1806

BOSTON COMMON

Beacon Hill

→ walking trail
★ registered landmark
R rest room
T transit

north

the colony of Indians and foreign invaders, was torn down once the settlement was adequately fortified. In 1768 the Sons of Liberty built a new beacon to warn the town of British hostilities (and to irritate the British), but after the Revolution it was blown down by the wind. At this point the city commissioned Charles Bulfinch, Boston's foremost architect, to design a monument for the site. This monument barely lasted twenty years. In 1807 John Hancock's heirs claimed part of the hill as their property and quarried gravel from it to sell for land fills. The monument literally had the ground carted away from under it. After it had been pulled down, the plaques and eagle were stored in the State House and then incorporated into the present monument, a copy of the Bulfinch original, which now stands in the State House parking lot.

Most of the building on Beacon Hill occurred in the first quarter of the 18th century and necessitated leveling the three hills of the area: Mount Vernon (north of Louisburg Sq.); Pemberton Hill (now the Pemberton Sq. area); and Beacon, or Sentry, Hill (now the State House parking lot). About sixty feet was sheared from each summit, and Beacon Hill as we know it today came into existence.

Residents of the Hill today take pride in living in the only downtown area of a large American city that has been residential since its founding. Of all the neighborhoods in traditional Boston, this is the most unswervingly traditional. Gas streetlights burn day and night, and the brick sidewalks were saved from destruction in 1947 by the ferocious ladies of West Cedar St., who sat upon them to prevent their removal. Conservatism is now law: the Beacon Hill Architectural Commission prevents any outward change, even a flashily painted door, if it offends the Hill's good taste.

You will, however, notice a difference in ambience from block to block. Mount Vernon, Chestnut and other south slope streets house well-to-do families and rising professionals: manicured gardens and small children abound. The north slope runs more to students and prosperous hippies, and the evidence of dogs—present everywhere—becomes alarmingly frequent. But the one emotion that unites Hill residents is a fierce love of privacy. Streets are narrow and one-way and restrooms are absent (except in the State House and Charles Street Meeting House) specifically because the Hill does not mean to make exploration easy. Remember as you walk that all the houses are private except the ones we note as museums.

Begin your tour from the MBTA station at **Park St.,** the first subway station in the country and now a National Historic Landmark. From here enter the Boston Common and walk up to the gold-domed Massachusetts State House.

Set aside by the Puritans in 1634, the **Boston Common** served as cow pasture, militia training ground and public park for over two hundred years. By the early 19th century, however, it became apparent that the cows, soldiers and ordinary citizens were incompatible. The militia accidently shot some cows while practicing for the War of 1812 and the cows in their turn (so complained Mayor Josiah Quincy) were not polite to the ladies. Eventually the cows and soldiers went elsewhere, but the people who just wanted a place to sit or stroll remained—and so it is today.

Exit from the Common in front of the **State House.** The building was designed in 1795 by Charles Bulfinch, but the distinctive gold-leaf on the dome was not added until 1861. You can enter the State House by the side-door in the right wing (the big double doors at the front entrance are opened only for important ceremonial occasions) and then head for Doric Hall, where you can ask questions and pick up pamphlets. In the House Chamber hangs the much-celebrated wooden codfish, "a memorial of the importance of the Cod Fishery to the welfare of this Commonwealth." After his visit to Boston, Davy Crockett commented that the codfish was a natural symbolic gesture for the people of Massachusetts to make, and that he kept bearpaws and a pair of antlers in his own house. The **Archives Museum,** which you reach by a convoluted path through the basement, houses some of the oldest and most important documents of American history. The Museum collection includes the Massachusetts Constitution, the oldest written constitution in the world still in effect, as well as Governor Bradford's *Of Plimoth Plantation,* a chronicle of the Pilgrims from their gathering in England through their first years in the New World. Americans thought they had lost the precious Bradford manuscript during the Revolution, but over a hundred years later it turned up in the library of the Bishop of London. (Nobody knows how it got there.)

After considerable haggling the document was returned to Boston. When you've finished with the sights inside the State House, exit by the Mount Vernon St. doors.

Henry James called **Mount Vernon** "the only respectable street in America." Stroll down it at an easy pace and pretend you're in the 19th century. 32 was once the home of Julia Ward Howe, who wrote "The Battle Hymn of the Republic." The Howes gave some of the best parties in Boston (among them a reception for General Grant and a breakfast for Bret Harte), at the end of which Julia sang "The Battle Hymn" if requested by her guests. **55 Mount Vernon,** now open to the public (Wed and Sat, 1pm to 5pm, $1 admission), was once the home of Rose Nichols, a writer and landscape architect.

After you tour the delightful Nichols house, continue a short way down the street to **57 Mt. Vernon.** This house was the residence of Daniel Webster for a short time, and afterwards the home of Charles Francis Adams. Adams was ambassador to England during the Civil War and did much to prevent an alliance between that country and the Confederacy. You may know him, however, as the father of writer Henry Adams. Henry Adams spent his boyhood in this house, whose location in the heart of Beacon Hill made it an excellent observation post for proper Boston. Apparently Henry observed very well. He once turned down a teaching job at Harvard because, he said, he knew "nothing of history, less about teaching, and too much about Harvard." As for Beacon Hill, it "lowered the pulsations of his heart."

At the intersection of Mount Vernon and Walnut Sts. is **14 Walnut St.,** built in 1802 for John Callendar. Dr. John Joy (after whom Joy St. is named) sold a corner of his garden to Callendar and later mentioned to a friend that Callendar wished to build "a small house finished for little money"—a phrase by which the house has been known ever since.

Continue down Mount Vernon. Pause for a second at **85 Mount Vernon,** the second of Harrison Gray Otis's three Beacon Hill homes. After only six years Otis moved from here to the more prestigious neighborhood overlooking the Common. More recently, this house attained fame as the abode of film heroes —in *The Thomas Crown Affair* and in television's "Banacek."

Now take a left down Willow St. until you come to a stone-lined trench. This is **Acorn St.,** one of the few old cobblestone streets left on Beacon Hill. Coachmen for nearby mansions used to live here, but now a more elite class fights for a chance to occupy these charming houses.

Once back on Willow continue to Chestnut and stop at **50 Chestnut,** the former home of historian Francis Parkman. Then go up West Cedar and turn right on Mount Vernon until you come to renowned **Louisburg Square.** (Pronounce the *s* in Louisburg.) The Square is one of the most popular sights in the city, and photographs of it turn up everywhere, including the cover of the Boston telephone directory. As you walk through, keep an eye open for 10 (the former home of Louisa May Alcott) and 20 (the place where Jenny Lind married her accompanist Otto Goldschmidt). The park itself is private; only the house owners have keys.

You are almost halfway through the south loop of the trail. If you want to do only the south loop today, continue with the text below. But if you plan to complete both the north and south loops in one day, start the north loop now from Louisburg Square by following the map to 62 Pinckney St., the Hillard house. Turn to p. 167 for the text of the north slope loop.

Turn left down Pinckney and left on Charles St. until you come to the **Meeting House** at 70 Charles. Back in the days when the waterline was closer (and the river was cleaner) the building housed the Third Baptist Church and baptisms took place in the Charles. But the Meeting House is best known as the forum for many anti-slavery speakers. William Lloyd Garrison spoke here, as did Wendell Phillips, Frederick Douglas, Harriet Tubman, and Sojourner Truth. Nowadays the building is still dedicated to radical causes (as you'll discover by the posters in the basement snack bar), but the main hall is closed to visitors unless you can persuade somebody to give you a quick tour.

Now turn onto the last leg of the trail, Beacon St. Oliver Wendell Holmes accurately described Beacon as "the sunny street for the sifted few"—the most exclusive section of Beacon Hill in the 19th century.

At **63-64 Beacon** you can see a few panes of the famous Beacon Hill purple glass. Between 1818 and 1824 some residents of the Hill installed ordinary glass from England in their windows, only to see their windows gradually become a rosy lavender color. Sunlight reacting with impurities in the glass caused this phenomenon. The windows created so much attention that the English manufacturers tried to duplicate their original error. When they finally succeeded, however, residents of the Hill without purple windows turned up their noses at the new batch of glass. It lacked tradition, they said, and tradition is the only thing that matters on Beacon Hill.

Stop at **Spruce St.** According to legend, this is the site of William Blackstone's original settlement. The river used to run close by here in Blackstone's day (where Charles St. is today), and if you compare the site with the river's present location, you'll get some idea of how much land has been filled in since the 17th century.

The Puritans moved to this side of the river for Blackstone's excellent spring, whose location historians speculated about for years. Most of them thought it was near Louisburg Square, even though that would have meant a long daily hike for Blackstone. But many years ago a spring broke through the cellar of a house near Chestnut and Spruce Sts. (that would be the second intersection from where you stand) and they asked: Is this Blackstone's spring resurfacing? The owner of the house was less impressed by the historical significance of the event. He had to pump out his cellar at considerable cost and (it is reported) his wife had to give up a new bonnet.

Now walk to **45 Beacon St.,** known as the third Harrison Gray Otis house (built in 1806 by Bulfinch). Otis was a rich landholder-merchant of the early 19th century, whose lavish parties and gold-trimmed clothes were the talk of the town. Every day his servants filled a Lowestoft punchbowl near the stairway with ten gallons of punch, so that his guests had something to sustain them on their way up to the second floor drawing room. Otis himself breakfasted on paté de foie gras, followed by lunch at noon, dinner around three, and supper at eight or nine. Although this high style of living appears not to have shortened his life—he lived to be eighty—Otis spent his last forty years suffering from gout.

From the Otis house continue up Beacon St. (past 42-43, the site of portraitist John Singleton Copley's house) to 39-40, the **Appleton-Parker houses,** now the Women's City Club (open Mon, Wed, and Fri, from 10am to 4pm, admission $1.50). You can tour the Appleton-Parker houses (and see the room where Longfellow married Fanny Appleton), but keep in mind that the house has not been restored to reflect the style of the 19th century.

Approaching the State House you'll pass double gates with plaques that mark the site of **John Hancock's house.** During the Revolution Mrs. Hancock, the formidable Dorothy Quincy, wrote a letter to British authorities and complained that the British soldiers training on the Common were disturbing her with all their noise. History does not record the British Army's reply.

Now that you've seen where the aristocrats lived, move on to the north slopes, historically the wrong side of the tracks. Not that *all* the residents of the north slopes were disreputable. Many well-to-do families lived on the eastern end of Cambridge St. (Harrison Gray Otis's first house is here) and black servants and artisans occupied the neighborhoods off Joy St. It was the area north of Louisburg Square which lacked respectability. Until 1823 it was the red-light district of Boston, unflinchingly called Mount Whoredom (sometimes spelled "Hoardam" on maps to spare the sensitive). In 1775 a visiting British officer commented about the city: "No such thing as a play house, they were too puritanical a set to admit of such lewd Diversions, tho' ther's perhaps no town of its size cou'd turn out more whores than this cou'd."

Of course this area aroused disapproval from the natives. As a Boston minister thundered, "Here, week after week, whole nights are spent in drinking and carousing; and as the morning light begins to appear, when others arise from their beds, these close their doors." The inhabitants, he pointed out, numbered "three hundred females wholly devoid of modesty and shame." But Boston's growth as a port proved stronger than Puritan fulminations. Even the development of the north slopes around 1800 failed to change the area's distinctive character. In 1823, however, after one-too-many sailors' brawls, Mayor Josiah Quincy locked up the inhabitants of Mount Whoredom in his new House of Correction, "cleaned up" the area, and began its transformation into a neighborhood for middle class and working people.

Begin your tour of the north slopes at **Pinckney St.,** the dividing line between the two slopes of the Hill. When the

Mount Vernon Proprietors began to develop the area, they were careful to insulate the elite of the south slopes from the masses settling in the north. Thus the Pinckney St. block is unusually long, with only three connecting streets between the two slopes.

Near the corner of Joy and Pinckney, pause at **5 Pinckney,** one of the oldest houses on the Hill. It was built in 1795 for George Middleton, a black coachman, and Louis Glapion, a black barber. Middleton fought in the Revolution. Farther up the street, at **20 Pinckney,** is the house Louisa May Alcott and her family occupied in their poorer days. Louisa's father, Bronson Alcott, was an idealistic philosopher who dabbled in utopian schemes but who was never quite able to support his family. A contemporary said of Alcott and his associates: "They dove into the Infinite, they soared into the Illimitable. And they *never* paid cash!" Fortunately Louisa was a practical person, and after she made money from her books the family moved to the more prosperous neighborhood of Louisburg Square.

Pause briefly at **62 Pinckney St.,** the home of the Hillard family in the days of the Underground Railroad. George Hillard was a U. S. commissioner whose job it was to issue warrants for fugitive slaves, and his wife was an abolitionist who reportedly hid slaves in their house without his knowledge. The stories about Mrs. Hillard's activities were unconfirmed until repairs were made at the turn of the century, and a hidden trapdoor in the ceiling fell on a workman's head. They found a cubbyhole under the roof large enough to hold several people, with two plates and two spoons on the floor.

Now return to the intersection at Anderson St., proceed along Anderson and then turn left on Revere. As you go down Revere you'll pass small private courts lined with red brick houses built around 1845. You might give a glance to **Goodwin Place,** at 73; **Sentry Hill Place,** at 79; and **Bellingham Place,** at 85.

From here continue to West Cedar St. and turn onto Phillips St. Then walk on to **66 Phillips,** formerly the home of abolitionists Lewis and Harriet Hayden. The Haydens were black leaders of the Underground Railroad and their home was one of the better-known "stops" in Boston. Although authorities knew about the Haydens' activities, they never searched their house for runaway slaves. The Haydens reportedly kept a keg of gunpowder in their basement and threatened to blow them all up if they ever came.

Walk on. Take a right on Anderson and then a left on Revere. Stop at **Rollins Place,** 27 Revere, a private court with red brick houses and (what looks like) an elaborate white porticoed house at one end. The white house is just a decorative wall—there's no house there. Years ago residents constructed the facade to prevent careless people from dropping off the 40-foot cliff behind it. After you've looked it over to your satisfaction, take a right at the end of Revere, and then a left on Myrtle.

Turn down South Russell St. until you come to 43, the **Ditson House,** built around 1797 by a trader named Joseph Ditson. It's one of the oldest houses on the Hill. Now walk up the street and look for an arched tunnel on your left. This is **Holmes Alley,** which was once used to hide fugitive slaves. Retrace your steps up South Russell, continue along Myrtle, and then turn left on Joy St.

The art studio at **40-42 Joy** was once a pair of stables, separate but identical, which were built by two brothers who didn't want to fight over sharing one. If you go in you can see the original stalls and feeders, now overflowing with artistic paraphernalia. A little farther down the street is **46 Joy,** where residents established the first black school in Boston around 1830. The school closed after ten years when the children were integrated into other Boston schools.

Now turn into **Smith Court,** one of the first settlements made by the blacks when they moved from the North End to Beacon Hill. The colonial brick building on your left, now the **Museum of Afro-American History,** was first used as a church and has been facetiously called "the haven from the loft"—the "loft" being the Old North Church, where blacks were allowed to sit only in the galleries. In 1832 William Lloyd Garrison held here the first meeting of the New England Anti-Slavery Society. At the conclusion of the meeting he said: "We have met tonight in this obscure schoolhouse; our numbers are few and our influence limited, but mark my prediction, Faneuil Hall shall ere long echo with the principles we have set forth. We shall shake the nation by their mighty power."

Once back on Joy St., continue down the street and turn right on Cambridge to 141 Cambridge, the first **Harrison Gray Otis House** (open Mon-Fri, 10am to 4pm, admission $1).

If you tour only one house on Beacon Hill, this should be it. The Society for the Preservation of New England Antiquities has painstakingly and lovingly restored it to the style popular in the early 19th century. All the details of the house are authentic, from the frivolous canary-yellow wallpaper to the mirror-panelled doors for reflecting candlelight. If you're lucky, your guide will demonstrate the art of pulling up 19th-century window curtains.

Also open to the public is the **Old West Church** next door. The original building was razed in 1775 when the British thought the Americans were using its steeple to signal Continental troops in Cambridge. In 1806 it was replaced by the present church, designed by Asher Benjamin.

Those of you who are walking both the north and south loops in one day should now return to Louisburg Square, off Pinckney St., and resume the south loop of the trail. (Pick up the text on p. 165.) But those of you who are finished for the day should walk up Hancock St. back to the State House. From there you can head for Tremont St., have an ice cream cone at Brigham's or Bailey's, and congratulate yourself for finishing the Beacon Hill trail.

SOUTH END—BAY VILLAGE TRAIL

(*Map, pp. 172–173*)

The South End has seen more demographic, economic, and even geographic changes than any other Boston district. Various ethnic groups have come and gone, factories have opened and closed, marshes have been converted into dry land. The South End's heyday came and went in the 19th century. After Beacon Hill reached full development and before Back Bay was rescued from its swamp, the South End enjoyed a very brief popularity. In the late 1840s and 50s, several handsome parks surrounded by townhouses—Union and Chester Parks—and a few honest-to-goodness mansions—the Allen and Deacon Houses on Washington St.—were completed. But when Back Bay opened, those who could afford the second move left and the South End fell to the *nouveau riche,* like William Dean

Howell's hero Silas Lapham, who "bought very cheap of a terrified gentleman of good extraction who discovered too late that the South End was not the thing." After the panic of 1873, the South End experienced a building boom, and the combination of these two events irretrievably transformed the neighborhood, opening it to industry and immigration. Many owners of residential property had been repossessed during the panic, and the banks sold their land to businessmen and divided homes into flats and boarding houses. Factories came, and the Irish, the Freedman, and the East European immigrant followed.

This is a tour for city-watchers, not for sight-seers. The South End is a grab-bag of ethnic and income groups: elderly people living on fixed incomes, newlyweds, and middle-aged millionaires share the same block. The black, Spanish-speaking, and Syrian and Lebanese communities are three of the most dynamic influences, but in a neighborhood composed of over forty different nationalities, no one of them can ever dominate. The South End has been an urban renewal project since 1965, which accounts not only for much of its special vitality, but also for its transitional struggles. New neighborhood organizations proliferate and continue to grope for political identity. Property values are rising—houses on Union Park sell for $120,000—but many of the poor still live in substandard housing. The South End hasn't decided whether to tempt the middle-class away from the suburbs or build low-cost apartment complexes; its future is open-ended.

The South End's problems are those which every city faces, but not all neighborhoods can command the same loyalty and concern from the residents. Neighborhood patrols have been organized, families are fighting for better schools, clean-up campaigns and tree-planting projects abound. It is no longer fashionable to move *out* of the South End.

Visit the South End late in the morning or early in the afternoon, when it's safe but lively. Women alone will be verbally harassed (in a wide selection of dialects), winos may appear on every other street corner, and restaurants and restrooms are few and on the tawdry side. But a visit to the South End will give you a richer picture of urban life than the view from the Hancock tower ever could. It is a neighborhood with a mind of its own. Robert Woods, Boston social

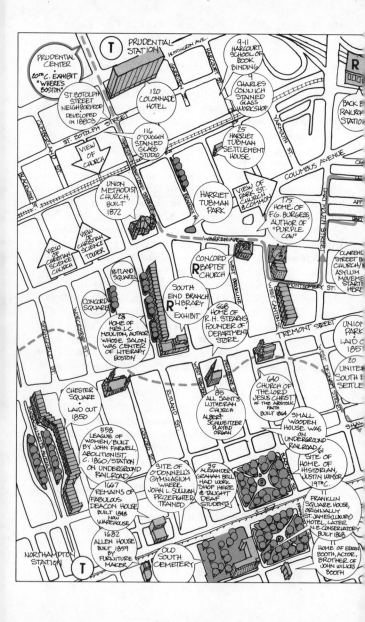

FIRST CORPS OF CADETS ARMORY, 1891

19TH C. EXHIBIT "THE GRAND EXPOSITION"

12 HAYNE'S FLUTE FACTORY, MAKERS OF WORLD FAMOUS FLUTES

SITE OF HOME OF CHILDE HASSAM ARTIST IN EARLY 1880'S

OUR LADY OF VICTORIES CHURCH, MARIST FATHERS

PIEDMONT

ARLINGTON STREET

FAYETTE

Bay Village

BAY ST. SHORTEST STREET IN BOSTON, WITH ONE OF SMALLEST HOUSES

BERKELEY STREET

85-89 MORGAN MEMORIAL GOLDMINE OF USED MERCHANDISE

HERALD STREET

SITE OF WILLIAM COLBURN'S PASTURE 17TH C.

CLARENDON STREET

539 CYCLORAMA BUILDING, 1884, HOUSED GETTYSBURG CYCLORAMA

NOW BOSTON CENTER FOR THE ARTS

R

41-43 FRANKLIN INSTITUTE ESTABLISHED THROUGH BEQUEST OF BEN FRANKLIN

SITE OF CASTLE ST. & STAGE COACH TO NEWPORT 1737

HOLY TRINITY ROMAN CATHOLIC CHURCH

SITE OF THREE PENNY LUNCH BREAD 1¢ SOUP 1¢ COFFEE 1¢

SITE OF FAMOUS 19TH CENTURY DUPLAIN'S FRENCH BAKERY

SOME OF LAST REMAINING 19TH CENTURY TENEMENTS

NATIONAL THEATER OLD VAUDEVILLE HOUSE 1911

GOOD VIEWS OF SOUTH END FROM ELEVATED TRAIN

"THE NECK" WATER EDGE IN 1630

DOVER ST.

EIGHT STREETS PARK

DOVER STATION

T

HOME OF S.S. PIERCE FAMOUS BOSTON FOOD MERCHANT

BERKELEY STREET

SITE OF TOWN GATE & FORT 1710

TRAVELER ST.

1303-1311 REMAINS OF ELEGANT OLD "CONTINENTAL" HOTEL

SYRIAN & LEBANESE SHOPS & CLUBS

WASHINGTON STREET

SITE OF FIRST TOWN GALLOWS 17TH C.

"REED BLOCK" HANDSOME 19TH CENTURY INDUSTRIAL BUILDING

60 EMPTY FIRE STATION MODELED AFTER PALAZZO VECCHIO IN FLORENCE

SITE OF DOVER STREET FLOATING BATH HOUSE, FIRST PUBLIC BATH HOUSE IN U.S.

ST. JOHN THE BAPTIST GREEK ORTHODOX CHURCH

HARRISON AVENUE

BANGOR ST.

SITE OF FIRST BRIDGE TO SOUTH BOSTON 1805

CATHEDRAL OF THE HOLY CROSS, KEELEY, ARCH. BUILT 1867-75

SITE OF SECOND TOWN GALLOWS/ANN HIBBENS HANGED HERE FOR WITCHCRAFT 1656

South End

UNION PARK ST.

← walking trail
★ registered landmark
R rest room
T transit

north

worker and social critic, had the South End in mind when he titled one of his books *The City Wilderness*. To enjoy your tour, you must also explore the community. Watch the street instead of the rooftops.

Start at the Prudential MBTA station on the Green line. You should visit the Boston 200 **Where's Boston** exhibit at the Pru before you begin walking. As you cross Huntington Ave., the modern austerity of the Colonnade Hotel separates downtown from the South End. Turn left on W. Newton St., typical of the faded gentility which the South End evokes. The community as a whole is coherent in design, due to the systematic planning and building which occurred during the mid-19th century. Like modest versions of the High Victorian homes of Back Bay, these buildings have considerable ornamentation but are more conservative in plan and elevation. The homes have withstood the neglect they met in the past, and even those buildings in bad internal condition appear solid from the outside. You will learn to read the character of a neighborhood by the freshness of the paint on the windowsills, the language spoken on the corner, the flowers in the window boxes, the display in the local delicatessen. Many of the streets look alike at first glance, but each has a distinct personality.

Farther down W. Newton, the railroad tracks cut a swath across the city and give a strange sense of openness to the densely populated South End. From this spot the city seems to rise around you, complete with views of the old and new Hancock buildings and Prudential Center. The coming of the railroad brought the immigrant and drove away those who could afford to escape the soot, noise and disease. These newcomers built churches whose style, form, and materials reflect the diversity of their religious beliefs. The Union Methodist Church, on the corner of W. Newton and Columbus, is such an example. Look to the right at Columbus for a view of the Common and the Park Street Church.

At W. Newton, where Columbus and Warren branch, turn left onto Warren and pass the **Harriet Tubman Park**, a small triangular green named after the "Moses of the South." Tubman, a runaway slave herself, organized the Underground Railroad, a network of abolitionists who helped thousands of slaves escape southern plantations. The South End was once dotted with Underground Railroad stations. Abolitionists in the area built secret passageways in their homes and held huge parties to cover the escape of their temporary "guests" on their way to find freedom in Canada. Many of the fleeing slaves decided to settle in the South End and formed communities here. The massive red brick **Concord Baptist Church,** on the corner of Warren and W. Brookline, represents the final stage of this community's expansion. Over the past century the congregation was forced to move from building to building as their numbers increased, but the church remained the focal point of the neighborhood, sponsoring schools, aid societies, and recreation programs. Concord Baptist's density disguises its size—to give you a sense of it, those purple stained glass windows on the cupola are six feet high.

Farther down Warren turn right at W. Canton St. and look at the steep stoops which rise above the basement apartments, flanked by lacy iron stair-railings. In this area, part of the Spanish-speaking community, street signs will be in Spanish as often as English. Turn left on Montgomery for a block and then left onto Dartmouth St. The signs of restoration on the side streets, the sounds of hammers and mounds of sawdust, impart a happy energetic quality to this section. Look down Dartmouth Place and note the even rows of projecting bay and oriel windows.

Turn right on Lawrence and right onto Clarendon. This area, including Berkeley, Clarendon, and Dartmouth Sts., is known as **Clarendon Park** and contains houses which look like miniature Back Bay and Beacon Hill homes. It has been said that these rowhouses were built expressly for the servants of wealthy Boston Brahmin families.

Across the street, facing Tremont, is the sprawling **Boston Center for the Arts.** This complex holds the Boston Philharmonic, the Associated Artists Opera Company, the Boston Ballet Company and School, the Community Music Center, the Theatre Company of Boston, and other performing arts groups and studios (see Theater, Music, and Dance). The National Theatre, which was built in 1911 as the largest vaudeville house in New England and once hosted stars like Gene Autry and Mae West, is being restored as a 3000-seat theater for concerts, dance and opera.

In the center of this complex, under one of largest domes on the continent, you will find the Cyclorama building, the nucleus of the BCA. The Cyclorama building was designed by Cummings and Sears to hold a gigantic circular painting (400 ft. by 50 ft.) of the battle of Gettysburg. After 1892, when the painting's novelty wore thin, the building was used for revivalist meetings, daredevil bicycle stunts, and sporting events (John L. Sullivan, one of the South End's favorite sons, fought here). In 1923, it was renovated into the Boston Flower Exchange and in 1970 it began its present function. Today, besides holding the central offices of the Boston Center for the Arts, the Cyclorama building houses the BCA Gallery, where the paintings displayed are less startling than the Cyclorama mural was, but certainly more appealing. During the Bicentennial, this will also be a place to rest, grab a snack, or untangle directions at the Boston 200 Visitor Information Center.

As you leave the Cyclorama building, turn right down Tremont St. and left onto **Union Park,** the South End's first residential square and once one of Boston's most prestigious addresses. Union Park is the inner sanctum of the South End; its exclusiveness heightens the contrasts of the neighborhood. The area has changed little since its completion in 1859. Most of the original lavish architectural detail remains—ornate keystone, intricate iron grillwork, cartouches framing the windows.

After strolling through Union Park, turn left on Shawmut for a block and watch the less genteel but more contemporary scene. This is the heart of the Syrian and Lebanese community. The restaurants, bakeries, and ethnic clubs point out that you have stepped into a Near Eastern enclave. Turn left onto Waltham, then right on Ringgold St., which is dominated by a black and white mural overlooking a sunken basketball court. Continue on Bond St. and turn left onto Milford, a quiet residential street with flat-facaded homes on one side and bay and bow-fronted homes on the other.

At the end of Milford you will again face the Boston Center for the Arts. Continue right on Tremont, past the Berkeley-Dover intersection. **Dover St.** used to lead to the "Neck", the site of the Puritans' town fortifications and gallows. You are now walking on land which is little more than a century old, for this area was filled in along with Back Bay. The Neck was originally an isthmus, forty yards wide at its narrowest point and flooded at high tide, which connected Boston and Roxbury.

By the 19th century, Dover St. had become anything but pastoral. This is the area where the last remaining Boston tenements (now empty) still stand. Mary Astin, a Russian immigrant, described them in her novel, *The Promised Land.* Dover Street, she wrote, is "heavy with the evil odors of degradation. . . . Nothing less than a fire or flood would cleanse this street." Today the **Castle Square** renewal project on Tremont and Dover, which provides housing for many of Boston's elderly citizens, atones for the sins of the past.

While you are standing at this intersection, glance down Berkeley at the Hancock building. From this angle, the tower looks one-dimensional, but, if you walk up the street, its diamond shape appears. Continue down Tremont for a few blocks and turn onto Arlington where the two streets part. Cortes St., on your left, is a short street of Victorian brick rowhouses which faces a multi-lane expressway. This street stands as a symbol of the confrontation of the 19th and 20th centuries which is ever-present in the South End. At the corner of Arlington and Columbus, visit Boston 200's **The Grand Exposition** at the First Corps of Cadets Armory. Here you can end your tour of the South End (the Arlington MBTA station is right across the street) or, if you are particularly energetic, begin your tour of Bay Village.

Originally mud flats, the **Bay Village** area was drained in the early 19th century and development began concurrently with building on Beacon Hill. If you've seen anything of Beacon Hill, you'll soon notice the resemblance between that part of Boston and Bay Village. The artisans who worked on Beacon Hill first settled here; they couldn't afford to live in the posh neighborhood of the Hill but they certainly knew how to build for themselves houses of similar quality and design. Although the district experienced some deterioration in the early part of this century (during Prohibition it was filled with speakeasies), history-conscious individuals bought the houses in the 1950s and restored them to their former elegance. Today you can admire their work—as well as the brick sidewalks and gas lamps, a more recent restoration effort— and enjoy the 19th-century ambience of this neighborhood.

After you've seen **The Grand Exposition** at the First Corps of Cadets Armory, continue on Arlington until you come to

Winchester, turn onto Winchester and then take a right when you come to Church St. From Church you can turn onto **Fayette St.**, the oldest street in the district and a remainder of the rash of streets and squares so named after Lafayette's visit to Boston in 1824. If you take a right to the end of Fayette you can see **Bay St.**, reputedly the shortest street in Boston. (The single house on Bay St. is supposed to be the smallest in the city.) Otherwise turn left on Fayette and continue up the street. You might take a look at the cat silhouettes on the shutters of 28 Fayette. The decorations supposedly date back to the Prohibition, when this area had a lively if unsavory reputation.

Slightly farther up the street is another Bay Village curiosity, the "half-house", which looks as if it was cut down the middle from the peak of the gable to the ground (it wasn't). After you've looked this over to your satisfaction, proceed to the end of Fayette (on your way you'll pass the site of Edgar Allen Poe's birthplace, near Jefferson St.), round the small brick park, and turn onto Melrose. At the end of Melrose you can turn right and retrace your steps up Arlington to the MBTA station.

CAMBRIDGE TRAIL
(*Map, pp. 180–181*)

Cambridge was settled as early as 1631 and semi-officially named Newtowne. Within seven years, its name and its future had changed. The Massachusetts Great and General Court decided to locate their recently founded college there, within the parish of "the holy, heavenly, sweet-affecting, soul-ravishing preacher," Rev. Thomas Shepard. The town was named Cambridge, in honor of the English university where many of the Puritan governors and clergy had been educated, and the "colledg" was named **Harvard** after the man who bequeathed half of his property and his library to the fledgling school. Though it is an industrial and commercial center as well, Cambridge's past and present are closely linked to the universities in its midst, especially Harvard and the Massachusetts Institute of Technology.

Cambridge is a pedestrian's haven, where jay-walking has been perfected to a fine art and where the twisting roads which intimidate the motorist bring delights around every corner to those who travel by foot. Start your tour at the Harvard MBTA station. As you exit, sedate Harvard Yard is behind you and bustling Harvard Square, the domain of Cambridge natives, students, transient and religious cultists, is in front. Cross Massachusetts Ave. and turn right, past the carpenter Gothic **First Parish Church, Unitarian,** on the corner of Church and Mass. Ave. Next to it is the **Old Burying Ground,** also called "God's Acre," dating from before 1635. The first eight Harvard presidents, as well as many Revolutionary soldiers and early Cambridge settlers, are buried here. Note the variety of gravestones in the Old Burying Ground: moving from the matter-of-fact to the sentimental, they chronicle America's changing attitudes toward death. Look by the fence at the corner of Garden St. to see a mileage marker dating from 1794.

Bear left onto Garden St. and visit **Christ Church,** the oldest existing church in Cambridge, completed in 1761. Christ Church had a congregation of Tory Anglicans who, as the rest of the Cambridge population let their patriotic fervor be known, thought it wise to seek refuge with the British General Gage, stationed in Boston. Little did they realize how useful their church would be to the patriots. During the Revolutionary War, it was used as a barracks and the organ pipes were melted down for much-needed ammunition.

You may want to cross the street and tour **Cambridge Common,** the focal point of the city's religious, political and social life for over 300 years. In 1740, during the great religious revival, George Whitefield chose this spot to preach to the Cambridge populace during his tour of America. Among his admirers was the actor David Garrick, who once said that Whitefield could bring his audience to penitent tears just by pronouncing the word "Mesopotamia." The Common also served as Washington's main camp in 1775-76. A bronze plaque and a scion of the Washington elm commemorate the spot where, according to legend, Washington took command of the 9000 men who had independently gathered there to form the Continental Army. The original elm died in 1923, but cuttings

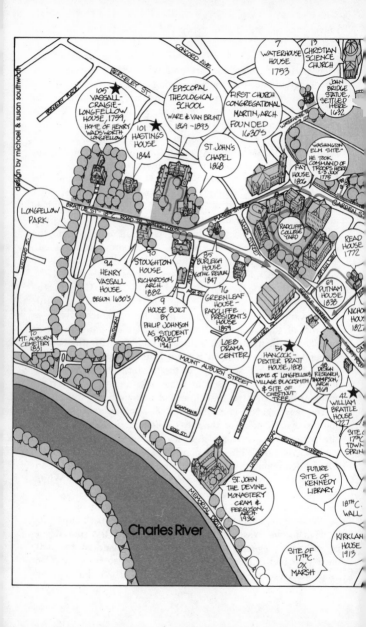

design by michael & susan southworth

7
WATERHOUSE
HOUSE
1753

13
CHRISTIAN
SCIENCE
CHURCH

JOHN
BRIDGE
STATUE,
SETTLED
HERE
1632

★ 105
VASSALL-
CRAIGIE-
LONGFELLOW
HOUSE, 1759,
HOME OF HENRY
WADSWORTH
LONGFELLOW

EPISCOPAL
THEOLOGICAL
SCHOOL
WARE & VAN BRUNT
1869~1893

FIRST CHURCH
CONGREGATIONAL
MARTIN, ARCH.
FOUNDED
1630'S

★ 101
HASTINGS
HOUSE
1844

ST. JOHN'S
CHAPEL
1868

WASHINGTON
ELM SITE-
HE TOOK
COMMAND OF
TROOPS HERE
3-3 JULY
1775

FAY
HOUSE
1806

LONGFELLOW
PARK

BRATTLE ST. TORY ROAD TO WATERTOWN

RADCLIFFE
COLLEGE
YARD

READ
HOUSE
1772

GARDEN ST.

94
HENRY
VASSALL
HOUSE
BEGUN 1630'S

90
STOUGHTON
HOUSE
RICHARDSON,
ARCH.
1882

85
BURLEIGH
HOUSE
GOTHIC REVIVAL
1847

69
PUTNAM
HOUSE
1838

BRATTLE STREET

NICHOL
HOUS
1827

TO
MT. AUBURN
CEMETERY
1831

9
HOUSE
BUILT BY
PHILIP JOHNSON
AS STUDENT
PROJECT
1941

76
GREEN-
LEAF
HOUSE-
RADCLIFFE
PRESIDENT'S
HOUSE
1859

LOEB
DRAMA
CENTER

MOUNT AUBURN STREET

54
HANCOCK-
DEXTER-PRATT
HOUSE, 1808
HOME OF LONGFELLOW'S
VILLAGE BLACKSMITH
& SITE OF
CHESTNUT
TREE

DESIGN
RESEARCH,
THOMPSON,
ARCH.
1969

★ 42
WILLIAM
BRATTLE
HOUSE
1727

SITE C
17TH C.
TOWN
SPRIN

CHAPMAN

BOG ST.

KENNEDY STREET

ST. JOHN
THE DEVINE
MONASTERY
CRAM &
FERGUSON,
ARCH.
1936

FUTURE
SITE OF
KENNEDY
LIBRARY

18TH C.
WALL

MEMORIAL DRIVE

UNIVERSITY ROAD

Charles River

KIRKLAN
HOUSE
1913

SITE OF
17TH C.
OX
MARSH

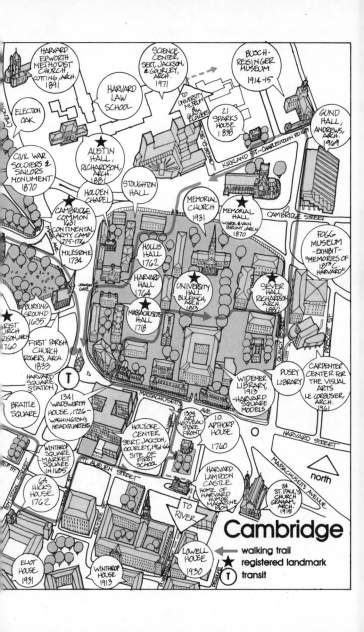

HARVARD EPWORTH METHODIST CHURCH, CUTTING, ARCH. 1891

SCIENCE CENTER, SERT, JACKSON, & GOURLEY, ARCH. 1971

BUSCH-REISINGER MUSEUM 1914-15

HARVARD LAW SCHOOL

TO UNIVERSITY MUSEUMS & FLOWERS

ELECTION OAK

21 SPARKS HOUSE 1838

GUND HALL, ANDREWS, ARCH. 1969

CIVIL WAR SOLDIERS & SAILORS MONUMENT 1870

AUSTIN HALL, RICHARDSON, ARCH. 1881

KIRKLAND ST.–CHARLESTOWN RD.

HOLDEN CHAPEL

STOUGHTON HALL

MEMORIAL CHURCH 1931

★ CAMBRIDGE COMMON 1631 –CONTINENTAL ARMY CAMP 1775-1776

★ MEMORIAL HALL WARE & VAN BRUNT, ARCH. 1870

CAMBRIDGE STREET

MILESTONE 1734

HOLLIS HALL 1762

★ HARVARD HALL 1764

★ UNIVERSITY HALL BULFINCH, ARCH. 1813

★ SEVER HALL RICHARDSON, ARCH. 1880

FOGG MUSEUM –EXHIBIT– "MEMORIES OF 18TH HARVARD"

JOHNSON GATE

★ BURYING GROUND 1635

★ FIRST PARISH CHURCH ROGERS, ARCH. 1833

MASSACHUSETTS HALL 1718

PUSEY LIBRARY

CARPENTER CENTER FOR THE VISUAL ARTS LE CORBUSIER, ARCH. 1961

HARVARD SQUARE STATION ⓣ

WIDENER LIBRARY 1913 –HARVARD SQUARE MODELS

HARVARD STREET

BRATTLE SQUARE

1341 WADSWORTH HOUSE, 1726 – WASHINGTON'S HEADQUARTERS

MASSACHUSETTS AVE.

1304 ART NOUVEAU STORE FRONT

10 APTHORP HOUSE 1760

O

▷ north

WINTHROP SQUARE MARKET SQUARE IN 1605

HOLYOKE CENTER, SERT, JACKSON, GOURLEY, 1964-66 SITE OF FIRST SCHOOL

MT. AUBURN STREET

HARVARD LAMPOON CASTLE HOME OF HARVARD HUMOR MAGAZINE 1909

2A ST. PAUL'S CHURCH GRAHAM, ARCH. 1915

MASSACHUSETTS AVENUE

6A HICKS HOUSE 1762

TO RIVER

Cambridge

ELIOT HOUSE 1931

WINTHROP HOUSE 1913

LOWELL HOUSE 1930

→ walking trail
★ registered landmark
ⓣ transit

were taken and nurtured at the Arnold Arboretum until one could withstand the gasoline fumes wafting over from Mass. Ave.

Now walk across Garden St. again and enter the **Radcliffe Yard,** the location of the administrative offices of Radcliffe College (the women's college associated with Harvard). The buildings on the Yard include Fay House, an 1806 mansion, the Radcliffe gymnasium, built in 1898, and Agassiz House, a multi-purpose building, named after the first Radcliffe president. Founded in 1879 as the "Society for the Collegiate Instruction of Women," Radcliffe was to provide its students with a Harvard education; that is, with instruction from those Harvard professors they could coax or entice into presenting lectures. Today the schools are essentially co-educational—in fact, all of the dormitories of both schools have been co-residential since 1970. However, Radcliffe does maintain several institutions of its own, particularly the Schlesinger Library, the most extensive library of women's studies in the country, and the Radcliffe Institute, which annually finances independent research projects for about forty talented women.

Continue down Garden and turn left on Mason St. The **First Church, Congregational,** on the corner, shares with the First Parish, Unitarian, the distinction of being the first congregation established in Cambridge. Both date from the 1630s. During the early 19th century, a feud flared up between the city's Unitarian and Trinitarian Congregationalists, and in 1829 Dr. Abiel Holmes (father of Oliver Wendell), who disapproved of these new-fangled Unitarian ideas, walked off with over half of the congregation. The rest chose a new pastor and built the First Parish Church, Unitarian, at the corner of Mass. Ave., and Church St. Finally, 35 years after Holmes' death, his congregation settled in this stone structure (dedicated in 1872) under the ministry of Rev. Alexander McKenzie. Look up at the church's spire for the ornamental weathercock of Shem Drowne, a devout church deacon who cast weathervanes as a hobby. One of America's earliest folk artists, Drowne also made the grasshopper on Faneuil Hall and the Indian, once atop the colonial governor's mansion, now in the Massachusetts Historical Society.

Down Mason St. on your right is the sweeping white limestone library of the **Episcopal Theological Seminary.** As you turn right onto Brattle you will see the modern library juxtaposed with the rest of the seminary buildings, which are all Gothic and ivy-covered, resembling a mediaeval cloister. The well-tended Greek revival **Hastings House,** next door, now holds apartments for the divinity students.

During the 18th century, **Brattle St.** was known as Tory Row. The same people who attended Christ Church, many colonial officials and most English sympathizers, lived here in Georgian country estates which stretched down to the river. When they fled, their homes were confiscated by the rebels and used as barracks, hospitals and headquarters for the Continental Army. Today, all of these 18th-century mansions still stand, sharing the street with more recent neighbors.

The **Longfellow National Historical Site,** at 105 Brattle, is such an example. Originally owned by John Vassall, Jr., whose loyalist sentiments led him to feel more secure on the other side of the Atlantic, this building was Washington's headquarters during the siege of Boston. In 1791 it was purchased by land-speculator and developer Andrew Craigie, but his good fortune proved precarious and Craigie spent his last years closeted away in his home, afraid to step outside for fear of being thrown into debtor's prison. After his death, his widow was forced to take in boarders and in 1836, when young professor Henry Wadsworth Longfellow came to Harvard, he rented rooms there. When Longfellow married the pretty, wealthy and socially prominent Fanny Appleton, her father gave the couple this house as a wedding gift. Here the poet lived until his death in 1882 and wrote such works as "Hiawatha" and "Evangeline," carried on his voluminous scholarly work, and completed his translation of Dante.

Now cross Brattle and return toward Harvard Square for a closer look at more of these stately homes. **Longfellow Park** on your right, once part of the Longfellow estate, gives a hint of Brattle's former expansive, pastoral setting. During the Revolution the **Henry Vassall House,** on the corner of Brattle and Hawthorne, was used as the medical headquarters of the American Army under Dr. Benjamin Church, who was imprisoned there after his arrest for traitorous correspondence with the enemy.

At the corner of Brattle and Appian Way is the **Harvard Graduate School of Education,** founded in 1920 and dominated by the modernistic **Gutman Library** with its eye-boggling interior colors. Continue down to **54 Brattle St.,** the home of

Dexter Pratt, Longfellow's "village blacksmith." His smithy was next door, and the site of the renowned "spreading chestnut tree" is marked with a granite tablet.

Pass the Design Research building and the **William Brattle House,** circa 1727, now the Cambridge Center for Adult Education. Brattle, a major general in the Cambridge militia, joined his neighbors in their flight from Tory Row, and his home was used by Major Thomas Mifflin, Washington's aide-de-camp and the Commissary General.

Cross the intersection of Mt. Auburn and Brattle, continue on Mt. Auburn for a block and turn right on Boylston. **Winthrop Square,** on the corner, was the original market square of old Cambridge. Now it is a pleasant place to sit and watch a variety of Cambridge faces pass. Farther down, on the corner of Boylston and South St., you will see the **Hicks House,** a simple wooden-frame, gambrel-roofed dwelling built around 1760. According to family tradition, its owner, John Hicks, participated in the Boston Tea Party, but he is best remembered as one of the three patriots shot in a skirmish with British soldiers returning from Lexington and Concord in 1775.

Now walk down South St., turn left on Dunster and right onto Mt. Auburn. You will catch the back view of **Holyoke Center,** a unified block of shops, offices, Harvard's Information Center and the University Health Services. Designed by Jose Luis Sert, former Dean of the Harvard Graduate School of Design, the building has added new cohesion and beauty to the Harvard Square area, thanks to its popular open-air plaza and walkway.

Farther down Mt. Auburn you'll pass **Lowell House,** one of the handsomest of the Harvard Houses. The bells inside the blue-domed tower came from the Danilov Monastery in Russia. A rather peculiar Russian bell-tuner accompanied the bells to America and proceeded to tune them by filing notches in the rims. When President Lowell stopped him, he began to think he was being persecuted and, sure someone was trying to poison him, drank ink as an antidote. At that juncture, Lowell sent him back to Russia. The bells were finally hung by a Harvard maintenance man, who, understandably enough, knew nothing about tuning them.

Cross Mt. Auburn and pass the **Lampoon Building,** a whimsical parody of a Flemish castle and the headquarters of the

Harvard humor magazine. The *Lampoon* is known for its annual spoofs of national magazines and such pranks as an abortive scheme to "invade" Cambridge *à la* Hannibal. The staff called it off when the circus informed them that the elephants they planned to rent might panic in a crowd.

Turn left on Linden St. and peer into the courtyard of Adams House to look at **Apthorp House,** built in 1760 for the rector of Christ Church. The non-Anglican Cantabridgians thought it was so lavish that they nicknamed it the Bishop's Palace, and eventually social pressure drove poor Apthorp out of the city. During the American Revolution, the house was confiscated and used as Burgoyne's place of detention after the Battle of Saratoga. Since 1916, Apthorp House has been the home of the master (or chief faculty resident) of this Harvard dormitory.

Now continue up Linden, turn left on Mass. Ave. and enter **Harvard Yard** through the gate opposite Holyoke Center. **Wadsworth House,** built in 1726, was the official residence of Harvard's presidents until 1849. Washington used it as one of his many headquarters, and supposedly the final plans to oust King George's troops from Boston were hatched in the Wadsworth parlor. Wander toward the center of Harvard Yard and look at elegant **University Hall**, designed by Bulfinch in 1816. Originally used as the student commons (dining hall), University Hall was the scene of some unscholarly shenanigans when the four classes used to compete against each other in food fights. The statue in front of University Hall, created by Daniel Chester French, is known as the "Statue of Three Lies." The inscription reads "John Harvard, Founder, 1638." In fact, the college was founded in 1636, Harvard was not the founder but an early contributor, and the model for the statue was Sherman Hoar, a Harvard student in 1885, since no one knew what the Rev. John looked like.

Behind University Hall, the **Harry Elkins Widener Library,** Memorial Church, and Sever Hall form a quadrangle. Widener, the third largest library in the country, contains fifty miles of book shelves and ten floors of stacks. The library is a memorial to Harry Widener, a young book collector who drowned in the sinking of the *Titanic*. Harry had indicated that he intended to donate his books to Harvard when the school had a sufficiently well-maintained library, so Mrs. Widener

185

gave the University a place to store Harry's books and room for about eight million more. As you walk down the granite steps of Widener you face **Memorial Church,** dedicated to the Harvard men killed in both World Wars. Built on a massive scale to counterbalance Widener, the Doric columns on Memorial Church's portico are so gigantic that they had to be made in a shipyard.

Now turn right, walk toward Quincy St. and confront **Carpenter Center for the Visual Arts,** home of Harvard's department of Visual and Environmental Studies. This glass and concrete structure, finished in 1963, is the only building in the U. S. designed by the great French architect, Le Corbusier. Conservative Bostonians compare it to "two pianos wrestling," but most agree that Le Corbusier turned his building into an abstract sculpture with a striking arrangement of angles and curves. (You can go up the ramp which allows you to pass through the building and watch the activities inside without disturbing the hard-working artists.) The ground floor, open to the public, exhibits the works of students and local artists.

Next door is the **Fogg Art Museum,** built in Harvard's familiar neo-Georgian style. The exhibits of this superb teaching museum change with the courses offered by the Fine Arts department. Farther down Quincy, on your right, is **Gund Hall,** designed by John Andrews for the Graduate School of Design, and **Memorial Hall,** on your left, facing Cambridge St. "Mem Hall," which Henry James called "the great bristling brick Valhalla," is a famous Victorian building designed by William Ware and Henry Van Brunt as a monument to the Civil War dead and finally completed in 1878. A fire in 1956 destroyed the wooden tower (which extended the building's height by a third), the pinnacles, and the clock, and they have never been replaced. Today Memorial Hall is used for large lecture classes, music and dramatic events, and the infamous freshman mixer. Walk inside before you leave to see Sanders Theater and the stained glass windows in the west hall.

Now pass the undergraduate **Science Center,** designed by Jose Luis Sert and associates, and turn left into Harvard Yard again, this time into the oldest part of the university, a former cow pasture which the Harvard overseers purchased in 1637. In 1810, when John Kirkland became president, he found the Yard an "unkempt sheep-commons," cluttered with a brewery and sundry privies. He is responsible for the tree-planting, the footpaths, and the tradition of care which still persists. In the farthest corner of the Yard, the freshman dormitories, **Hollis, Lionel, Stoughton,** and **Mower** form a square to the north of Harvard Hall. Hollis, built in 1763, and Stoughton, in 1805, boast such famous former residents as Emerson, Thoreau, Oliver Wendell Holmes, and Edward Everett Hale. **Holden Chapel** between Lionel and Mower, Harvard's first official chapel, was completed in 1744. It was the first home of the Medical School, and is now the headquarters of the Harvard-Radcliffe Chorus. Since Holden was a commoner, it is Mrs. Holden's coat of arms you see above the entrance.

Next to Hollis is **Harvard Hall,** today a classroom building which stands on the site of the original Harvard Hall, destroyed by fire in 1764. On the night of the fire a student had snitched a book from the library, and the next day, realizing that it was the only surviving volume from John Harvard's library, went to President Holyoke, expecting an ample reward. Holyoke thanked him, took the book, and expelled him for breaking the rules. **Massachusetts Hall,** built facing Harvard Hall in 1720, is the oldest Harvard building still standing. The upper two floors are used as a freshman dorm, and the building also contains the office of Harvard's President.

You now end your tour facing **Johnson Gate,** the main entrance to Harvard Yard. Before you take the subway back to Boston, stroll through Harvard Square, the most eclectic block in New England. There you'll find shops selling everything from saris to imported coffee, and the largest number of bookstores per square foot in the country. Before you leave listen to the troubadors who congregate in front of Holyoke Center, check the wares of the local craftsmen, and compare the techniques of the street hawkers, canvassers and evangelists.

BACK BAY TRAIL

(*Maps, pp. 190–192*)

The Back Bay trail is divided into two loops which—unless you are a stalwart walker—might best be taken separately. To get a sense of the unique historical development of this district, you should take the east loop first and strike out in the early afternoon to get to the Gibson Museum during its open hours.

Choose a sunny afternoon to take the MBTA to Copley Station, where the east loop begins. Named for portraitist John Singleton Copley, Copley Square was Boston's religious and intellectual center at the end of the last century. As you emerge from the Dartmouth St. exit of the subway station you face the **Copley Plaza Hotel,** which was the site of the Museum of Fine Arts until it moved to the Fenway in 1909.

Cross the street and head diagonally across the modern plaza to the striking glass **Hancock Tower,** one of the unluckiest buildings in Boston. Growing pains began in 1965 when I. M. Pei was commissioned to design a home office for the John Hancock Mutual Life Insurance Company. Following their "good neighbor" policy of urban design, Pei and his partner Henry Cobb drew up plans for a 60-story rhomboidal building sheathed in mirrors to reduce its apparent size. What followed was a less than neighborly battle, with the Boston Society of Architects claiming the building would destroy the serenity of 19th-century Copley Square. Hancock won, the zoning law was changed, and construction got underway in 1968. No sooner was the excavation made than sidewalks and streets shifted, damaging water and sewage mains. Later some 3,500 of the 10,344 windows cracked and had to be replaced with plywood sheets. But the building is intact now and, as one architect observed, "It really is an excellent (neighbor), because it looks like it isn't there."

Enter the Hancock Building on Clarendon St. and stop at the **Boston 200 Visitor Information Center** to check on special events. Next take the elevator to the **observatory,** where photomurals, a taped commentary, a model of the city in 1776 and a filmed helicopter ride provide orientation to Boston topography. Below you, laid out like a graph, is the most orderly set of streets you will ever find in Boston. Parallel to the river are five broad avenues, the middle one, Commonwealth Avenue (or, as Bostonians say, Comm. Ave.) marked by a Parisian-style mall.

Long the home of Boston's First Families, the Back Bay still cradles a few Cabots and Lowells among its current population of students and young professionals. While other Americans boast of connections with the Mayflower, these First Families trace their rise to the fortunes of the 19th-century merchant princes. For a hundred years now they have been cultivating that endearing provinciality which (as Oliver Wendell Holmes put it) "carr(ies) the Common . . . as the unit of space, (and) the State House as the standard of architecture."

Back Bay was once a bay or estuary of the Charles River that cut back behind the city, almost isolating it from the mainland. In a prospectus appealing directly to the people, early developers proposed damming the bay to provide water power for mills located on a smaller cross dam:

> *How shall the citizens of Boston fill their empty stores?* The answer is easy,—ERECT THESE MILLS, AND LOWER THE PRICE OF BREAD. If the public do not have all these improvements it will not be the fault of
> URIAH COTTING

Over objections that the "beautiful sheet of water" would become an "empty mud-basin, reeking with filth," the dams were in operation by 1821. But the number of mills envisioned by the planners never appeared, and—much to their chagrin—the Back Bay became a stinking mudflat. Only the giant frogs who took up residence in the marsh were happy. As described by a visiting writer, "Some, when they sit upon their breech, (were) a foot high, and some as long as a child one year old." So clamorous were they that Bostonians named Frogg Lane (the present Boylston St.) in their honor.

A menace to public health, the land was divided in 1856, with small parcels going to private developers and the largest portion going to the Commonwealth. With gravel brought from West Needham, the filling of the bay started at Arlington St. in the late 1850s. Filling and building activity proceeded apace until the late 1880s, when the new district reached the Fens.

Now return to ground level and cross the street to **Trinity Church.** If you are here between 10:30am and 3:30pm, go in and pick up a fact sheet detailing the history and architecture

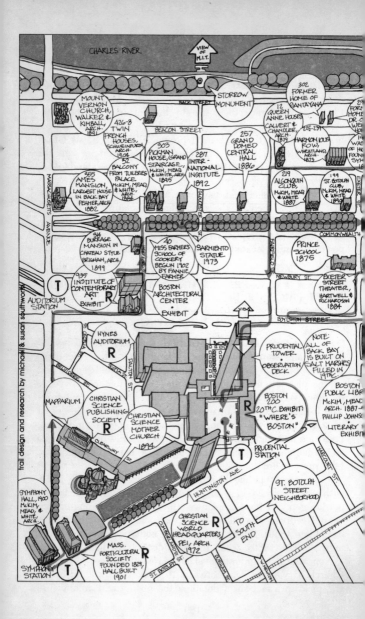

CHARLES RIVER

VIEW OF M.I.T.

trail design and research by michael & susan southworth

MOUNT VERNON CHURCH, WALKER & KIMBALL ARCH. 1891

426-8 TWIN FRENCH HOUSES, SCHWEINFURTH ARCH. 1904

303 PICKMAN HOUSE/GRAND STAIRCASE, McKIM, MEAD & WHITE, ARCH. 1895

BALCONY FROM TUILERIES PALACE

STORROW MONUMENT

BACK STREET

BEACON STREET

257 GRAND DOMED CENTRAL HALL 1886

2817 INTER- NATIONAL INSTITUTE 1892

302 FORMER HOME OF SANTAYANA

12 QUEEN ANNE HOUSE, CALVERT & CHANDLER, ARCH. 1879

HARMON HOUSE ROW, WHEATLAND ARCH. 1873

219 ALGONQUIN CLUB, McKIM, MEAD & WHITE 1887

199 ST BOTOLPH CLUB, McKIM, MEAD & WHITE 1890

355 AMES MANSION, LARGEST HOUSE IN BACK BAY FEHMER, ARCH. 1882

314 BURRAGE MANSION IN CHATEAU STYLE BRIGHAM, ARCH. 1899

935 INSTITUTE OF CONTEMPORARY ART EXHIBIT

40 MISS FARMERS SCHOOL OF COOKERY, BEGUN 1902 BY FANNIE FARMER

SARMIENTO STATUE 1973

BOSTON ARCHITECTURAL CENTER • EXHIBIT

PRINCE SCHOOL 1875

COMMONWEALTH

NEWBURY ST.

EXETER STREET THEATER, HARTWELL & RICHARDSON 1884

BOYLSTON STREET

MASSACHUSETTS AVENUE

AUDITORIUM STATION

HYNES AUDITORIUM R

MAPPARIUM

CHRISTIAN SCIENCE PUBLISHING SOCIETY R

CLEARWAY

DALTON ST.

CHRISTIAN SCIENCE MOTHER CHURCH 1894

PRUDENTIAL TOWER • OBSERVATION DECK

BOSTON 200 20TH C. EXHIBIT: "WHERE'S BOSTON"

NOTE: ALL OF BACK BAY IS BUILT ON SALT MARSHES FILLED IN 1912

BOSTON PUBLIC LIBRARY McKIM, MEAD ARCH. 1887- PHILIP JOHNSON • LITERARY EXHIBIT

PRUDENTIAL STATION T

SYMPHONY HALL, 1900 McKIM, MEAD, WHITE ARCH.

MASS. HORTICULTURAL SOCIETY FOUNDED 1829, HALL BUILT 1901

CHRISTIAN SCIENCE WORLD HEADQUARTERS PEI, ARCH. 1972 R

HUNTINGTON AVE.

ST. BOTOLPH STREET NEIGHBORHOOD

TO SOUTH END

SYMPHONY STATION T

ST. BOTOLPH ST.

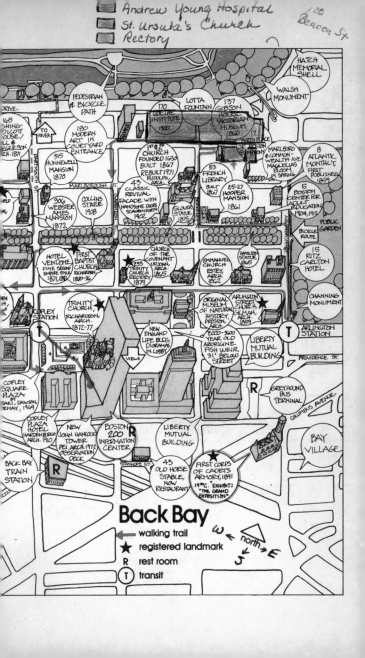

Andrew Young Hospital
St. Ursula's Church
Rectory

100 Beacon St.

Back Bay

← walking trail
★ registered landmark
R rest room
T transit

W ← north → E
S

HATCH MEMORIAL SHELL

WALSH MONUMENT

PEDESTRIAN & BICYCLE PATH

168 WASHINGTON HOUSE, H.H. EGERSON, ARCH. 1871

DRIVE

TO RIVER

180 MODERN ART IN COURTYARD ENTRANCE

170 GOETHE INSTITUTE 1900

LOTTA FOUNTAIN

137 GIBSON HOUSE VICTORIAN MUSEUM 1860

17 BOSTON PLACE SYMPHONY

8 ATLANTIC MONTHLY, FIRST PUBLISHED 1857

MARLBORO & COMMON-WEALTH AVE. MAGNOLIAS BLOOM IN SPRING

315 HUNNEWELL MANSION 1870

15 & 20 CHURCH FOUNDED 1630 BUILT 1867 REBUILT 1971 RUDOLPH, ARCH.

53 FRENCH LIBRARY BUILT 1867

6 BOSTON CENTER FOR ADULT EDUCATION 1904, 1912

306 WEBSTER MANSION 1872

COLLINS STATUE 1908

43 CLASSIC REVIVAL FACADE WITH HANDSOME DOORS SCHULTEN-ROTH 1902

GLOVER STATUE 1875

25-27 HOOPER MANSION 1861

PUBLIC GARDEN

BICYCLE ROUTE

15 RITZ CARLTON HOTEL

HOTEL VENDOME FINE SECOND EMPIRE STYLE 1871, 1881

FIRST BAPTIST CHURCH RICHARDSON 1870-76

CHURCH OF THE COVENANT UPJOHN, ARCH. 1865

233 TRINITY CHURCH RECTORY 1879

EMMANUEL CHURCH ESTEY, ARCH. 1862

HAMILTON STATUE 1865

CHANNING MONUMENT

COPLEY STATION

TRINITY CHURCH, RICHARDSON, ARCH. 1872-77

NEW ENGLAND LIFE BLDS. DIORAMAS IN LOBBY

VIEWS

ORIGINAL MUSEUM OF NATURAL HISTORY, PRESTON, ARCH.

ARLINGTON STREET CHURCH, GILMAN, ARCH. 1859

LIBERTY MUTUAL BUILDING

ARLINGTON STATION

3,000-3,600 YEAR OLD ABORIGINE FISH WEIR 31' BELOW STREET

PROVIDENCE ST.

COPLEY SQUARE PLAZA SASAKI, DAWSON, DEMAY, 1969

GREYHOUND BUS TERMINAL

R

COLUMBUS AVENUE

COPLEY PLAZA HOTEL HARDENBURGH, ARCH. 1910

NEW JOHN HANCOCK TOWER PEI, ARCH. 1972 OBSERVATION DECK

BOSTON 200 INFORMATION CENTER

R

LIBERTY MUTUAL BUILDING

R

BAY VILLAGE

BACK BAY TRAIN STATION

R

STANHOPE ST.

43 OLD HORSE STABLE, NOW RESTAURANT

FIRST CORPS OF CADETS ARMORY, 1891 19TH C. EXHIBIT: "THE GRAND EXPOSITION"

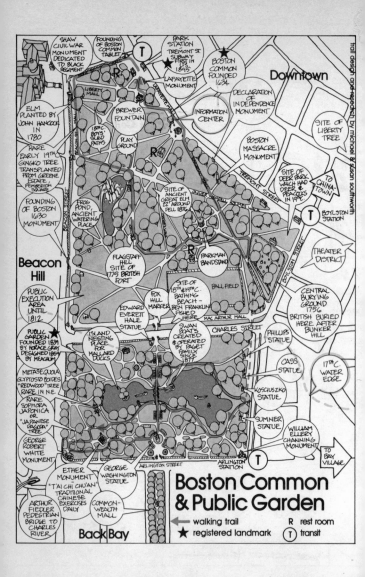

trail design and research by michael & susan southworth

SHAW CIVIL WAR MONUMENT DEDICATED TO BLACK REGIMENT

FOUNDING OF BOSTON COMMON TABLET

PARK STATION TREMONT ST. SUBWAY FIRST IN 1895

★ BOSTON COMMON FOUNDED 1634

Downtown

LAFAYETTE MONUMENT

LIBERTY MALL

BREWER FOUNTAIN

ELM PLANTED BY JOHN HANCOCK IN 1780

18TH C. BOY'S SLED PATHS

INFORMATION CENTER

DECLARATION OF INDEPENDENCE MONUMENT

SITE OF LIBERTY TREE

RARE EARLY 19TH C. GINGKO TREE TRANSPLANTED FROM GREENE ESTATE, PEMBERTON SQUARE

PLAY GROUND

BOSTON MASSACRE MONUMENT

FOUNDING OF BOSTON 1630 MONUMENT

FROG POND, ANCIENT WATERING PLACE

SITE OF DEER PARK WHICH HAD DEER & PEACOCKS IN 1914

TO CHINA-TOWN

TREMONT STREET

OLIVER WENDELL HOLMES

SITE OF ANCIENT GREAT ELM 22' AROUND FELL 1876

BOYLSTON STATION

Beacon Hill

FLAGSTAFF HILL SITE OF 1775 BRITISH FORT

PARKMAN BANDSTAND

THEATER DISTRICT

PUBLIC EXECUTION AREA UNTIL 1812

FOX HILL MARKER

SITE OF 18TH & 19TH C. BATHING BEACH - BEN FRANKLIN FISHED HERE

BALL FIELD

BOYLSTON STREET

CENTRAL BURYING GROUND 1756 BRITISH BURIED HERE AFTER BUNKER HILL

PUBLIC GARDEN FOUNDED 1839 BY HORACE GRAY DESIGNED 1869 BY MEACHAM

EDWARD EVERETT HALE STATUE

MAC ARTHUR MALL

CHARLES STREET

PHILLIPS STATUE

METASEQUOIA GLYPTOSTROBOIDES "REDWOOD" TREE RARE IN N.E.

ISLAND NESTING PLACE FOR MALLARD DUCKS

SWAN BOATS CREATED & OPERATED BY PAGET FAMILY SINCE 1877

CASS STATUE

17TH C. WATER EDGE

RARE SOPHORA JAPONICA OR "JAPANESE PAGODA" TREE

KOSCIUSZKO STATUE

GEORGE ROBERT WHITE MONUMENT

SUMNER STATUE

WILLIAM ELLERY CHANNING MONUMENT

ETHER MONUMENT

GEORGE WASHINGTON STATUE

ARLINGTON STREET

ARLINGTON STATION

TO BAY VILLAGE

"T'AI CHI CHU'AN" TRADITIONAL CHINESE EXERCISES DAILY

COMMON-WEALTH MALL

Boston Common & Public Garden

ARTHUR FIEDLER PEDESTRIAN BRIDGE TO CHARLES RIVER

Back Bay

◄── walking trail
★ registered landmark
R rest room
T transit

of the church. Designed by H. H. Richardson, the church is a free adaptation of 11th-century French Romanesque style.

From its consecration in 1877 the church was under the superb leadership of Phillips Brooks, composer of the carol "O Little Town of Bethlehem." A bronze statue of Reverend Brooks now stands outside the north transept of the church. Erected by the citizens of Boston, it is inscribed with a Bostonian's idea of the four cardinal virtues:

> Preacher of the Word of God
> Lover of mankind
> Born in Boston
> Died in Boston

Across the plaza, which was designed in 1969 by Sasaski, Dawson and Demay, the graceful Renaissance Public Library faces the square. Save it for the end of the loop and look across the street, behind the newspapers and flowers, for the New Old South Church. For the story behind its name and other tidbits, read the handout available inside the Boylston St. entrance (open 8:30am to 5pm).

Leaving Copley Square, head one block up Dartmouth and take a right on Newbury St. Originally lined with fine homes, Newbury St. is now known for its elegant shops, galleries, and sidewalk cafés. At the end of the first block is Richardson's ivy-covered Trinity Rectory, built as a two-story house in 1879. As you continue down Newbury St., New England Life appears on your right. Beneath this mammoth building workmen in 1913 and 1939 found buried deep in the silt some 65,000 decayed, upright stakes interlaced with wattling. According to archaeologists this was an ancient fish weir, used by aborigines 2,000 to 6,000 years ago to trap fish for food.

At the corner of Berkeley and Newbury Sts. is the Church of the Covenant, where poet and philosopher George Santayana used to walk from his boyhood home on 302 Beacon to see "a bit of genuine Gothic." The building opposite was built in 1862 for the Boston Society of Natural History, one of the first such societies in America, whose membership list included scientists like Louis Agassiz. When the Society moved to the present Museum of Science, the building was taken over by Bonwit Teller.

Follow Newbury to Arlington St., which forms the western

border of the Public Garden. Just south of you is the Arlington Street Church. Designed by Arthur Gilman, projector of the Back Bay plan, this was the first building constructed on the newly filled land. The Mother Church of American Unitarians, the Arlington Street Church was first ministered by the abolitionist William Ellery Channing, of whom Jonathan Phillips said, "I have studied his character. I believe him capable of virtue." Several blocks down Arlington at the Stuart Street Armory is Boston 200's The Grand Exposition (see p. 103). If you decide to see the exhibit later, walk up Arlington past the Ritz Carlton to the beginning of the Commonwealth Avenue Mall.

Back in 1856 the Back Bay Commissioners under architect Arthur Gilman set aside the mall and the Public Garden for recreation. Although the Public Garden had boasted a greenhouse and a conservatory for birds and plants in the 1840s, it wasn't until 1861 that the present design, with its continental fountains, trees, and pond, was approved. For the area west of the Public Garden, zoning restrictions set limits on building heights, confined materials to masonry and brick, and stipulated setbacks of 20 to 25 feet from the curb.

You can stop for tea or lunch at the Boston Center for Adult Education, 5 Comm. Ave. (Call 267-4430 for hours.) Then turn right on Berkeley St. to see an extraordinary church graft. The original First and Second Church was built in the English Gothic Revival Style and admired as the "Westminster Abbey of Boston." In 1969 a fire swept the church, leaving only the tower intact. Paul Rudolph's addition incorporates the spire in a novel design that preserves the architectural character and skyline of Back Bay.

Continue down Berkeley past the French Library (main entrance at 53 Marlborough) to Beacon St., formerly the toll road over the Mill Dam. Veiled by late afternoon mist, this was a popular promenade for young lovers. At 137 Beacon is the Gibson House. The first Mr. Gibson was a merchant in the China trade; later Gibsons are noted only for having turned their house into a museum. If you arrive between 2pm and 5pm any day except Monday or a holiday, you can see the interior of their Victorian home preserved just as it was at the tunr of the century.

Leaving the museum, resume your stroll as far as the Goethe Institute at 170 Beacon. Open to the public, the first two floors are filled with contemporary German art and literature. For modern sculpture, look around the courtyard of 180 Beacon.

Now turn left on Clarendon St. Two blocks up, at the corner of Comm. Ave., is the First Baptist Church. Another work by Richardson, this church with its austere, unadorned interior forms a striking contrast to the richness of the contemporary Trinity Church. On the tower is Bartholdi's frieze of famous Bostonians. You won't have to squint to see why irreverent Bostonians dub this the "Church of the Holy Bean Blowers."

Proceed up Comm. Ave. past 128-130, an elaborate French Baroque building which makes its more sedate bedfellows look conservative indeed. The most reactionary of the lot is the club on the corner of Commonwealth and Dartmouth Sts. Bastion of Boston's Female Society, the Chilton Club admits members through its front door, members with guests at the side door, and servants and deliveries by the alley door. The public is not admitted through any door.

For nonmembers, the best vantage point is the Vendome across the way. For decades the city's foremost hotel, it was patronized by the Louis Tiffanys, Sarah Bernhardt, Oscar Wilde, and other international luminaries.

From Dartmouth turn right onto Newbury and pick out Hartwell and Richardson's Exeter Street Theater. Built as a temple for the Progressive Spiritualists, the building was converted into a theater, and was the only movie house a Proper Bostonian woman would enter. This was no doubt because its proprietor was a woman of high culture who spoke with a British accent and showed only foreign films.

Now as you turn onto Exeter St., Phillip Johnson's 1971 addition to the Boston Public Library will appear to your left. Resist the temptation to go in, and walk down Boylston St. to the main entrance in Copley Square. Here is the most imposing view of the main building, which was completed in 1895. With the vision of "an apparatus that shall carry this taste for reading as deep as possible into society," early Bostonians created the first lending library in the world. Go in to see the Literary Boston Exhibit, and stop at the information desk for a pamphlet that will guide you through richly decorated rooms to the murals by Puvis de Chavannes and J. S. Sargent. (For library hours, see p. 110.)

If you want to start the west loop of the trail now, walk up Boylston St. to Prudential Center (or take the MBTA to Prudential station). Stop in the Prudential pavilion to see Where's Boston, Boston 200's exhibit on the city today (see p. 105). Then head for the world headquarters of the Christian Science Church. Founded by Mary Baker Eddy in 1879 to "reinstate primitive Christianity and its element of healing," the First Church of Christ, Scientist is framed by its new center, designed by architects Pei and Cossutta.

Walk beside the reflecting pool past the quadrant-shaped Sunday School (tours of church and school are available; see p. 228) and around to the neighboring Horticultural Hall. Since 1900 this has been the home of the Massachusetts Horticultural Society, which introduced the cultivation of apples to the United States. Its outstanding library is open to visitors Mon-Fri, 9am to 4:30pm in winter, 8:30am to 4pm in summer.

Across the street is Symphony Hall, home of the Boston Symphony Orchestra. Unlike most of the country's orchestras, which were organized by groups of citizens, the B.S.O. was founded in 1881 and financially supported by one man, Major Henry Lee Higginson, for its first 37 years. Since 1918 when the Major relinquished his control, Symphony (as a Proper Bostonian would say) has been supported by contributing "Friends," many of whom can be seen in their customary stalls wearing their customary garb at Friday concerts. (For concert information, see p. 294.)

Now loop back around to the main entrance of the Christian Science Center. Running obliquely at its side is the Christian Science Publishing Society, which prints the international daily newspaper *The Christian Science Monitor*. Faithful to its promise "to injure no man," the *Monitor* has been known to sketch diapers onto the picture of a nude baby before releasing it for publication. While you're here visit the Mapparium—a unique chance to view the world from the inside (see p. 228 for hours.)

Leave the Christian Science Center via Mass. Ave., which took on the name of the Cambridge street after it was extended across the river by the Harvard Bridge. Turn right on Boylston St. and pay tribute to Dr. Zabdiel Boylston, who first inoculated Bostonians against smallpox and unwittingly instituted a new fad, the smallpox party. Naturally, tea and music were included.

955 Boylston is the home of the Institute of Contemporary Art, which restored the exterior of this century-old police station and turned the interior into an exciting gallery (open Mon-Sat, 10am to 5pm; Sun, 2pm to 5pm; $1.) As you turn down Hereford St. the exclusive **Tennis and Racquet Club** will be on your right.

At 40 Hereford hunt for the modest sign marking **Miss Farmer's School of Cookery**. Perhaps best known for her *Boston Cooking School Cook Book* (which was refused by leading publishers and had to be printed privately), Fannie Farmer gave the world its first recipes using standard and level measurements, ensuring consistent results time after time.

Heading back down Comm. Ave., you will be following the route of the Boston Marathon, the 26-mile foot race that has taken place every spring since 1897. As you pass the **Andrew House**, 32 Hereford, notice the cast-iron balconies over the first story windows. They came from the Tuileries Palace in Paris which burned during the 1874 revolt. Nearby is the **Pickman House**, 303 Comm. Ave., whose austere classical facade belies the extravagance of its original owners. For one daughter's debut the Pickman home was transformed into a garden, for the other a Parisian café with sidewalk tables, lampposts, and simulated stars. Number 287 is the **International Institute** where foreign visitors can stop between 9am and 5pm weekdays for orientation and good fellowship. Farther down the mall pause in front of 217 or 199 and count the Cadillacs doubleparked on the street. This is the sign of Boston clubdom.

Not far beyond the clubs at **191 Comm. Ave.** is the home of Major Henry Lee Higginson, a Boston institution himself, who was as generous with advice as he was with money. Declaring, "Any well-trained businessman is wiser than the Congress and the Executive," the Major saw fit to honor Presidents T. Roosevelt, Taft, and Wilson with his opinions. A sobering reminder of the public's fickleness is the statue of William Lloyd Garrison, the abolitionist-reformer who was dragged through the streets of Boston only fifty years before this monument was placed on the mall. Even then the statue was so controversial that nearby residents talked of moving out of their homes.

After turning left at the Webster-Ames mansion (306 Dartmouth, built 1872), you can take a side trip to the end of Dartmouth, where the grassy Esplanade borders the banks of the Charles River. (For ways to divert yourself, see Outdoor Boston.) Then resume your path up Marlborough to a delightful set of row houses. Numbers 225-231 form a "group house" of individual units, which are joined to their neighbors 233-239 by rhythmic repetition of oriel windows, dormers, and simple doorways. Somewhat less serene, though certainly more fun, is the house at the end of the block, 12 Fairfield. Built in the Queen Anne Style, this building has picturesque chimney stacks, gables, and brick cut in playful tinker toy shapes.

As you head left on Fairfield St. look down the alleys that run the length of Back Bay. Part of Gilman's original scheme to save the district from urban blight, the alleys provided inconspicuous access to kitchen doors for deliveries. Today they are used for parking by residents and treasure hunting by local indigents.

If you are feeling adventurous, this is a good time to poke around some shops on Boylston and Newbury Sts. Hunt for toy models of McDonald's or organic Fritos; or check Shopping for specific items.

Climax your day with a trip to the top of the Pru. From the Skywalk on the 50th floor (Admission $1) you can see the effect this urban renewal project has had on the Back Bay. To begin with it was built over train yards that had been a terrific eyesore. But these yards had also protected Back Bay from contact with the less desirable South End and Huntington Ave. Though a great civic improvement, the modern center, by its design which allows fluid movement of people, also provides a bridge between the South End and Back Bay, thus jeopardizing the social insularity and domestic character of the Back Bay. But development is always a two-sided issue. In losing its domestic scale, the area has gained a dramatic tower that links Back Bay to the rest of Boston's spine of skyscrapers.

FANEUIL HALL MARKETPLACE

is coming back to life!

Since 1742, Faneuil Hall has been Boston's traditional market district. In 1825, Alexander Parris
designed the imposing granite "Quincy Building" and
side blocks for the city's expanding commerce. Today, a full-scale redevelopment program is reviving
this historic area as an exciting contemporary center,
bringing together fine shops and restaurants, a food
market, nightlife and entertainment — for a true
modern marketplace in downtown Boston.

The first black Bostonians arrived in 1638 aboard the ship *Desire* from the port of Providence in Barbados, the West Indies. The Puritans paid for them through the sale of "troublesome Indians." A second vessel, the *Rainbowe*, the first American slave ship, left Boston in 1645 for the Guinea coast of West Africa. Available slaves were scarce as the British had traded there earlier. The Americans provoked a quarrel with a coastal village, landed their cannon, and attacked. Those Guineans who were not killed were taken captive and brought to Massachusetts for sale. Stories of the massacre had drifted back to Boston, however, and the ship was met by indignant citizens who had its officers seized and its human cargo returned home at public expense.

By 1705 there were well over four hundred slaves in Boston, most of whom were house servants. Others were responsible for transporting farm produce from the outlying areas to the markets of North Square and Haymarket, where they bargained and traded on their masters' behalf. Cotton Mather, colonial Boston's most influential minister, reputedly first learned of smallpox inoculation from his Senegalese slave who had been immunized by African doctors. Mather led the fight to introduce the practice among a reluctant Boston population.

The first free black settlement was at the foot of Copp's Hill in the North End and was known as "New Guinea." The Snowhill St. side of nearby Copp's Hill Burying Ground bears the bodies of over 1,000 colonial Boston blacks, including Prince Hall, the founder of the Black Masons. Blacks are also to be found in the Central Burying Ground on the Common. By 1829 the handful of free blacks in the city had risen to relative prosperity with new jobs as street laborers, coachmen, window cleaners, sailors and barbers. As Irish immigrants poured into the North End, Afro-Americans moved out to better quarters on the north slope of Beacon Hill. Most of the social and religious organizations of Boston's present black population have their origins with the Beacon Hill colony.

The 19th century saw a portion of that community move across the Charles River to Cambridge in search of better schools. Others who were servants followed their employers into the new townhouses of the South End and Back Bay. With the end of the century and the deterioration of the north

slope of Beacon Hill, the heart of the black community next moved to the South End and Roxbury. The post-World War II northern migration and West Indian influx have expanded that settlement until now most of Roxbury, North Dorchester and parts of Mattapan are predominantly black communities.

Black Bostonians have been around for over three hundred years and have amassed a history as varied and interesting as that of any of the city's other long-term ethnic groups. Ironically enough, much of that history has been a struggle with a liberal Boston social conscience which has supported social change elsewhere but has resisted advancement at home. Take the Black Heritage Trail to explore that history.

To begin the Black Heritage Trail, take the Blue line of the MBTA to the Bowdoin stop. Exit onto Cambridge St. and walk to the right until you reach Joy St., which intersects Cambridge on your left. Once on Joy St., climb up a block until you reach Smith Court. When the north slope of Beacon Hill was black, this was the heart of the community. As you enter the Court, on your left is the **Old African Meeting House,** the first black church in Boston and one of the earliest educational centers for persons of African descent. It was constructed in 1805 by Boston blacks who refused to continue to sit in the galleries of the white churches. William Lloyd Garrison founded the New England Anti-Slavery Society here. The building today houses the Museum of Afro-American History—the center for many Black Heritage activities. Stop here to pick up a more detailed brochure about the trail including a walking tour and a schedule of events. Notice also the marker outside the building. It is the Black Heritage Trail logo and will appear on every site in Boston relevant to black history. Some of the more important of these include:

Abiel Smith School on Smith Court. The first public school for black children in Boston. It was reluctantly established by the city in March of 1834 after black citizens, tired of paying taxes to support public schools which their children could not attend, protested and demanded equal educational facilities. Forty years later, overcrowding prompted parents to petition for integration into the regular public school system.

George Middleton House, 5 Pinckney St. This wooden structure on Beacon Hill was built in 1795 by Middleton and a barber named Lewis Glapion, both free blacks. Middleton was

Look For This Sign as You Walk the Black Heritage Trail

BLACK HERITAGE TRAIL

1. **Old South Meeting House**, Milk and Washington Streets, Boston
2. **Tremont Temple**, Tremont Street, Boston
3. **Old Granary Burying Ground**, Tremont Street (Adjacent to Park Street Church), Boston
4. **Park Street Church**, Tremont and Park Streets, Boston
5. **Crispus Attucks**, site of Boston Massacre, Boston Common
6. **Boston Common**
7. **Civil War Monument**, Boston Common
8. **The State House**, Beacon Street, Boston (Beacon Hill)

9. **The George Middleton House**, 5 Pinckney Street, Boston (Beacon Hill)
10. **The African Meeting House**, Smith Court, Boston (Beacon Hill)
11. **Abiel Smith School**, Smith Court, Boston (Beacon Hill)
12. **John J. Smith House**, 86 Pinckney Street, Boston (Beacon Hill)
13. **The Lewis Hayden House**, 66 Phillips Street, Boston
14. **Dr. George F. Grant House**, 108 Charles Street, Boston
15. **Charles Street Meeting House**, Charles Street, Boston
16. **Site of Boston Massacre**, Washington Street

a colonel who led a black Massachusetts company called the "Bucks of America" at the Battle of Bunker Hill. Also at Bunker Hill was Peter Salem of Framingham, the black soldier who killed the leader of the British forces, Major Pitcairn.

Lewis and Harriet Hayden House, 66 Phillips St. The Haydens were two abolitionists whose home served as an important station on the Underground Railroad. Lewis was a runaway slave from Kentucky who escaped to Boston in 1848. He and his wife aided John Brown with plans for the raid on Harper's Ferry and William and Ellen Craft with their escape from slavery.

Charles Street Meeting House, Charles and Mt. Vernon Sts. The site of many 19th-century abolitionist meetings, the meeting house saw a famous controversy over the seating of black servants in the family pews. Outraged members withdrew to form the Tremont Temple, the first integrated church in Boston.

Boston Massacre Monument, Tremont St. side of the Boston Common. This memorial to the five victims of the Boston Massacre bears the name of Crispus Attucks, a former slave, at its top.

Robert Gould Shaw Monument, the Common at Park and Beacon Sts. The 54th regiment was a company of free Massachusetts blacks who fought in the Civil War. Sgt. William Carney, a member of the regiment, was the first black American to win the Congressional Medal of Honor. The flag of the regiment is on display in the Hall of Flags in the State House.

Granary Burying Ground, Tremont St. The graves of Attucks and the other Massacre victims are here, to the right of the main entrance gate.

Boston Massacre Site, in front of the Old State House. The official site of the Massacre of 1770 is marked by a circle of cobblestones. For a full account of the event see the Freedom Trail: Downtown.

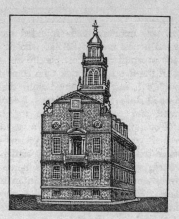

We're proud to say our famous neighbor is looking better than ever.

Since 1831, when we opened our doors at 28 State Street we've been fortunate enough to live across the street from the Old State House. So when we were asked to contribute to the restoration of this great historic shrine, we were glad to be the one private organization to help. Along with HUD and other public bodies, we are helping by contributing to the renovation of this beautiful building, including internal and external work as well as display facilities and extra staffing to make it more accessible to visitors. Now more than ever, the Old State House should be on everybody's tour of historic Boston.

New England Merchants National Bank ⓘ

OTHER BOSTON NEIGHBORHOODS

East Boston

East Boston was unintentionally founded around 1630 by "One Noddle, an honest man of Salem" who drowned offshore when his canoe overturned. He lost his life but gave his name to the largest of the five islands that then comprised East Boston; and Noddle's Island it remained until the area's official settlement in 1833. Like the other islands, Noddle's Island has been obliterated and connected to the mainland by 19th-century landfill operations. You may get some idea of its location, however, if you remember that present-day Maverick Square was once the property of an early settler on the island, Samuel Maverick, who lived up to his name by being an Episcopal royalist in a predominantly Puritan community. Of the other islands, Hog or Breed's Island is now the area of Orient Heights, and Bird, Apple and Governor's Islands have been levelled to accommodate Logan International Airport.

In the 19th century East Boston was a lively business district whose shipyards were world-famous. The Donald McKay shipyard alone produced 21 clipper ships, as well as a good number of ocean packets, schooners, warships and steam vessels. With the decline of the shipyards in the latter half of the century, East Boston became more residential than commercial. The neighborhood was mostly Irish in the 1880s (with pockets of Portuguese, Greeks, Scandinavians, Russians and Germans here and there), but it has been predominantly Italian since an influx of immigrants in 1905.

Brighton

Brighton was originally the home of the Nonantum Indians, a friendly tribe converted to Christianity by the Puritan missionary, John Eliot. Along with Christianity (they were the first tribe converted in British America), the Nonantums adopted agriculture and rejected their former nomadic ways. Unequipped and untrained, the Nonantums could not adjust to their new lifestyle and, as they put land under cultivation, drove away the wildlife that had once sustained them. The Puritans, afraid that the starving tribe would become hostile during King Phillip's War, sent them to Deer Island. They were never to return.

Welcome to our neighborhoods!

Like America, Boston is made up of many different parts. Neighborhoods. Each with a history, a flavor of its own. Throughout Boston, some twenty neighborhoods want to show you what makes them special. And they're using as their local "showcase" libraries, schools or community centers. As one of this city's oldest and largest banks, with roots of our own in Boston's neighborhoods, we're delighted to sponsor this program for Boston 200. So please, in order to really participate in the Bicentennial celebration, stop in at the neighborhood exhibits and see the real Boston. It's the neighborly thing to do.

The National Shawmut Bank of Boston

Participating neighborhoods:
South End, Brighton, the Waterfront, Fenway, the North End, Beacon Hill/West End, South Boston, Chinatown, West Roxbury, East Boston, Jamaica Plain, Roslindale, Hyde Park, Mission Hill, Dorchester, Roxbury.

The British settlers, however, succeeded in forming a flourishing market and agricultural center here. Before the era of transcontinental railroads and Chicago's boom, thousands of barrels of Brighton beef were salted and shipped across the country each week. Merchants also sent fruit trees, seeds, and flowers west by the Boston-Albany Line and stocked downtown shops with May Day bouquets for the city's gentlefolk. Here the strawberry and the Brighton pine were first cultivated, as was the first asparagus plant in the U.S. Some of Brighton's famous fruit reached the public in a more potable form—currant wine became a best-selling beverage. Today Brighton's organic days are over and it is a bustling commuter town composed of families, students, and elderly citizens with a variety of ethnic backgrounds.

South Boston

South Boston achieved fame during the Revolution—Washington set up his guns on Dorchester Heights here, laid siege to the city and forced the British to evacuate Boston on March 17, 1776—but it did not experience its most vigorous growth until the beginning of the 19th century. At that time glass, iron and shipping industries moved into the area and attracted Irish immigrants looking for work. They stayed, built fine houses (one of which became the Perkins Institute for the Blind, where Helen Keller was educated), and laid out the neat streets and parks you can still see today. This has been and still is the most predominantly Irish neighborhood in Boston, a close-knit community that brags about the L Street Brownies, a group of hardy men who defy freezing winter temperatures and go swimming every day.

Dorchester

Around 1630 the Rev. John White of Dorsetshire, England, rallied together some of his parishioners and urged them to found a settlement in the New World. They made elaborate plans with him for the new colony, set sail, and founded Dorchester, the Dorsetshire of the newly established Massachusetts Bay Colony. (The Rev. John White himself stayed home in England.) After initial setbacks the settlement of

Dorchester thrived, first as a fishing port and then as a ship-building community.

In the early 19th century the first pottery works in the country was established in Dorchester, and mills—grain, paint, copper, textiles—cropped up in the lower falls area. Undoubtedly the most pleasant aspect of industrialization was the fragrance of chocolate that once floated from the famous Walter Baker chocolate factory.

Dorchester also developed as a suburban residential and recreational area. In 1822 Savin Hill—once fortified for the Revolution—became a seaside resort area complete with luxury hotel. Today it is better known for its "three-deckers," typical 3-family dwellings in Boston and the passion of domestic architecture buffs. Equally prominent is the Ashmont Hill area, which developed as a suburb for the well-to-do in the late 19th century.

Dorchester is now a quiet residential community proud of its long history. Five of its historic houses remain: the Blake house, the two adjoining Clap houses, the Ball-Hughes house and the Pierce house. (George Washington not only slept in the Pierce house, he reportedly lost a pistol there.)

Mattapan

Mattapan was described by Captain John Smith as the "Isle of the Mattahunts," the Indian tribe who lived in the area. (The name Mattapan means "a good sitting-down place.") Originally the part of Dorchester referred to as "the Pasture," Mattapan was declared separate in 1630 and quickly became a mill center. Leather, corn meal, steel nails, chocolate and paper were produced by water-powered mills and factories along the Neponset River. The Hollingsworth Paper Mill, built in 1773, is the oldest paper mill in America still standing.

In 1800, Mattapan was a sparsely settled community with a "hay scale and drinking trough" in the center of town. It grew slowly throughout the next century, until the Chelsea Fire of 1907 brought an influx of Jews in search of new homes. By 1930, Mattapan was the largest Jewish center in Massachusetts. Since then, however, the Jewish inhabitants have been moving steadily to more remote suburbs, to be replaced by blacks and other ethnic groups. Modern Mattapan is predominantly a middle-class black community, with neighborhood associations working to preserve local history and character.

Roxbury

Roxbury was one of six harbor villages founded in 1630 by the Massachusetts Bay Colony. It was located on the mainland, but connected to the settlement of Boston on Shawmut peninsula by the "Neck," a strip of land about a mile long and barely 200 feet wide. On the 18th of April in '75, William Dawes made his midnight ride over the Neck through Roxbury to Lexington, warning the countryside that the British were coming. (His friend Paul Revere took an alternate route, was captured by the British between Lexington and Concord, but achieved immortality anyway.) The Neck disappeared with 19th-century landfilling, but Washington St. still follows Dawes's route from the peninsula over the Neck through Roxbury.

Until after the Revolution Roxbury was a sparsely populated farming community, whose heart was Eliot Square (named for Puritan missionary John Eliot). The square is the site of the First Church of Roxbury, whose original building was used as a signal station for the patriots during the Revolution and was William Dawes's starting point. Also on the square is the Dillaway-Thomas House, the former home of Rev. Charles Dillaway, who taught the first Japanese students to come to this country. The house, which was used to quarter Revolutionary soldiers, now belongs to the city of Boston and is being restored as an adjunct to the Museum of Afro-American History.

For about a hundred years Eliot Square was also the home of the Roxbury Latin School (now located in West Roxbury), which boasts such alumni as Revolutionary hero Joseph Warren, cardiologist Paul Dudley White and historian Walter Muir Whitehill. Other famous Roxburyites are the portraitist Gilbert Stuart, Boston's foremost abolitionist William Lloyd Garrison, and Black Muslim leader Malcolm X.

Besides Eliot Square, a visit to Roxbury should include the Shirley-Eustis House on Shirley St., built by Governor William Shirley in 1750 and later bought by Governor William Eustis.

Roxbury today is a predominantly black residential district and the center of black culture and politics in Boston. On Elm

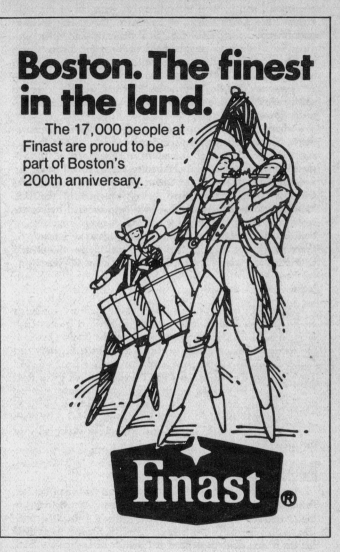

Hill Ave. is the National Center of Afro-American Artists, an educational and cultural institution that grew out of the well-known Elma Lewis School of Fine Arts. The Center sponsors performances and classes for the community and often provides scholarships to neighborhood children for instruction in the arts. For information on performances, see p. 291, p. 295 and p. 296. Other outstanding community groups include Circle Associates and the Roxbury Action Program, which underwrite small neighborhood businesses and invest in the area's economic growth.

Roxbury has also been a center of the civil rights movement. Neighborhood parents organized in the 1960s to persuade the Boston School Committee to close Roxbury's Boardman School and send local children to Peter Faneuil School on Beacon Hill. The movement, known as Operation Exodus, was the first community-organized busing program in the U.S. Mandatory city-wide busing has now been ordered by a state court, as a result of political action that stemmed from Operation Exodus. Another outpost of civil rights in Roxbury is Freedom House, an activities center opened by Muriel and Otto Snowden which has been in operation for 25 years.

Mission Hill

Mission Hill, a multi-racial section of old Roxbury bordering on Boston's medical complex, started as a working-class Irish neighborhood created by immigration in the 1840s. Later in the century German factory workers joined the community and founded Mission Church, the first basilica in North America. You can visit the basilica at 1545 Tremont St. and get a first-hand look at its famous building material, Roxbury pudding stone. (Legend has it that the giants who used to live in Roxbury got angry one night during a feast and threw their plum pudding at each other, scattering these unique stones all over the area.)

Jamaica Plain

There are two theories about the origin of the name Jamaica Plain. The first is that it celebrates Cromwell's victories in the Caribbean. The second is that it states the drinking preferences of Boston's 17th-century dock workers: they liked Jamaican rum, and they liked it "plain."

The coming of the Boston-Providence Railroad converted Jamaica Plain from a country retreat to a streetcar suburb. Tanneries and breweries sprang up, manned by newly arrived Irish and German workers. But the town retained much of its rural character thanks to the expansion of Frederick Law Olmsted's park system. In 1880 James Arnold, a New Bedford merchant, established the 500-acre Arnold Arboretum as the "link in the emerald necklace" of Olmsted parks. This spectacular garden, together with Franklin Park, the Arborway and Jamaicaway, make Jamaica Plain the greenest community in Boston.

Although the Arboretum is Jamaica Plain's most conspicuous attraction, the neighborhood also contains the delightful Children's Museum, the home of Mayor Curley (now in use by the Oblate Fathers), and Bromley-Heath, the first tenant-run housing project in the U.S.

West Roxbury

West Roxbury, positioned on the eroded cone of a volcano (it's been dead for 100 million years), was not recognized as a community distinct from Roxbury proper until 1851. Part of this neighborhood rests on land granted to Captain Joseph Weld in 1643 for services rendered to the Massachusetts Bay Colony. West Roxbury is most famous as the former home of Brook Farm, a utopian experiment in clean living and high thinking. This community, founded by such transcendentalists as George and Sophia Ripley, William Ellery Channing, and Margaret Fuller (with occasional support from Emerson, Hawthorne and Theodore Parker), suffered a spiritual and financial collapse after five years. Still, this "French Revolution in miniature," as Emerson dubbed it, lingers in the minds of American reformers and intellectuals.

Roslindale

Roslindale was a part of West Roxbury until 1870 (when it was named after the vacation spot of Roslyn in Scotland) and grew as a streetcar suburb, settled mostly by Germans and Irish. In Roslindale's Forest Hill Cemetery are buried General Warren, who was killed at the Battle of Bunker Hill, and Eugene O'Neill, the great American playwright.

Hyde Park, incorporated in 1868, is the most distant suburb of Boston, pocketed between West Roxbury and Dorchester. It was also one of the first commuter towns in the area, its growth encouraged by the Boston-Providence Railroad. But Hyde Park had noteworthy industries of its own. The Neponset River and its tributary, Mother Brook, powered the town's cotton and woolen mills. People still reminisce about the George Clark paper mill which once produced the distinctive red-and-blue-threaded paper used for U.S. currency.

After its first pioneer settlement, Fairmont Heights, was established in 1856, Hyde Park was the chosen residence of many writers, artists and reformers. Angelina and Sarah Grimke, fervent abolitionists and women's rights advocates, lived here, and J.J. Enneking, the famous rural painter, drew inspiration from the picturesque landscapes that surrounded his home. During the Civil War, this neighborhood was the site of Camp Meigs, an Army training camp. 5000 troops were readied for battle on the former pasture of Ebenezer Paul, among them the Union's first black regiment under the command of Colonel Robert Gould Shaw.

ENTERTAINING YOURSELF

FESTIVAL AMERICAN CALENDAR

Boston will celebrate the Bicentennial by organizing neighborhood festivals and city-wide galas, and by looking ahead to the future as well as back on the past. Boston is already known as an exciting place to live, and this aspect of the city will be accentuated during the Bicentennial by hundreds of events ranging from talks on current issues to neighborhood parades. One special Bicentennial program will be "The Bicentennial Forums: Boston Examines the American Experiment," sponsored by the New England Mutual Life Insurance Company in cooperation with Boston 200 and the Parkman Center for Urban Affairs. Beginning in early 1975 and continuing through 1976, this series will feature nationally-known leaders who will engage in public dialogues about the country's historic principles and their implications for the future. In addition, the Ford Hall Forum, America's oldest public lecture series, will continue to present free talks by controversial personalities at the Alumni Hall at Northeastern University. For more information on the Bicentennial Forums call 338-1975 (Boston 200 information) or check the Boston 200 newspaper; for the Ford Hall Forum call 426-0725.

You may also want to look into the lecture series of two Boston 200 Task Forces. The Task Force on Law and Civil Liberties will deal with constitutional issues of current interest by presenting mock trials at Faneuil Hall; and the Task Force on Health Care will sponsor the Lowell Lectures in Medicine for 1975 and 1976, talks by nationally acclaimed health leaders on milestones in medicine and on the issues affecting health care delivery today.

Last but not least, the city will honor its own citizens, all its neighborhoods, and members of the ethnic groups which give Boston its special diversity and cultural richness. Each month of the Bicentennial the Mayor's Office of Cultural Affairs will pay tribute to a different nationality with special cultural programs as well as dance, musical and dramatic performances; and Boston 200 will set up exhibits in City Hall every week (from May to Sept) which will feature a different Boston neighborhood. Boston 200 will also sponsor special events in the neighborhood for that week. Be sure to inquire about these programs during your visit, and watch for traditional neighborhood events, such as the street processions in the North End on feast days. You can also go to the Children's Festival, held every Sunday afternoon in Copley Square, where your children can meet Boston children, teach each other regional games and listen to folk singers.

The Mayor's Office of Cultural Affairs' most sweeping project is Summerthing, a treat to the native and the visitor alike. An ambitious effort to make the city a more enjoyable place to live, Summerthing works hand-in-hand with Boston neighborhoods to sponsor festivals, creative workshops, block parties and performances. For information on specific Summerthing and ethnic-month events call the ARTSLINE at 261-1660. When Summerthing is not in season, ARTSLINE is an information source for all of Boston's cultural goings-on. For specific dates of the above events and changes which may occur in the following festivals, consult the Boston 200 newspaper or call Boston 200 information at 338-1975(6).

MARCH 1975

5   Boston Massacre Day—205th anniversary celebrated by procession led by Charlestown Militia from the Massacre site to City Hall Plaza.

17   St. Patrick's Day and Evacuation Day Parade—procession begins at Andrew Sq., marches through South Boston to East Broadway.

APRIL 1975 is Irish Month in Boston

14-24   First ten days of U.S. Bicentennial Celebration. Opening of all Boston 200 exhibits and trails. Call 338-1975 for information.

America,
You've got 200 good wishes coming

So when they light the candles on our cake,
celebrate with an ice-cold bottle of delicious Coca-Cola.
In our entire history there hasn't been a more
refreshing tradition than enjoying Coca-Cola.

Paul Revere House by Robert Kennedy

Old North Church by Robert Kennedy

18 Lantern Service at Old North Church commemorating the 200th anniversary of Paul Revere's ride. Re-enactment of Paul Revere's ride begins at Paul Revere Mall in North End and ends on Lexington Green. Re-enactment of William Dawes' ride from John Eliot Sq. in Roxbury to Lexington Green.

19 Patriots Day—Parades in Lexington and Concord, and in Boston from Old City Hall to Revere Mall to Old North Church. Parade by Ancient & Honorable Artillery Co. in Back Bay. City Ring, to which all Boston is invited to bring bells and join area high school bands and church chimes in ringing in Patriots Day.

20 Bike race along Paul Revere's route, sponsored by State Bicentennial Commission.

21 Boston Marathon—26-mile run form Hopkinton to Prudential Center

MAY 1975 is Albanian Month in Boston

Four Elements Air Festival—Kite Festival sponsored by the Committee for Better Air

19 Black Solidarity Day—celebration at Franklin Park
20 Lafayette Day—ceremony at Lafayette Monument on Boston Common
26 Memorial Day—ceremony at Copley Sq.

JUNE 1975 is Afro-American Month in Boston

Four Elements Earth Festival—"plant-in" and folk song fete at the Fenway

2 First Muster Ancient and Honorable Artillery Company Parade—Faneuil Hall to Boston Common to Copley Square
7-8 June Art in the Park—Boston Common
13-14 Celebrate—Jubilee—The Black Triumph—all night cabaret, cultural events and entertainment at the National Center of Afro-American Artists
15 Bunker Hill Day Parade—from corner of Vine and Tufts Sts. in Charlestown.
17 Bunker Hill Re-enactment—Bunker Hill Monument, Charlestown. 200th anniversary of historic battle.

JULY 1975 SUMMERTHING

Four Elements Fire Festival—demonstrations by the Fire Department and fireworks displays

4   Independence Day—parade begins at City Hall, proceeds through historic sections of Boston and ends with extensive exercises at Faneuil Hall. Declaration of Independence read at Old State House. Fireworks over Dorchester Bay.
5-6   Independence Day festivities continue in the neighborhoods
11-13 Feast of Madonna del Carmine—North End
18-20 Feast of St. Rocco—North End
25-27 Feast of St. Joseph—North End

AUGUST 1975 SUMMERTHING

Four Elements Water Festival—celebration on the Esplanade

1-3   Feast of St. Agrippina—North End
8-10   Feast of Madonna della Cava—North End
15-17 Feast of Madonna del Soccorso—North End
22-24 Feast of St. Anthony—North End
29-31 Feast of St. Lucy—North End
30-31 Festival of the August Moon—Chinatown

SEPTEMBER 1975 is Lithuanian Month in Boston

OCTOBER 1975 is Italian Month in Boston

9   Leif Erickson Day—celebration at Leif Erickson Statue on Commonwealth Ave.
13   Columbus Day—ceremony at Columbus Statue in Louisburg Sq. Parade in North End.
27   Veteran's Day—parade circles Boston Common and the Public Garden

NOVEMBER 1975 is Jewish Month in Boston

Whole World Celebration opens at Hynes Auditorium

21   Christmas Festival of Lights opens at Boston Common

DECEMBER 1975 is Hispanic Month in Boston

16   Boston Tea Party Day—observance on the Boston Tea
        Party Ship at Congress St. Bridge

JANUARY 1976 is Arab Month in Boston

1-6   Christmas Festival of Lights continues on Boston Common
15   Martin Luther King, Jr. Day—celebration at City Hall
19   Benjamin Franklin Day—ceremony at Franklin Statue
        at Old City Hall

FEBRUARY 1976 is Chinese Month in Boston

12   Lincoln's Birthday—ceremony at Lincoln Statue in Park
        Sq.
16   Washington's Birthday—celebration at Equestrian Statue
        on Boston Common

MARCH 1976 is Polish Month in Boston

5   Boston Massacre Day—the Charlestown Militia leads a
        procession from the Massacre Site to City Hall Plaza.
        206th anniversary of Massacre.
14   St. Patrick's Day and Evacuation Day Parade—procession
        begins at Andrew Sq., marches through South Boston
        to East Broadway. 200th anniversary of British
        evacuation of Boston.

APRIL 1976 is Armenian Month in Boston

19   Patriots Day—re-enactment of rides of Paul Revere and
        William Dawes. Parades. (see April 1975)
        Boston Marathon—a 26-mile run from Hopkinton to
        Prudential Center

MAY 1976 is Greek Month in Boston

Four Elements Earth Festival—"plant-in" and folk song fete
Committee for Better Air.

19   Black Solidarity Day—celebration at Franklin Park
20   Lafayette Day—ceremony at Lafayette Monument on
        Boston Common
26   Memorial Day—ceremony at Copley Sq.

JUNE 1976 is Haitian Month in Boston

Four Elements Earth Festival—a "plant-in" and folk song fete at the Fenway

5-6	June Art in the Park—Boston Common
7	First Muster Ancient and Honorable Artillery Company—parade from Faneuil Hall to Boston Common to Copley Sq.
11-12	Celebrate—Jubilee—The Black Triumph—all night cabaret, cultural events, and entertainment at the National Center of Afro-American Artists
17	Bunker Hill Day—re-enactment of historic battle at Bunker Hill Monument
20	Bunker Hill Day parade—begins at Vine and Tufts Sts. in Charlestown to the Boston Common

JULY 1976 SUMMERTHING

Four Elements Fire Festival—demonstrations by the Fire Department and fireworks displays

Operation Sail brings ships from many countries to Boston harbor

3	Washington's arrival in Boston—re-enactment at Boston Common
4	Independence Day (see July 1975)
9-11	Feast of Madonna del Carmine—North End
16-18	Feast of St. Rocco—North End
23-25	Feast of St. Joseph—North End
30-31	Feast of St. Agrippina—North End

AUGUST 1976 SUMMERTHING

Four Elements Water Festival—celebration on the Esplanade

1	Feast of St. Agrippina continues—North End
6-8	Feast of Madonna della Cava—North End
13-15	Feast of Madonna del Soccorso—North End
20-22	Feast of St. Anthony—North End
27-29	Feast of St. Lucy—North End
29	Festival of the August Moon—Chinatown

SEPTEMBER 1976 is Native American Month in Boston

OCTOBER 1976 is Portuguese Month in Boston

9   Leif Erickson Day—celebration at Leif Erickson Statue on Commonwealth Ave.

11   Columbus Day—ceremony at Columbus Statue in Louisburg Sq.

27   Veteran's Day—parade circles Boston Common and the Public Garden

NOVEMBER 1976 is Yankee Month in Boston

Whole World Celebration opens at Hynes Auditorium

19   Christmas Festival of Lights opens and continues through Jan. 5 on Boston Common

DECEMBER 1976 is Multicultural America Month in Boston

16   Boston Tea Party Day—observance on the Boston Tea Party Ship at Congress St. Bridge.

MUSEUMS AND ATTRACTIONS

If you want to gaze on some great art, see the physical remnants of America's past, or indulge an idiosyncratic interest, Boston has a museum for you. The following listings are divided into three parts: first, the major sights which appeal to the general audience and the connoisseur alike; second, those which cater to more specialized interests; and third, those located on the outskirts of the city. Devote a day to the Museum of Fine Arts, take an avid stamp collector to the only philatelic museum in the world, or pack a picnic lunch and leave for the country, visiting on your way the former home of Bronson Alcott's utopian community.

MAJOR MUSEUMS AND ATTRACTIONS

Boston Tea Party Ship and Museum, Congress St. Bridge on the Tea Party Path (338-1773). T-South Station; by car from south, Southeast Expressway to Downtown-Chinatown exit; from north, Expressway to High St.-Congress St. exit. The exhibit includes the brig *Beaver II*, a full-scale copy of one of the ships involved in the Tea Party. The Tea Party Museum houses audiovisual presentations and historical documents relevant to the Tea Party. Visitors may explore the entire ship and throw chests of tea overboard, creating their own Boston Tea Party. Open daily, 9am to 5pm in winter, 9am to 8pm in summer. Adults $1.50, children 14 or under, 75¢.

Children's Museum, Jamaicaway, Boston (522-5454). T-Arborway, get off at Buttle St. Take the kids to a museum where everything can be touched. Play with computers, participate in a Japanese tea ceremony, visit an Algonquin wigwam, see what the frequently changing "What's New" exhibit has to offer. Films and arts and crafts demonstrations change weekly. All the guides are friendly, well-informed and helpful. Open Tues-Fri, 2pm to 5pm, Sat, Sun and school vacations, 10am to 5pm, Fri, 6pm to 9pm. Adults $1.60, children 3-15 80¢, Fri eve. free.

Chinatown. From T-Boylston, walk down Boylston St., continue on Essex, turn right on Harrison Ave. to the heart of Chinatown, identified by the pagoda-shaped telephone booths. Oxford Pl., off Harrison, is the spot where the Chinese first settled about one hundred years ago. Until after World War

From the
Creators
of Citygames

More Participatory
Fun for the whole
Family at the
World-famous
children's
Museum
☼ see page (224) for details

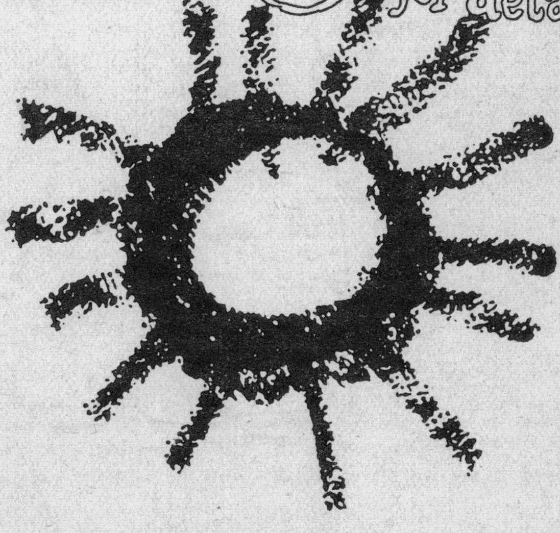

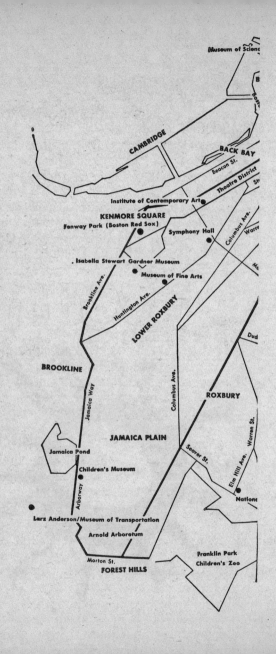

Museum of Science

CAMBRIDGE

BACK BAY

Beacon St.

Theatre District

Institute of Contemporary Art

KENMORE SQUARE

Fenway Park (Boston Red Sox)

Symphony Hall

Columbus Ave.

Warre

Isabella Stewart Gardner Museum

Museum of Fine Arts

Brookline Ave.

Huntington Ave.

LOWER ROXBURY

Dud

BROOKLINE

Columbus Ave.

ROXBURY

Jamaica Way

JAMAICA PLAIN

Jamaica Pond

Seaver St.

Children's Museum

Elm Hill Ave.

Warren St.

Arborway

Nationa

Larz Anderson/Museum of Transportation

Arnold Arboretum

Franklin Park

Children's Zoo

Morton St.

FOREST HILLS

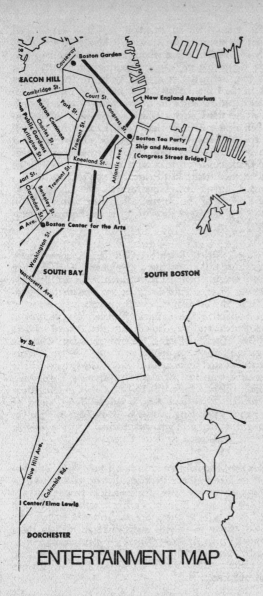

Boston Garden

New England Aquarium

BEACON HILL

Cambridge St.

Court St.

Congress St.

Boston Tea Party
Ship and Museum
(Congress Street Bridge)

Park St.

Boston Common

Charles St.

Tremont St.

Public Garden

Arlington St.

Kneeland St.

Atlantic Ave.

Tremont St.

...ert St.

...arendon St.

Berkeley St.

... Ave.

Boston Center for the Arts

Washington St.

SOUTH BAY

SOUTH BOSTON

...tachusetts Ave.

...by St.

Blue Hill Ave.

Columbia Rd.

... Center/Elma Lewis

DORCHESTER

ENTERTAINMENT MAP

II, when the tense political situation in China encouraged many families to emigrate to America, Chinatown was composed mostly of transient males who came to work in the whaling industry, the textile mills or in laundries and restaurants, areas where they were not competing with Westerners. They would work in the United States, send money to their families and, with luck, return home in a few years. Today Boston's Chinatown is the third largest Chinese settlement in the nation, after San Francisco and New York. Explore for yourself the myriad specialty shops and groceries and discover the best bargains on brocade jackets, jade crafts, porcelain, exotic teas and spices. Complete your tour with a meal at one of the many excellent restaurants in the area. If you're here in February or August, attend one of the festivals—the Chinese New Year or the Festival of the August Moon—and watch colorful dragon dances and fireworks displays. (See the Festival American calendar.)

First Church of Christ, Scientist, Christian Science Center (262-2300 ext 2078) T-Prudential or Symphony. The Christian Science Center consists of the First Church of Christ, Scientist and the Christian Science Publishing Society. The church building, called The Mother Church by its members, consists of two distinct buildings: the Original Edifice, first permanent home of the church, and the domed Extension, where services are held today. The Publishing Society publishes Christian Science magazines, books, pamphlets and the *Christian Science Monitor*, an influential international daily newspaper. While you are there, be sure to visit the Mapparium, a huge walk-through colored globe. Tours of The Mother Church: Mon-Fri, 10am to 5pm; Sat and Sun, noon to 5pm. Tours of Mapparium and Publishing Society: Mon-Fri, 9:30am to 11:30am and 1pm to 3:30pm. Mapparium only: Mon-Sat, 8:15am to 4pm; Sun, noon to 3pm. Free.

Franklin Park Zoo, Franklin Park, Boston (442-0991) T-Egleston Station, then take Franklin Park bus; by car, take exit 17 off Southeast Expressway. A part of Frederick Law Olmsted's Boston park system, now Franklin Park is a rather shabby zoo but getting better all the time. Special features include the Children's Zoo, where attendants allow children to help them feed the animals, and "A Bird's World", a giant aviary. Open May-Nov, daily, 10am to 5pm. Main Zoo free. Children's Zoo, adults 75¢, children 25¢. Bird's World, adults 25¢, free to accompanied children.

The Isabella Stewart Gardner Museum, 280 The Fenway, Boston (734-1359). T-Arlington, stop at Museum of Fine Arts. Mrs. Jack's Palace is a more appropriate name for this museum, the art collection of one of Boston's great eccentrics. In the eyes of the proper Bostonians, Mrs. Gardner committed her first indiscretion by being born in New York. For those which followed Mrs. Jack took gleeful responsibility. She drank beer instead of tea, walked a pet lion (named Rex) instead of a dog, and drove her sleigh along the sidewalk when she had a mind to. She collected jewels and had her two favorite diamonds set on gold springs to wear in her hair like butterfly antennae. And each Lent she absolved herself—her sins were rumored to be well worth the penance—by scrubbing the steps of the Church of the Advent. Her greatest self-indulgence, however, was collecting art, not to mention artists. To house her collection she reconstructed a Florentine palace, shipped stone-by-stone from Italy. Although in her sixties when the building began in 1910, she rarely missed a day at the site and was always accompanied by her personal trumpeteer who summoned malingering workmen.

Her collection reflects her personality as clearly as her home does. One of the most magnificent private galleries in the world, it includes one of the finest Titians extant ("The Rape of Europa"), one of the world's thirty-six surviving Vermeers, and works of Botticelli, Tintoretto, Corot, Sargent and Whistler.

Sadly, her good taste was exceeded only by her cosmic ignorance of design and exhibit skills. She crammed a tiny room full of Manets and gave the central position to William James' portrait of his brother. Her own portraits by Sargent and Whistler have rooms to themselves, while the only Vermeer in New England is lost in the clutter of a heavily decorated room.

None of this ineptness would be so irritating if Mrs. Gardner hadn't insisted to posterity that she knew what she was doing. But she bequeathed her collection to the public on condition that none of her pieces ever be moved. If so much as an ashtray is re-arranged, the land, building, and all of its contents are to be sold and the money donated to Harvard. Everyone is afraid to test the strength of her will in court.

Despite these foibles, perhaps even because of them, the Gardner is one of Boston's guaranteed delights. Every city has its art patrons, but only this one had a Mrs. Jack. Open Tues, 1pm to 9:30pm; Wed-Sun 1pm to 5:30pm. Free. Free concerts September through June, Thurs and Sun at 4pm and Tues at 8pm.

Government Center—New City Hall (722-4100) T-Government Center. Tours of City Hall are given Mon-Fri 10am to 4pm, starting every half hour. Begin at the information desk. The Main Art Gallery on the fifth floor has frequently changing showings of major artists. Ask at the information desk for the location of the other four exhibit spaces which feature local talent. Tours and galleries are under the auspices of the Mayor's Office of Cultural Affairs. For further details see Freedom Trail, p. 119.

Harvard University Museums, 11 Divinity Ave., Cambridge (495-1000) T-Harvard. The University museums are composed of four distinct collections. The Museum of Comparative Zoology (entrance on Oxford Street) displays stuffed specimens and skeletons of a wide variety of animals, extinct and surviving. The North American Bird collection, the oldest known dinosaur egg, the "Harvard" Mastodon, and the only known skeleton of a Kronosaurus, a 42-ft marine reptile, are among its attractions. The Mineralogical and Geological Museum houses 150,000 mineral samples. Of special interest are the stalactites and fluorescent minerals. The Botanical Museum holds the famous glass flower collection, the work of Leopold Blaschka, who created these life-like models as teaching tools for Harvard students. The display includes 164 families of flowering plants as well as models depicting the life cycle of many non-flowering species, the pollination process and the effects of disease on plants. The Peabody Museum of Archaeology was the first museum of its kind in the country. Its collection includes artifacts from Eskimo, South Sea Island, Mayan and Southwest American Indian cultures. A fine exhibit on traditional and contemporary aspects of Tlingit Indian (an Alaskan tribe) life opened in 1974. The special Bicentennial exhibit is an ethnographic study of American Indian culture, emphasizing the Revolutionary period. Open Mon-Sat, 9am to 4:15pm. Free; Glass Flower exhibit, 25¢.

Institute of Contemporary Art, 955 Boylston St., Boston (266-5151) T-Auditorium. Founded in 1936, the ICA continues to be the leading force in Boston contemporary art through its exhibitions, public art program and related educational activities. Excellent changing exhibits in a renovated 19th-century police station. Tours of artists' studios every first Thursday of the month. Open Mon-Sat 10am to 5pm, Sun 2pm to 5pm.

The Massachusetts State House, Beacon Street, Boston (727-2121) T-Park St. The seat of the Massachusetts government overlooks Boston from the city's highest hill, once the property of John Hancock, Revolutionary financier and the state's first elected governor. Completed in 1795, the central red brick, white-columned section was designed by Charles Bulfinch, under the inspiration of classical temples. The dome, now covered with 23 karat gold, was first sheathed with copper by Paul Revere in 1802. Atop the dome is a gilded pine cone, a symbol of the forests that helped the early settlers survive. Here you can watch the State Senate and House of Representatives in action and visit the governor's office if he's not around. The Archives Museum in the basement holds documents and maps significant in Massachusetts history, including Bradford's manuscript of the history of Plimoth Plantation, the 1630 Massachusetts Bay Company Charter, Indian treaties and some of Paul Revere's engravings. Tours are available; phone for the schedule.

Museum of Afro-American History, Smith Court off Joy St., Boston (723-8863) T-Bowdoin. A restored African meeting house, the oldest black church building in U.S. The museum displays exhibits of Afro-American history in New England. Guided tours of the Black Heritage Trail may be arranged by appointment. Open daily 1am to 4pm. Adults $1, children 50¢.

Museum of Fine Arts, 465 Huntington Ave., Boston (267-9377) T-Arborway (Huntington Ave.). Streetcar stops in front of the MFA.

The MFA, an imposing granite palace, occupies twelve acres of land, making it one of the few Boston sights which are not crowded between other buildings. The museum has eight structurally separate departments—Egyptian, Classical, Decorative Arts (European and American), Asiatic (Chinese, Japanese, Indian, Islamic, and Korean), Prints and Drawings, Textiles, Paintings, Contemporary, and a non-circulating library, open to the public, which contains 145,000 books and pamphlets.

The collection of Egyptian architectural casts and artifacts is the most complete one outside of Cairo, and the Japanese art collection has no rival in the nation. You will pass through endless rooms devoted to early American furnishings—Duncan Phyffe chairs, Paul Revere silver, canopied four-posters—more than enough Americana to please the most finicky Daughter of the American Revolution. In the hemicycle, on the second floor, an array of Impressionist paintings (mostly Monet)

For the next two years we'll show you the past two hundred.

Museum Highlights, 1975-1976:

FRONTIER AMERICA,
January 24 – March 12, 1975

PAUL REVERE'S BOSTON
April 18 – October 12, 1975

COPLEY, STUART, WEST
July 22 – October 17, 1976

NEW ENGLAND PROVINCIAL PAINTERS
July 22 – October 17, 1976

BOSTON MUSEUM OF FINE ARTS
479 Huntington Avenue, Boston

creates a mood of light and color which will follow you through the entire museum.

During the Bicentennial the Museum of Fine Arts has planned several special exhibits, including a collection of 18th century art treasures called "Paul Revere's Boston: 1735-1818" (Apr-Oct, 1975), an exhibition of paintings by Copley, Stuart, and West (July-Oct, 1976), New England Provincial Painters (July-Oct 1976), and a massive diorama of the Battle of Bunker Hill, complete with 5200 toy soldiers (June-Sept, 1975).

When you are either footsore or eyesore, stop for a gracious lunch at the MFA restaurant. The food is good and the interior view exquisite. A trip to the MFA is an absolute must. Don't sweep through; spend at least half a day there. Open Mon, Wed, Fri, Sat, Sun, 10am to 6pm, Tues, Thurs, 10am to 9pm. $1.50, free Sun morning.

Museum of Science and Hayden Planetarium, Science Park, Boston (742-6088) T-Lechmere to Science Park. An action-oriented museum featuring live animals, natural history and technical science exhibits, visitor-operated demonstrations, audio-guided tours. Hayden Planetarium offers programs twice daily as well as lectures, courses, and special evening demonstrations in astronomy. Special Bicentennial exhibits on "Yankee Ingenuity" and "Medicine and Health in Boston." For people with children, a must, for those without, a treat. Cafeteria on premises. Open Mon-Sat 10am to 5pm, Fri until 10pm, Sun 11am to 5pm. Adults $2, children $1.

Museum of Transportation, Larz Anderson Park, 15 Newton St., Brookline (521-1200) T-Cleveland Circle, then bus to Forest Hills. Once the estate of Larz Anderson, wealthy world traveler, diplomat and car buff, who used to buy a car every year (starting in 1898) and never sold one. Twenty to thirty autos are displayed at any one time, plus sleighs, carriages and a fire engine (rides available on weekends). The antique bicycle collection is the best on the East Coast. Slide shows and silent films continuously on weekends and during the summer. Open Tues-Sun, 10am to 5pm. Adults $1.50, children and senior citizens 25¢.

New England Aquarium, Central Wharf, Boston (742-8870) T-Aquarium. All the bizarre, colorful and amusing specimens of marine life are on display here. Watch scuba divers feed the fish in a 200,000 gallon ocean-water tank, visit the salt-

water tray which covers the entire first floor where aquatic mammals and birds show off, and admire the new mammal barge. Gallery guides are located at each major exhibit; underwater movies are shown daily. You can also watch a historical film, "Boston and the Sea," made by the Museum of the American China Trade. Open Mon-Fri, 9am to 5pm; Fri till 9pm; Sat, Sun, holidays, 10am to 6pm. Adults $2.50; students, senior citizens and servicemen, $1.25; children 6-15, $1.00.

Harrison Gray Otis House, 141 Cambridge St., Boston (227-3956) T-Charles or Government Center. Built in 1796 and designed by Bulfinch, this house gives you a picture of Boston high life in the days of the early republic. Exact reproductions of the furniture, wall paper and paint colors have been created through extensive research, making the interior as exact a facsimile of the original interior as is possible. The Society for the Preservation of New England Antiquities, an organization which restores and protects fine historic houses, has headquarters in the Otis house and maintains its library and museum here. Contact their office for more information on SPNEA homes in the area. Open Mon-Fri, 10am to 4pm. $1.

Charlestown Navy Yard and "Old Ironsides," T-Community College on the Orange Line. The Boston Navy Yard, founded in 1800, covers 43 acres. It is located on historic Moulton's Point, where the Charles and Mystic Rivers merge, the spot where the British launched their attack in the Battle of Bunker Hill. The installation originally cost $19,350, appropriated from funds for the construction of six 74-gun ships. It proved to be a good investment, for today the complex is worth $450 million. In 1833 the drydocks, the first in the nation, were completed under the guidance of Col. Laommi Baldwin, "the father of American Civil Engineering." The Naval Yard has built, outfitted, and launched ships for every American war since 1812. Part of it has now been designated a National Historic Site, maintained by the National Park Service.

The most conspicuous sight in the Navy Yard is certainly the U.S.S. *Constitution* or "Old Ironsides." This, the most famous ship in American history, was built in 1797 by Joshua Humphrey. 175 feet long, and holding 400 men, the *Constitution* was an innovation in its time. It was longer than most ships and had more cannon, but its maneuverability allowed it to run from the enemy when out-gunned. "Old Ironsides" was intended as the showpiece of the Revolutionary War Navy,

Come aboard the Discovery. It's a showboat full of sea lions, whales and bottlenosed dolphins.

Right in Boston harbor, right next to Central Wharf is the only floating mammal amphitheatre in the world! It's the New England Aquarium's *Discovery*. Walk across the gangway and take a seat in the stadium above the quarter of a million gallon pool.

That's where the sea lions, dolphins and small whales perform for you. Trained in Florida, they're ready to show New Englanders what they know. You'll see them jump through hoops, play ball, and echo locate objects with blindfolds on. They're so smart they could even throw tea into the harbor to celebrate the bicentennial!

During their performance, you'll see an open-ocean film on a large screen above the pool. It's a movie that the Aquarium has put together from locations all around the world. While you watch, you'll learn how these mammals live in their natural environment.

Come aboard the showboat *Discovery* for a water ballet, a ball game, a movie and an out-at-sea education. The sea lions, whales and dolphins will applaud you when you're there.

New England Aquarium
The Fins of Man

but did not see action until the unofficial war with the Barbary pirates at Tripoli in 1803. But it was during the War of 1812 that the U.S.S. *Constitution* gained its fame and its nickname. On August 19, 1812, the *Constitution* engaged in its first full-scale sea-battle with the British frigate, the *Guerriere,* off the Nova Scotia coast. After an hour of cannon fire the *Constitution* was nearly unscathed while the *Guerriere* could barely limp into port. The British soldiers, astounded by the fact that their cannon fire didn't dent its sturdy oaken sides, dubbed the ship "Old Ironsides."

The *Constitution* has suffered more threats from the U. S. Navy than from enemy guns. It was decommissioned in 1830 and the Navy was about to destroy it when Oliver Wendell Holmes rallied the nation to its defense with his poem "Old Ironsides." The Navy then rebuilt it and kept it on active duty until 1882. Again in 1905 the Navy flew in the face of public sentiment and proposed that the *Constitution* be used for target practice. Instead, through funds raised in a nation-wide campaign, the *Constitution* was completely rebuilt in 1925. Today "Old Ironsides" has undergone a third reconstruction, this time with a $45 million Senate appropriation, and rests safely in the Navy Yard, the oldest commissioned ship in the Navy. One of the Navy Yard buildings houses the Constitution Museum, devoted to the ship's history.

Other sights in the Charlestown Navy Yard include the Rope Walk, the Commandant's house and the Alexander Parris building. The Rope Walk, a remarkable building almost a quarter of a mile long, was the place where all the rope for the U.S. Navy was manufactured until 1971. The Commandant's house, a graceful square brick Federal mansion, designed in 1809 by Samuel Nicholson, has been the home of the Navy Yard's commandant since its completion. The Rope Walk, along with the granite laboratory buildings and the wood-and-metal shop, was designed by Alexander Parris. His simple, well-proportioned style set an example for many American architects. During the Bicentennial, a multi-media exhibit of the Battle of Bunker Hill will be presented on Hoosac Pier.

ADDITIONAL MUSEUMS AND ATTRACTIONS

Boston Fire Museum, 20 Eustis St., Roxbury, T-Dudley. This is the oldest surviving firehouse in Boston, originally built in 1819. The present structure has been restored to its original decor, complete with models and a photographic history of early fire departments. Exhibits tell the history of fire departments from colonial times to the present. Open Mon-Fri, 9am to 5pm; Sat-Sun, 10am to 4pm. Free.

Busch-Reisinger Museum, Harvard University, 29 Kirkland St., Cambridge (495-2338). T-Harvard; parking difficult. Germanic art from the Middle Ages to the present with an especially excellent collection of German Expressionist works. Every Thursday at noon organ concerts are given. Tours may be arranged in advance. Open Mon-Sat, 9am to 4:45pm; in the summer closed Sat. Free.

Mary Baker Eddy Museum (Longyear Historical Society), 120 Seaver St., Brookline. T-Kenmore, take Chestnut Hill bus to Fisher Ave. By car, Huntington Ave. outbound, follow signs for Fisher Ave. This 100-room turn-of-the-century mansion contains memorabilia of the founder of Christian Science, Mary Baker Eddy—portraits, photos, manuscripts, personal possessions. Stroll through the gardens and grounds, maintained by the Longyear Historical Society. Tours available. Open daily, 9am to 5pm (earlier closing in winter.) Adults $1, under 20, 25¢.

Fogg Art Museum, Quincy St., Cambridge (495-2387) T-Harvard. Teaching museum of Harvard University. The best university art museum in the country, the Fogg shows an excellent selection of period and genre. Three exhibits under the title "Memories of Eighteenth-Century Harvard" are planned for the Bicentennial: Benjamin Franklin (Apr 17-Sept 22, 1975), Lafayette (Winter 1975-76), and Harvard Divided (May-Sept, 1976). Open Mon-Sat, 9am to 5pm; Sun 2pm to 5pm. Free.

Grand Lodge of Masons in Massachusetts, 186 Tremont St., Boston (426-6040), T-Boylston. Exhibit on the Masonic fraternity with particular reference to Masons in Boston from the colonial period to the present. Exhibits include material on Lafayette, Joseph Warren, Paul Revere, John Hancock and Washington. Open Mon-Fri 10am to 4pm. Free.

Hayden Gallery, MIT Library, Memorial Drive, Cambridge (253-4680) T-Central Square. A small gallery with fine rotating exhibits of contemporary painting and sculpture. Note the giant Calder stabile outside. Open during the academic year. Mon-Sat, 10am to 4pm, closed Sun. Free.

John F. Kennedy National Historic Site, 83 Beals St., Brookline (566-7937) T-Cleveland Circle line to Coolidge Corner. The 35th President of the United States was born in this house in 1917, and it is furnished with pieces which belonged to his family. Open daily 9am to 5pm. Adults 50¢, children under 16 free.

London Wax Museum, 179 Tremont St., Boston (542-6882) T-Boylston. 125 life-size wax figures by Madame Josephine Tussaud. The museum includes that chamber of horrors without which no wax museum would be complete. Open Mon-Sat, 10am to 9:30pm, Sun, 1pm to 9:30pm. Adults $1.95, children $1.

Museum of the American China Trade, 215 Adams St., Milton (696-1815) T-Ashmont, then Mattapan streetcar. The former home of Captain Robert Bennet Forbes, this museum includes a collection of China Trade art objects, documents and artifacts which capture the spirit of America's participation in the Far Eastern sea trade. Open Tues-Sat, 2pm to 5pm. Adults $1.50, children 50¢.

OUT-OF-TOWN ATTRACTIONS

Cardinal Spellman Philatelic Museum, Regis College, Weston (894-6735) T-Riverside, taxi to college. By car, Mass Pike to Weston exit, turn onto Rt 128. This is the only museum in the world devoted exclusively to stamp collecting. Guided tours may be arranged by appointment. Open Tues and Thurs 9:30am to 2:30pm, Sun 2pm to 5pm. Adults 50¢, children 25¢.

De Cordova Museum and Park, Sandy Pond Road, Lincoln (259-8355). Rt 128 to Trapelo Rd. (exit 47W). Julian De Cordova, 19th-century glass manufacturer, bequeathed his home to the town as a museum. The 30-acre park is decorated with outdoor sculpture, while inside the mansion graphics, painting and sculpture are displayed. Arts and crafts classes, films and demonstrations are offered regularly. Call to arrange a gallery talk. Open Tues-Sat, 10am to 5pm, Sun, 1:30pm to 5pm, closed Mon. Adults $1.50, children 50¢.

Fruitlands Museums, Prospect Hill, Harvard (456-3924). Take Rt 2 to Harvard exit, south on Old Shirley Rd., turn onto Prospect Hill. Fruitlands includes the remains of Bronson Alcott's utopian community, a Shaker museum representing another communal experiment, an Indian Museum, and an art gallery of American landscapes and portraits, featuring works by members of the Hudson River School. Fruitlands is housed in an 18th-century farmhouse where Alcott founded his Transcendentalist community in 1843. Artifacts of Alcott and his friends—Emerson, Thoreau, and Fuller—are on display. Open Tues-Sat, 1pm to 5pm. Adults, $1, children 25¢.

GALLERIES

Gallery-hopping on Newbury Street could while away a day if you aren't careful, and much more if you are a serious art patron. You'll find art suited to every taste and pocketbook, primitive to contemporary, graphics, sculpture, watercolors, oils, ranging in price from expensive to modest (forget about cheap—just browse if you're broke). Gallery talks are offered at many places, especially if a special exhibit is featured. Most galleries are open from 10am to 5pm Mon-Sat but some close Mondays and keep erratic hours during the summer, so call if you want to visit a specific one. The Copley MBTA station brings you within a few blocks of all of the following galleries, plus many more:

Alpha Galley, 121 Newbury (536-4465) offers fine contemporary art with an emphasis on graphics by modern masters.

Childs, 169 Newbury (266-1108), exhibits fine American painting of the eighteenth, nineteenth and early twentieth centuries, as well as art objects of the China trade.

Doll & Richards, 172 Newbury (266-4477), is the nation's oldest gallery. Its general policy, which is waived today, was to carry only works by living artists. It specializes in twentieth-century American sculpture, prints, and painting.

Graphics 1 and Graphics 2, 168 Newbury (266-2475) has an outstanding selection of original prints by 20th-century artists.

Harcus Krakow Rosen Sonnabend, 7 Newbury (262-4483), also has a branch at the Chestnut Hill Mall. It concentrates on contemporary painting, graphics, sculpture and tapestries.

Pucker/Safrai, 171 Newbury (267-9473), exhibits African and Eskimo sculpture, the polished bronze works of Kieff, and graphics by twentieth-century masters like Chagall, Matisse and Picasso.

Rolly-Michaux, 125 Newbury (261-3883), exhibits Impressionist and post-Impressionist works. Contemporary artists of international repute are represented, among them Calder and Picasso. The oils and sculpture are expensive but some drawings, lithographs, and even some watercolors are within reach.

Shore Galleries, 8 Newbury (262-3910), features recent works by New England artists and nineteenth and early twentieth-century American art.

Vose Galleries of Boston, Inc., 238 Newbury (536-6176), has been directed by the Vose family with taste and integrity for five generations. Some of their paintings by Thomas Cole, John Singleton Copley and Gilbert Stuart circulate to museums. The gallery has a large collection but insufficient wall space to display all of it. Therefore, describe the types of painting which interest you and the attendant will assist you.

There are a number of galleries in the Harvard Square area, although they cannot compare with Newbury Street's. **Art/Asia** at 8 Story Street, and **Art Explorers,** at 1804 Massachusetts Ave. (specializing in Eskimo art), are well worth a visit. If you'd like to rent a picture or attend an art class go to **Cambridge Art Association** at 23 Garden Street or call 876-0246.

The **Boston Visual Artists Union Gallery,** Three Center Plaza, sells the works of its 700 Boston area artist-members. The BVAU Gallery brings together artists dealing with a variety of styles and media and gives the public access to the art created in its midst, by means of one of the finest new galleries in the U.S. The gallery usually closes for a few weeks in late summer, so call first if you're in town then (227-3076). T-Government Center.

SHOPPING IN BOSTON

DOWNTOWN BOSTON

Hustle-bustle-rush-rush. For energetic shoppers. Before Christmas beware mounted policemen hired to protect cars from pedestrians. Besides being the locus of a thriving jewelry business, Washington Street is famous for its large clothing and department stores. Charles Street, backyard shopping district for Beacon Hill, excels in rare antiques and exotic plants. Neighborhood specialties for Chinatown, North End and Waterfront listed below. Late nights Monday and Wednesday. T-Park, State or Washington.

ANTIQUES: Elegant antiques on Charles St.; nautical artifacts and Americana along the Waterfront.

BOOK SHOPS:
Special Collections (Antiquarian):

Brattle Book Shop, 5 West St. Since 1825. Oldest continuously run rare book store in Boston. Proprietor George Gloss was

honored as a walking library of knowledge and dispenser of philosophy in the Commonwealth's 1973 Golden Dome Citation.

Goodspeed's Book Shop, 18 Beacon St. and 2 Milk St. Specialties are antique maps and autographs.

Starr Book Co., Inc., 37 Kingston St. Superb collections of American and English literature.

General Selection:

Lauriat's, Inc., 30 Franklin St. and 1 Washington Mall. Large, deals in fine bindings and complete sets. Also cards and party supplies.

The Old Corner Bookstore, 50 Bromfield St. Boston's oldest, originally on corner of School and Washington Sts.

U.S. Government Printing Office Boston Bookstore, G-25 JFK Building, Government Center. Everything the government wants you to read. Open Mon-Fri, 8am to 4pm.

COMESTIBLES: Fresh fish from Fish Pier off Northern Ave. and lobster companies on Commercial St. (all on Waterfront). Italian wine, cheese and pastries on Hanover and Salem Sts. in North End.

DEPARTMENT STORES:

Filene's, 426 Washington St. Wide selection of high-quality goods. Lively battle in Automatic Bargain Basement, where clothes, linens, gifts sell at reduced prices. Unforgettable.

Gilchrist's, 417 Washington St. Boston's oldest department store. Popular prices. Famous for almond macaroons baked hourly.

Kennedy's, 32 Summer St. Wide choice of men's, women's, boys' clothes.

Jordan Marsh, 450 Washington St. Boston's largest store. High quality; bargain basement.

R. H. Stearns Co., 140 Tremont St. Fine-quality men's, women's, children's clothes; household articles.

F. W. Woolworth Co., 350 Washington St. Complete department store with moderate prices.

OLD COINS, STAMPS: Poke around Bromfield and Province Sts.

76 years after the shot heard 'round the world, Eben Jordan and Ben Marsh opened the doors of a new retail establishment in downtown Boston. The year was 1851 and the corner of Washington and Summer streets has been the busiest corner in New England ever since.

124 years later Jordan Marsh is, as it was then, the leading store in town for fashions and home furnishings. Our growth has been constant (from one store to ten in four New England states). But our roots remain in downtown Boston, where our home office and major store are still located.

We invite you to visit all our fine stores. Boston, Framingham, Malden, Peabody, Braintree, Burlington, Worcester, Bedford, N.H., South Portland, Maine and Warwick, R.I. But for nostalgia's sake, we direct you downtown, where it all began.

JORDAN MARSH

OPEN MARKETS:

The Boston Flea Market, Quincy Market. Antiques and crafts, old-time music and entertainment every Sunday, Apr-Oct, 1pm to 6pm.
Faneuil Hall Flower Market, adjacent to Faneuil Hall. Cut flowers, plants at market prices. Open daily.
Haymarket, Faneuil Hall area. Fruit, vegetables, meat at wholesale prices. Jostling crowds, Italian mamas. Take a shopping bag. Fri and Sat, dawn to dusk.
Italian North End, Hanover and Salem Sts. Barrels of squid, eels; fresh oregano, fruit, and nuts in open air markets; tantalizing whiffs from bakeries. Practice your Italian before going. A daily happening.

AMERICANA:

Faneuil Hall Gift Shop, Faneuil Hall First Floor. Boston 200 information and Bicentennial commemorative items. Open daily 10am to 6pm.
Faneuil Hall Heritage Shop, Faneuil Hall Basement, #5. Early American reproductions in pewter and silver. Open 9am to 7pm daily.

NEWBURY AND BOYLSTON STREETS

Boston gone continental. Elegant, prestigious and expensive. Check the galleries (see Galleries p. 242) and plant boutiques or feel European in a sidewalk café. Exciting cluster of shops in Prudential Center. Best for couture, coiffures, and fashionable imports from Europe and New York. Open late Monday and Wednesday nights. T-Arlington, Auditorium, Copley or Prudential.

ARTS, CRAFTWORK: Leatherwork, American Indian arts. On Newbury St. from Clarendon to Hereford.

Buffalo Days, 221 Newbury St. Native Indian arts.
The Santa Fe Shop, 167 Newbury St. American Indian arts and crafts.
Sojourn, 254 Newbury St. Artisan showcase. Delightful stuffed animals.

FINE APPAREL, SHOES: Brand-name clothes, branches of top New York stores. Along Newbury St. from Arlington to Dartmouth and the entire length of Boylston St.

Brooks Brothers, 46 Newbury St. Fine-quality men's clothes.
Bonwit Teller, 234 Berkeley St. Choice women's apparel. Also **The Twig at Bonwit Teller,** 73 Newbury St. Bonwit's junior shop.
Joseph Antell, 0 Newbury St. Elegant shoes and bags for women.
I. Miller Guild House, 37 Newbury St. Chic women's shoes and bags.
Lord and Taylor, 750 Boylston St. First-class clothes for men, women, and children.
Louis, 470 Boylston St. Distinctive men's apparel, designer clothing.
Peck and Peck, 500 Boylston St. Impeccable selection of women's wear.
Saks Fifth Avenue, Prudential Center. Exclusive clothing for men, women, children.

FUN AND GAMES:

Boston Chess Studio, 335 Newbury St. Largest selection of chess games and books in New England. Tables for playing, 40¢ per hr. Open Tues and Fri, noon to 8pm; Wed, Thurs and Sat, noon to 6pm.
Brentano's Book Store, Prudential Center. Hand-carved chess and backgammon sets, gallery of sculpture, jewelry, prints. Books, too.
F.A.O. Schwarz, 40 Newbury St. Toys, toys, toys! Many imported or made specially for F.A.O. Riotous stuffed giraffes.

INTERIOR DECORATION, DESIGN, FURNISHING: Along Newbury St. from Berkeley to Exeter and Boylston St. from Arlington to Exeter.

Decor International, 171 Newbury St. Hand-woven rugs, tapestries. Folk art from New Guinea, Africa, 35 countries in all.
MaKanna, 416 Boylston St. Trousseau items, especially fine linens.
Pan-tree, Inc., 380 Boylston St. Gourmet cookware. Men welcome.
Rug Gallery, Inc., 112 Newbury St. Rya rugs, Polish and Yugoslavian peasant designs. For walls and floors.

Walls and the Coverings Thereof, 164 Newbury St. Fine wallpaper, matching fabrics.

INTERNATIONAL FLAVOR: Interior furnishings, assorted crafts. Many on Newbury St. between Clarendon and Exeter.

Artisans, 165 Newbury St. Yucatan jewelry, Japanese tureens, much more. Affordable prices.
Aladire Ltd., 156 Newbury St. Handprinted Nigerian textiles.
Alianza, 140 Newbury St. Mexican handcrafted design. Furniture, wall hangings, jewelry.
The Wandering Piper, 167 Newbury St. Scottish crafts and clothes, including kilts, tartan skirts, Harris tweed jackets.

JEWELRY: Custom design work in silver and gold. In the Arlington to Berkeley block of Newbury and on Boylston from Arlington to Dartmouth.

Shreve, Crump and Low Co., 330 Boylston St. Where proper Boston brides register silver and china patterns. Check for special Bicentennial section.

THE LATEST THINGS: Stereo equipment, natural cosmetics, organic foods, contemporary costumes. Newbury St. above Dartmouth and all along Boylston St.

Erewhon Trading Co. Retail Store, 342 Newbury St. Organic groceries, picnic makings.
The Face and Body Shop, 217 Newbury St. Natural-care body products, tea blends, herbs and spices.
Organic Food Cellar, 297 Newbury St. Organic foods, bulk grains. *Tofu* ice cream sandwiches for natural food epicures.
Tao Book Store, 303 Newbury St. Eastern culture and religion, getting-your-head-together books and miscellania.

HARVARD SQUARE

Young and fun. Street music, Hari Krishna, and yogurt cones. No discernible logic to location of shops; of necessity the fun is in the search. Best for boutiques, books, and fine crafts. Very special shops mentioned below. Open late Thursday night. T-Harvard.

ARTS, CRAFTS: Work in leather, clay, wood, gold, silver, and gems.
Contemporary Crafts, 10 Arrow St. Intriguing gallery and shop with work in wood, glass, etc.

Spoons for a Boston Tea Party

Landmarks of the American Revolution are richly reproduced in four teaspoons of heavy silver plate by Reed & Barton. (Left to right): Faneuil Hall and Bunker Hill Monument; Old North Church and Paul Revere's Ride; John Hancock House and the Boston Tea Party; Old State House and the Minute Man. Order several sets. As elegant Bicentennial commemoratives, ideal gifts, handsome additions to your personal silver collection. Four 6-inch spoons, gift boxed, $17.95 plus $1.50 postage and handling. (Mass. residents add 3% sales tax.)

SHREVE, CRUMP & LOW CO.

S C L

330 Boylston St., Boston, Mass. 02116 (617) 267-9100
The Mall at Chestnut Hill, Mass. 02167 (617) 965-2700

BOOKS: Bookstores are indigenous here. Good general selections at:

Harvard Coop Book Annex, Palmer St.
Harvard Bookstores, Inc., 1248 Mass. Ave.
Paperback Booksmith, 25 Brattle St.
Phillips-Brentano's Book Store, 7 Holyoke St. Also games.
Reading International Corp., 47 Brattle St. Foreign periodicals, too.

Special collections at:

Book Case and Annex, 41 and 42 Church St. Huge assortment of second-hand books.
Grolier Bookshop, 6 Plympton St. Modern poetry.
Logos Bookstore, 58 Boylston St. Contemporary Christian books and oddments.
Mandrake Book Store, 8 Story St. British and American art, architecture, psychiatry, philosophy.
Pangloss Bookshop, 1284 Mass. Ave. Second-hand books, obscure literary magazines.
Schoenhof's Foreign Books, Inc., 1280 Mass. Ave. Foreign-language books and art prints.
Sphinx Book Store, 111 Mt. Auburn St. Good books on philosophy, the occult, and organic cooking.
Starr Book . Shop, Inc., 29 Plympton St. Second-hand books, especially American and English literature.
Temple Bar Bookshop, 9 Boylston St. Poetry, literature, and photography are specialties.
Thomas More Book Shop, 6 Holyoke St. Modern religion, theology, moral philosophy.

CONTEMPORARY FURNITURE:

Children's Workbench, 1033 Mass. Ave.
Fluid Dynamics, 99 Mt. Auburn St. Water beds, of course.
Hooper-Ames, 40 Boylston St.
The Upper Story, 1045 Mass. Ave.

OLD THINGS, USED THINGS:

Dazzle, Inc., 11 Boylston St. (second floor). "Experienced" jeans, jackets, and more.
Goodwill Thrift Center, 1116 Mass. Ave. Recycled clothes, furniture.
Keezer's Harvard Community Exchange, 1221 Concord Ave. New and used clothes bought and sold. "Poor Man's Brooks Brothers" (15-minute walk from Harvard Sq., or take Belmont Center bus.)

THE OMNIBUS:

The Harvard Coop, 1400 Mass. Ave. Any and everything.

PLACES TO MOSEY AROUND:

Design Research, 48 Brattle St. Scandinavian contemporary design and Marimekko fabrics. 6 departments (including furniture and houseware) in a labyrinth of glass and color.
The Garage, 36 Boylston St. Over 25 shops. Folk art, houseware, funny boxes, beer-making stuff. far-out clothes.
Truc, 40 Brattle St. Unique gifts for others—and yourself. Fancy candles, soap, cookware and more.

OUTDOOR BOSTON

Parks

For Frederick Law Olmsted, the father of the Boston Park system and previously the designer of New York's Central Park, the public park fulfilled a particular need. It produced a healthfully soothing and refreshing effect upon people escaping the bustle, confinement, and disturbance of the city into spacious natural scenery. Implementation of Olmsted's concept of an "emerald necklace" adorning Boston is a glittering example of far-sighted land use policy by 19th-century government.

Below are brief descriptions of seven major parks you are likely to see. For further information on these or other parks and specific events held within them, call the Boston Dept. of Parks and Recreation (722-4100) or the MDC Park Office (727-5250).

Boston Common, the oldest public park in the nation, dating from 1634, provides green space and shaded walking paths in the heart of downtown Boston. On summer Sundays a bandstand concert is held from 2pm to 4pm, and at Christmastime live reindeer are on display near the intersection of Park and Tremont Sts. as part of the famous Christmas festival featuring lighted trees all over the Common. Beneath the Common is the Underground Parking Garage, which has reasonable rates and is open 24 hours a day. MBTA stations are at Park St. and Boylston.

Adjacent to the Common, across Charles St., is the Public Garden which contains fountains, formal flower beds, and carefully labelled rare trees. Of special interest is the Swan Boat Ride, a thoroughly enjoyable break from sightseeing or shopping and something no child visiting Boston should miss. The boats, shaped like swans and pedalled by strong-legged summer employees, navigate the duck and goose infested waters of the Garden's pond. The ride costs 40¢ for adults, 25¢ for children, and is open daily Apr-Sept.

The Back Bay Fens follow Muddy River and lie between Park Drive and the Fenway. Hundreds of rose varieties grown in formal plantings are best seen in June and July, and private citizen plots, the remnants of Boston's wartime Victory Gardens, are the interesting individual expressions of city gardeners.

Charlesbank Park and the Esplanade border the Charles

River and lie along the Back Bay residential section. The Community Boating concession for Boston residents is located in the park next to the Longfellow Bridge. Model boats can be sailed in Storrow Lagoon, and playground and picnic facilities are available. The Hatch Shell, a bandstand, is the site of pleasant evening concerts by the Boston Pops and Boston Symphony Orchestra (see Theater, Music, and Dance). Take the MBTA to Charles.

Arnold Arboretum in Jamaica Plain is open daily from sunrise to sunset. Administered by Harvard University in conjunction with the Boston Dept. of Parks and Recreation, the Arboretum is an extraordinarily beautiful 265-acre park containing over 6,000 varieties of ornamental trees, flowers, and shrubs. Middle May is the most splendid time; hundreds of lilacs, dogwoods, azaleas, and rhododendrons are in bloom. All plants are labelled. There is no admission charge and parking is free. Take the MBTA to Forest Hills, then walk two blocks west to the entrance. By car follow Route 1 south to Jamaica Plain.

Franklin Park, the largest park of the system, is accessible from the Egleston MBTA station. Every night of the summer, from July 4 to Labor Day, it is the home of the Elma Lewis Playhouse in the Park, a program of the National Center of Afro-American Artists. The free performances range from music and dance to dramatic presentations, gospel, and rock music. In the past, Duke Ellington, Odetta and the Billy Taylor Trio have participated. The park also houses the Franklin Park Zoo, open daily year-round. Admission to the main Zoo is free; the children's Zoo costs 75¢ for adults, 25¢ for children.

OUTDOOR ACTIVITIES

Beaches

Crane's Beach, Argilla Rd., Ipswich. 30 miles north of Boston. Take Rt 128 exit 18. A 5½ mile white sand beach with large dunes. Can be crowded in mid-summer. Parking $2.50 weekdays, $3.50 weekends.

Nahant Beach, Nahant Beach Parkway, Nahant. 15 miles north of Boston near intersection of Rts 1A and 129. T-Haymarket, then bus. Firepits and playground. Surfing allowed.

We're Exploring Alternatives to World Hunger.

United Brands has long shared the widespread concern over adequate world-wide production and distribution of food. As major producers of nutritious foods, we continually seek new ways and means to develop high protein food sources; new fields, new technologies are constantly being explored.

Food production is not the only business we're in, but it's one of the most rewarding. Meats, bananas, lettuce, shortening and cooking oils, poultry and livestock feeds are just some of the areas where we are working to improve and increase production.

Maybe hunger can't be erased everywhere in the world... but we intend to keep trying.

Nantasket Beach, Rt 228, Hull (925-0054). 18 miles south of Boston. T-Fields Corner, then bus. Also reachable by Mass. Bay Line boat from Rowe's Wharf on Atlantic Ave. (T-Aquarium). Two round trips daily; $4.75 adults, $3.25 children under 12. Call 542-8000 for department times. Paragon Park is at the beach and surfing is allowed.

Plum Island, Parker River Wildlife Refuge, Newburyport. 35 miles north of Boston. Take Rt 1 to Newburyport, then follow signs to Plum Island Turnpike. Beautiful 6½ mile sand beach with abundant water fowl. Surf-fishing allowed. Parking is $1 and admission 50¢ per person over 16.

Revere Beach, Revere Beach Parkway, Revere (284-0038). Off Rt 1A, T-Revere Beach. Bathhouse facilities.

South Boston Beaches. Along Day Blvd. in South Boston. T-South Station, then bus for Castle Island, City Point, Pleasure Bay and M Street Beaches. T-Columbia for Carson Beach, which has bathhouse facilities and rental lockers.

Beaches: Freshwater

Cochituate State Park, Rt 30 near Mass. Pike interchange, Natick. Picnic tables and firepits in the woods surrounding the lake.

Walden Pond Reservation, Rt 126, Concord. Swim in the pond Thoreau lived by and explore the adjacent woods. Open June 15-Labor Day.

Boat Rentals

Simpson's Pier, 90 Broadsound Ave., Revere (284-9656). T-Revere Beach. Fishing boats with outboard motor; $4 per hour, $24 per day. Open May-Sept, 7am to 7pm.

Hurley's Boat Rental, 136 Bay View Ave., Quincy (479-1239). T-Quincy, then Hough's Neck bus to Sea St. 16-ft. fishing boats with outboard motor; $17.50 per day. Open Apr-Oct, 6am to 6pm daily.

Jamaica Pond Boat House, 507 Jamaicaway (Rt 1), Jamaica Plain (524-3321). T-Arborway line to Pond St. Rowboats at 75¢ per hour. Fishing is allowed on the pond with license. Open Apr-Oct, from 5am to 8pm weather permitting.

South Bridge Boat House, Main St. (Rt 62), Concord (369-9438). Canoes and rowboats available for use on a 24-mile stretch of the Concord River which passes by the revolutionary battleground. $2 per hour, $10 per day weekdays. $3 per hour, $15 per day weekends. Open 9am to 6pm weekdays, 9am to dusk weekends. Closed Mon.

Winthrop Sailboat Rental, 541 Shirley St., Winthrop (846-2497). T-Orient Heights, then bus to Crystal Cove Marina. 10-ft. to 17-ft. sailboats; $20-$35 per day. Instruction available. Open May-Nov.

Bicycle Rentals

Beacon Hill Bike Shop, 303 Cambridge St., Boston (523-9133). T-Charles. 3-speed bicycles; $1.50 per hour, $6 per day. Open 8am to 7pm daily.

Bicycle Peddlar, 832 Commonwealth Ave., Boston (731-2550). T-Commonwealth Ave. line. 3-speed bicycles; $1.25 per hour, $3.50 per day weekdays, $4 per day weekends. Open 10am to 5pm. Closed Thurs.

Herson Cycle Co., 1250 Cambridge St., Cambridge (876-4474). T-Harvard/Lechmere bus line. 3-speed bicycles; $3 per day, $12 per week. 10-speed bicycles: $6 per day, $25 per week. Large deposit required on 10-speeds. Open Mon-Fri, 9am to 8pm; Sat, 9am to 5pm.

Fishing

Tackle, bait and advice as to what is running are available from:

Bill's Bait and Sport Shop, 1400 Dorchester Ave., Dorchester (436-9473).
Frisky Bait and Tackle Service, 291 Watertown St., Newton (244-9682).
Mass. Bait Shop, 466 American Legion Highway, Revere (284-8400).
Neponset Circle Bait Shop, 6 Redfield St., Dorchester (436-9231).
New England Bait and Tackle, 323 Meridian St., East Boston (567-9326).

A license is required to fish in fresh water anywhere in the Commonwealth of Massachusetts. 7-day non-resident permits are available from the Division of Fisheries and Game at 100 Cambridge Street, Boston (727-3158) or from any town clerk for $8.25. The following ponds are conveniently located and are stocked with trout.

Horn Pond, Woburn. Between Rts 3 and 38.

Houghton's Pond, Blue Hill Reservation, Milton. Near Rt 128, exit 65.

Jamaica Pond, 507 Jamaicaway (Rt 1), Jamaica Plain. T-Arborway line to Pond St. Rental rowboats available. Special Jamaica Pond permit required; is available at Jamaica Pond Boat House.

Upper Mystic Lake, Mystic St. (Rt 3), Winchester.

Salt water fishing does not require a license. There is a new 250 ft. fishing pier at Castle Island in South Boston (T-South Station, then City Point bus) and North and South Shore communities often allow fishing from the shoreline. Small fishing boats with outboard motors can be rented to increase mobility (see Boat Rentals). Deep sea fishing is available through **Boston Harbor Cruises Inc.** The boat leaves daily at 8am from Long Wharf (at State St. and Atlantic Ave., T-Aquarium) and returns at 4pm. The price of $10 includes bait and tackle. For more information call 227-4320.

SPECTATOR SPORTS

Baseball

Boston Red Sox Baseball Club, 24 Jersey St., Boston (267-2525). T-Kenmore. American League professional baseball. Games are at Fenway Park, perhaps the best major league park in the nation for spectators due to its relatively small size and high proportion of good seats. The crowd is always large, loud, partisan, and friendly. 81-game season runs Apr-Oct with day and night games. Tickets are $1.25-$4.50.

Basketball

Boston Celtics Basketball Club Inc., Boston Garden, Boston (523-6050). T-North Station. NBA professional basketball featuring the greatest dynasty in the history of professional sports, 12 times world champions. The Celtics are always among the best teams in the league; they play intelligent, fast-break basketball, and have developed a winning tradition of excellence. 40 games in an Oct-May season with most games Wed and Fri nights and Sun afternoons. Night games begin at 7:30pm, afternoon games at 2pm. Tickets $3-$8.

Football

New England Patriots Football Club, Rt 1, Foxboro (262-1776). Take Southeast Expressway to Rt 128 to Rt I-95 then Foxboro exit. Buses also available. NFL professional football with three exhibition and seven regular season home games played Aug-Dec. Games are played at the new Foxboro Stadium. Tickets can be difficult to obtain, so check well in advance. Tickets cost $5-$8.

Hockey

Boston Bruins Hockey Club, North Station, Boston (227-3200). T-North Station. The NHL professional team in a hockey-crazy town. If you are from out-of-town, don't cheer too hard for the other team—Boston fans are highly partisan and imbued with Bruin pride. Many games are sellouts so inquire about the availability of seats. 40 games plus playoffs in a season running Oct-May. Most games on Thurs and Sun. Tickets $6-$10.

Soccer

Boston Astros, Boston University Nickerson Field, Babcock St., Boston (262-2807). T-Commonwealth Ave. line. ASL professional soccer with 20-game season running May-Sept. Most games on weekends. Starting time 7:30pm. Tickets $1-$3.

Boston Minutemen, Boston College Alumni Stadium, Chestnut Hill (227-5474). T-Commonwealth Ave. line to the end; NASL professional soccer. 20 game season May-Aug with most home games Sat at 7:30pm. Tickets $1-$4.

Tennis

Boston Lobsters Tennis Club, Walter Brown Arena, Babcock St., Boston (266-9682). T-Commonwealth Ave. Line. WTT professional tennis. 22 home matches played at night, May-Aug. Tickets $4-$6.

Boxing

AAU Amateur Boxing, the Harbor House Hotel, 830 The Lynnway (Rt 1A), Lynn (742-2248). Boxing every Mon night June-Labor Day. Admission $3. From Sept-Jan the action shifts indoors to the Wonderland Ballroom, 1290 N. Shore Blvd., Revere. T-Revere Beach.

Dog Racing

Wonderland Race Track, Wonderland Park, Revere (284-1300). T-Wonderland. Races at 8pm, May to September. Perfectas, Trifecta, and daily double. $1 admission. Closed Sun.

Horse Racing

Bay State Raceway, Rt 1, Foxboro (361-4900). Take Southeast Expressway to Rt 128 to Rt I-95, then Foxboro exit. Gray Line buses also available. Harness racing June-Sept, Tues-Sat at 8pm, Sunday at 2pm. Admission $1. Closed Mon.

Suffolk Downs, McClellan Highway, East Boston (567-3900). T-Suffolk Downs. Thoroughbred racing Sept-July with 9 races weekdays, 10 races weekends and holidays. 1:30pm post time. Admission $2-$3. Closed Tues.

RESTAURANTS

We have chosen restaurants with the intention of providing a varied list which covers a wide price range and contains places to eat in each major section of the city. You will find that restaurants are arranged by area and not by specialty, although certain styles of food are often concentrated in certain parts of town: the North End, for instance, is the home of Italian cooking in Boston. If you are seeking a certain style of restaurant—French, Indian, kosher, vegetarian—consult the index of the book to find the pages on which those entries occur.

This list is limited by space, and does not by any means contain all the fine restaurants in Boston. In addition, many new restaurants will open during the Bicentennial, too late to make our publishing deadline. We urge you to discover your own favorites. Also, because of the time lapse involved in publishing this book, you should not be surprised by a 5-10% rise in prices due to inflation.

Finally, keep in mind that Boston contains large and excellent hotels, which serve food commensurate with their other facilities. We have made it a practice not to list hotel restaurants except for a few which are particularly famous, but you may want to sample other hotel fare on your own.

DOWNTOWN

Athens Olympia, 51 Stuart St. (426-6236). T-Boylston. The Olympia serves Greek food, particularly lamb, in a friendly European atmosphere. Meals cost $2.50 to $6.25. Children's menu available on request. Liquor. No reservations needed. American Express. Handy to theaters and downtown cinemas. Open daily, 11am to midnight.

Benihana of Tokyo, 201 Stuart St. (542-1166). T-Arlington. At Benihana's your meal is cooked at the table. This unique experience in Japanese dining draws a varied clientele; prices range from $5.50 to $10 (the Benihana special which also includes sake wine). Credit cards accepted and reservations required. Liquor. Open Mon-Fri, noon to 2:15pm, 5:30pm to 9:30pm; Sat, 5:30pm to 10:30pm; Sun, 4:30pm to 8:30pm.

Bette's Rolls Royce, One Union St. (227-0675, 523-8409). T-Government Center or Haymarket. All the food at Bette's is homemade; specialities include oysters, steaks, home-fries, Reuben sandwiches, Greek salad, chili, pastries. Dress is informal. Sunday nights from to 7pm to 11pm you'll find honky-tonk piano, sing-alongs, and Dixieland bands. Free hors d'oeuvres, Mon-Fri, 5pm to 7pm. Prices range from $1.25 to $5.95, all à la carte. Open daily, 11:30am to 2am. Liquor license; credit cards accepted. No reservations.

Delimaster, 150a Tremont St. (825-3688). T-Park St. or Boylston. Take-out or sit-down delicatessen meals. Stuffed cabbage, pepper steak, Hungarian goulash, and all of the traditional New York deli items. Open daily, 7am to 3am. Prices from 60¢ to $7.80 (half portions for children). No credit cards or reservations. Beer and wine.

Dini's, 94 Tremont St. (227-0380). T-Park St. Good seafood in the center of downtown Boston. Lunch and supper can be ordered à la carte or as complete meals, ranging from $6 to $10. Steaks, chops and chicken are also served; a children's menu is available. Reservations are recommended; American Express and Master Charge accepted. Liquor. Open daily, 10:30am to 10:30pm; Sun, 11:00am to 10:30pm.

Dunfey's Last Hurrah, Tremont and School Sts. (227-8600). T-Park St. or Government Center; parking around corner at Province Street Garage. Schrod, steak, shrimp or chicken matched with your choice among seven sauces. All entries include potato and Parker House rolls. Salad from a varied salad bar. Stews and sandwiches also available. The atmosphere is exuberant Gay Nineties. Liquor. Major credit cards accepted. Meals cost $2 to $10. Open daily, 11:30am to 2am. No reservations.

Durgin Park, 30 North Market St. (227-2038). T-Government Center or Haymarket. Durgin Park is famous for many things, particularly its rude waitresses, long communal tables, and roast beef. The menu is huge, the atmosphere loud and friendly. Luncheon specials at $1.25 until 2:30pm. Other items are à la carte, ranging from $3.50 to $9.00. Open Mon-Sat,

11:30am to 9pm. No credit cards or reservations accepted. Liquor.

Fatted Calf Saloon and Eatery, 4 Beacon St. (523-8721). T-Park St. or Government Center. Full meals available from $1.75 to $4.95. Specializing in beef dishes. Liquor. American Express and BankAmericard accepted. Open Mon-Fri, 11:30am to 10pm.

Havah Nagila Restaurant, 280 Cambridge St., Boston (523-9838); T-Charles. 1653 Beacon St., Brookline (277-3433). T-Cleveland Circle line to Washington Sq. Informal, inexpensive ($1.00-$3.75) Israeli and Middle Eastern specialties. Sandwiches, shish kebab and good Turkish coffee are the staples. Beer and wine. No reservations or credit cards. Open daily, 11:30am to midnight.

Jacob Wirth's, 31-37 Stuart St. (338-7194, 8586). T-Boylston. A traditional German restaurant, famous for its good beer. Floor is sprinkled with sawdust. Lunches from $1.50 to $2.25; dinners, $1.50 to $3.75. Open Mon-Sat, 10:30am to 9:15pm. Liquor. No credit cards; no reservations.

Locke-Ober Cafe, 3-4 Winter Place (542-1340). T-Washington; parking under Common or in Bedford St. Garage. One of Boston's most famous restaurants—and certainly its most traditional. Women may now dine in its elegantly paneled downstairs room, once reserved for men. Both dining rooms are faithfully Victorian in decor. The cuisine is French and American, and meals cost from $5 to $18. Liquor. The restaurant accepts American Express, Bank-Americard and Master Charge. Open Mon-Sat, 11am to 10pm. Reservations recommended. Jackets required.

Maison Robert, 45 School St. (227-3370). T-Park St. or Government Center. One of Boston's newer excellent restaurants, located in the Old City Hall. French-style veal leg of lamb, Dover sole, filet mignon are among the specialties. The Maison has two floors, with food upstairs slightly more expensive ($15 for a full dinner). Outdoor cafe in summer. Open Mon-Fri, noon to 2:30pm, 6pm to 10pm; Sat, 6pm to 10:30pm; Sun, 6pm to 10pm. American Express, Master Charge, and BankAmericard accepted; reservations required. Liquor. Jackets and ties required for dinner.

Maitre Jacques, 10 Emerson Place (742-5480). T-Charles St. or Science Park. Maitre Jacques is "a classical French restaurant in a modern setting." All items are à la carte, luncheon prices ranging from $4 to $8, dinner from $5 to $10. Specialties include lamb, veal, Dover sole, and of course, onion soup gratinée. Open Mon-Fri, noon to 2:30pm, 6pm to 10pm; Sat, 6pm to 10:30pm. Credit cards accepted; reservations desired. Liquor. Jackets and ties required for dinner.

One Dock Square, 16 North St. (723-9887). T-Government Center. Serves both lunch and dinner. Thick market-style sandwiches and salad bar; fish and meat dishes served too. Dinners from $2.25 to $6.95. Open Mon-Sat 11:30am to 11:30pm, Sun 9am to 9pm. Sunday brunch 11am to 2:30pm. American Express, BankAmericard, and Diner's Club accepted. Reservations suggested for dinner. Liquor (2 bars).

Patten's Restaurant, 173 Milk St. (227-8775). T-State or Aquarium; adjoining parking. Located in a Bulfinch building, Patten's emphasizes seafood and steaks served in an early American setting. Schrod, prime rib, stuffed shrimp and big sandwiches (crab, club, Reuben) are specialties. There's a $1.95 luncheon plate; other choices go from $2.50 to $10. Liquor. Master Charge, American Express and Diner's Club are accepted. Open Mon-Sat, 11am to 1am.

Pete's or Sabia's Cafe, 82 Broad St. (338-9666). T-Aquarium or State; parking at Harbor Tower Garage. Large, relaxed place with a long list of daily specials, most of them ranging from $2 to $4.50 and including potato. Many kinds of meat, fish and sandwiches. No freezer: all food is fresh. Known for its big drinks. No credit cards. Open Mon-Fri, 11:30am to 10pm (last food order 9pm).

Union Oyster House, 41 Union St. (227-2750). T-Haymarket or Government Center; parking in Government Center garage. A Boston landmark in its own right, the Oyster House has been doing continuous business since 1826 in a building which dates from 1742 or earlier. In colonial times the building was a fashionable draper's shop, selling imported silks. *The Massachusetts Spy,* a periodical "Open to All Parties But Influenced by None," was published in the upper stories. During the Revolution Ebenezer Hancock, paymaster of Washington's army, kept his office here. When the restaurant opened, it soon became a favorite of Daniel Webster, who could polish off six plates of oysters and as many brandy-and-waters at a sitting. It was also briefly the home of Louis Philippe, later king of the French, who once gave French lessons to Bostonians for a living. Now Boston's oldest restaurant, the Oyster House is most proud of its baked stuffed lobster, shore dinner, oyster stew and fresh schrod, though other excellent seafood and prime meats are available. Lunch prices range from $1.15 to $3.25, dinners from $3.50 to $11.25 (though less expensive sandwiches are available). Liquor. American Express, BankAmericard, Diner's Club and Master Charge accepted. Open Sun-Thurs, 11am to 9pm; Fri, 11am to 9:30pm; Sat, 11am to 10pm. Children's menu available.

CHINATOWN

China Pearl, 9 Tyler St. (426-4338). T-Boylston; parking next door. Large, good, Chinatown restaurant featuring Cantonese and Polynesian food. Specialties include Moo Goo Gai Pan, Champagne Duck and The Four Happiness. Prices range from $5 to $8.50. Liquor; all major credit cards accepted. Open daily, 11am to 2am.

Fung Won, 8 Tyler St. (542-1175). T-Essex. Cantonese-style food, specializing in Peking Duck ($12—serves 3 or 4). Luncheon specials, 11am to 3pm, weekdays. Open Mon-Fri, 9am to 3pm; Sat-Sun, 9am to 4pm. Prices start at $1.60. No credit cards; no liquor. Reservations required for large groups.

The Shanghai, 21 Hudson St. (482-4797). T-Boylston. Shanghai, Szechuan, and Mandarin fare. Peking Duck is especially good. Patrons are given chopsticks, and must ask for forks. Prices range from $1.95 to $13.50. Open daily, 11am to 3pm for lunch, 5pm to 10pm for dinner. Tea and pastries served Sat and Sun, 11:30am to 2pm.

NORTH END

Cantina Italiana, 346 Hanover St. (742-9851). T-Haymarket. Good, inexpensive Italian food in an informal atmosphere. Specialty of the house: shrimp fra diavolo. Dinners from $2.50 to $5.50, children's portions on request. Liquor. Reservations required on weekends; American Express accepted. Open daily, 11:30am to midnight.

Felicia's, 145A Richmond St. (523-9885). T-Government Center. Northern Italian cooking, including chicken virridicio (boneless chicken) and cannelloni (homemade crepes filled with meats and covered with white cream sauce). Wed-Sat you can watch Felicia cooking in the kitchen. Full dinners from $6.50 to $8.95; à la carte items also available. Beer and wine; children's menu; reservations accepted, except on Sat; American Express and Diner's Club. Open Mon-Sat, 5pm to 10:30pm; Sun, 4pm to 10:30pm. Jackets and ties required in winter.

Giro's, 464 Hanover St. (523-8420). T-North Station. Large selection of Italian-American dishes, including steaks, chops, lobster, chicken, pasta. Lunch prices start at $1.90; all dinners are a la carte. Credit cards and reservations are accepted. Liquor. Open daily, 11:30am to 1am.

Joe Tecce's, 53 North Washington St. (523-8975). T-Haymarket or North Station. One of Boston's most famous Italian restaurants. Specialties include veal scallopini and chicken cacciatore; reasonable prices attract a very mixed clientele. Open Mon-Fri 5pm to 11pm, Sat 5pm to midnight. No credit cards or reservations. Liquor.

Mother Anna's, 211 Hanover St. (523-8496). T-Haymarket. Italian food, including veal scallopini, chicken and shrimp. Full dinners average $6.25; half-portions available for children. Open Tues-Sun, 5pm to 11pm. No credit cards or reservations; wine and beer.

Polcari's, 283 Causeway St. (742-4142). T-North Station. Polcari's Italian-American cuisine attracts a large crowd of Boston businessmen and politicians. A la carte meals start at $2.50. Specialties include shrimp scampi, lobster fra diavolo, lasagna, steaks, and filet mignon. Open Mon-Fri, 11:30am to 1am; Sat, 5pm to 1am; Sun, 11:30am to 1am. Credit cards accepted. Liquor. Reservations not required.

CHARLESTOWN

Warren Tavern, 2 Pleasant St. (241-8500). T-Community College. It's typical Boston fare of seafood, beef and poultry in an old New England atmosphere. The building dates from 1780. Master Charge accepted. Reservations suggested on Fri and Sat, jackets after 6pm. Prices from $4.50 to $7. Open Mon-Sat in summer, daily in winter, 11:30am to 2:30pm, 6pm to 9pm.

WATERFRONT

Anthony's Pier 4, 140 Northern Ave. (423-6363). T-South Station or take the Fish Pier bus; parking available. Anthony's is one of the most famous seafood restaurants in Boston. The food is expensive, but of high quality. Specialties include fresh seafood, lobster, steaks and roast beef. Reservations are not accepted, so you'll probably have to wait a while and enjoy the free cheese and crackers in the bar. Try to get a table with a view of the Boston skyline and harbor. Liquor. Credit cards are accepted. Open Mon-Sat, 11:30am to 11pm; Sun and holidays, 12:30pm to 10:30pm. Jackets and ties required.

The Chart House, 60 Long Wharf (227-1576). T-Aquarium; parking at restaurant. Steaks, chicken and seafood dinners from $6 to $9; sandwiches served at the bar, hamburgers available for children. Lunch prices range from $2 to $4. Open Mon-Fri, 11:30am to 2:30pm; Mon-Thurs, 5pm to 11pm; Fri-Sun, 5pm to midnight. BankAmericard, Master Charge, and American Express accepted; no reservations. Liquor.

Dom's, 236 Commercial St. (523-8838). T-Aquarium or Government Center; parking lot across street. Located near the wharves in an old beer warehouse with the original beam-and-brick interior, Dom's serves northern Italian meals, specializing in seafood, pasta, chicken and veal dishes. Lunch runs $1.75 to $4.50; dinner, $3.50 to $10.75. Children under ten get free spaghetti, meatballs and beverage at dinner. Liquor. Master Charge and BankAmericard accepted. Open Sun-Fri, noon to 2:30pm; Mon-Sat, 5:30pm to 1:30am; Sun, noon to midnight.

Jimmy's Harborside, 242 Northern Ave. (423-1000). T-South Station; street parking and valet service. A fine seafood restaurant located on the Fish Pier, with a large seating capacity and a romantic harbor view. Limited reservations are accepted; otherwise, you wait in the bar. All kinds of fish and shellfish, though baked stuffed filet of sole and lobster Newburg are specialties. Prices range from $2.25 to $9. Limited children's menu. American Express, Master Charge, Diner's Club, Carte Blanche and house credit cards accepted. Open Mon-Sat, 11:30am to 9:30pm. Jackets required.

No-Name Restaurant, 15½ Fish Pier (338-7539). T-South Station, then City Point bus. Seafood at low prices is the specialty of this waterfront restaurant. Fish is freshest possible, pastry is homemade. Meals from $2 to $3. Clientele is mainly families, businessmen. Open Mon-Fri, 8am to 9:30pm. No reservations.

BEACON HILL

Au Beauchamp, 99 Mt. Vernon St. (523-6720). T-Charles St. Typical French food and atmosphere in lovely setting on historic Beacon Hill. The fare includes coq au vin, chateaubriand, coquilles St. Jacques, soft shell crabs amandine. There is a children's menu. Entrees from $6.25 to $10. Open noon to 2:30pm, 6pm to 9pm; Sun, 5:30pm to 9pm. Wine and beer. Reservations required on weekends.

The Charles, 75A Chestnut St. (523-4477). T-Charles, Arlington, or Park St. A Beacon Hill restaurant that caters to a young office crowd, it offers beef Cordon Bleu, stroganoff and other dishes from $5.50 to $9.50. Don't be surprised to run into local politicians. Credit cards are accepted and French and Italian wines are available. Open every day except Sunday for dinner, 4:30pm to 11pm. Also open for lunch. Reservations required on Sat.

The Townhouse, 84 Beacon St. (227-9600). T-Park St. or Arlington. It's popular with young business people and combines a seafood and steak menu. "Biggest burger in town." Sunday brunch. Credit cards are accepted and there is a bar, where prices start at $2.50. The Bull and Finch Pub is a separate cocktail section with sandwiches and snack foods. Open 11:30am to 2am.

BACK BAY

Cafe L'Ananas, 281 Newbury St. (353-0176). T-Auditorium. French/Continental cooking—lunch may be eaten outdoors. Complete lunches from $3 to $5, dinners from $8 to $13. No credit cards. Reservations accepted. Liquor (including 70 wines). Open Mon-Sat, noon to 2:30pm, 6pm to 11pm.

Cafe Budapest, 90 Exeter St. (734-3388). T-Copley, located in the Copley Hotel; parking at Prudential Center. One of Boston's most elegant restaurants, offering Hungarian food and romantic decor. Iced cherry soup, goulache, mixed grill à la Hongroise and Hungarian strudel are the particular specialties. Excellent Viennese coffee. Meals from $10 to $16. Liquor. Major credit cards accepted. Reservations recommended. Open Sun-Thurs, noon to 10:30pm; Fri-Sat, noon to midnight. Jackets and ties required.

Cafe Florian, 85 Newbury St. (247-7603). T-Arlington or Copley. A sidewalk cafe which serves an exclusive line of French omelettes; specialty dishes include Hungarian goulash, Shrimp Arrogada; full line of Espresso and Viennese coffees, European pastries. Prices range from $2.50 to $5. Clientele is predominantly shoppers, businessmen, and families. Open Mon-Thurs, noon to midnight; Fri-Sat, noon to 1am; closed Sun.

Casa Romero, 30 Gloucester St. (261-2146). T-Auditorium. The simple, tasteful decor of Casa Romero promises good food, and you won't be disappointed. But beware of the spices! Specialties include enchiladas verdes (tortilla and chicken in green sauce), shrimp, stuffed peppers, cactus salad, chocolate-cinnamon coffee, and rich mango soufflé. Prices from $4 to

$17 (dinner for two). Open 7 days a week, 6pm to 11pm; lunch is served Tues-Fri, noon to 2:30pm. No credit cards; reservations not accepted Fri and Sat. Liquor.

Charley's Eating and Drinking Saloon, 344 Newbury St. (266-3000). T-Auditorium. Also Chestnut Hill Mall, Chestnut Hill (244-1200). Charley's friendly Gay Nineties pub atmosphere is complemented by some of the best beef this side of the Charles River. Specialties include New York sirloin, prime ribs, and sliced London broil; Charley's also brings back the nickel beer, served with dinner entrees. Full bar service. Prices range from $1.95 for one of Charley's heaping sandwiches to $6.50 for 16 oz. of sirloin steak. Open daily, 11:30am to 3:30pm for lunch, 3:30pm to 1am for dinner, drinking until 2am. American Express and Carte Blanche accepted. Charley's serves a large mixed crowd, but does not take reservations, so get there early on weekends.

Copley's, Copley Plaza Hotel, Copley Sq. (267-5300). T-Copley. A stately restaurant in one of Boston's most luxurious hotels. Four menus rotate daily, offering quiche, schrod, Carpetbagger Steak (wrapped in bacon and served stuffed with mushrooms, peppers and onions), Black Forest Cake, and other specialties. Extensive salad bar. Lunches average $3.65, dinner entrees from $4.95 to $8.95. Soft, live music nightly. A conservatory and tea court are also on the premises. Open Mon-Fri, 11:30am to 3pm, 6pm to midnight; Sat, 6pm to midnight; Sun, noon to midnight. Reservations taken for dinner. Jackets and ties required.

The English Room, 29 Newbury St. (262-8631). T-Arlington, one half block from the Ritz Carlton Hotel. Service is fast and unrefined at the English Room, but there's plenty to eat. Rolls, salad, dessert and beverage are included in the price of each of the twenty entrees. Prices from $2.90 to $4.50. The dinner crowd is largely students. No credit cards, no liquor. No reservations, either, so it's a good idea to get there before 6pm on the weekends. Open daily, 11am to 9pm.

Falstaff Room, Sheraton Hotel (236-2000). T-Prudential Center. Sunday brunch is a bargain at the Falstaff Room—wide selection of dishes from bagels and lox to Boston cream pie, all for $4.33 ($2 if you are under 12). Bloody Mary fountain provides an endless supply of Bloody Marys . . . they're weak, but they're free. All-American steak and brew dinners also available, 5:30pm to 11pm, 7 days a week. Sunday brunch,

9:30am to 3pm; Mon-Fri, breakfast and lunch, 7:30am to 2:30pm. Full liquor license; credit cards accepted.

Greenhouse I, 385 Boylston St. (261-1050). T-Arlington. Syrian sandwiches are the specialty in this small Near Eastern/American sidewalk cafe. It also creates its own new sandwiches, priced from $1.25 to $2.50. Open daily, 11am to 6pm (8:30pm during the Bicentennial). Plants are sold in the greenhouse in the rear.

Hai-Hai, 423 Boylston St. (536-8474). T-Arlington. One of Boston's few Japanese restaurants, Hai-Hai ("Yes-Yes") offers tempura, katsu (fried cutlets), steak teriyaki, soba (a soup/stew), and daily specials at prices you can afford (lunch, $1.50-$3, dinner, $2.50-$4). Open Mon-Sat, noon to 2:30pm, 5pm to 10pm; Sun, 4pm to 9pm. Beer and wine. No credit cards; no reservations.

Half-Shell, 743 Boylston St. (423-5555). T-Copley. Seafood restaurant with branches in Denver and L.A. Prices from $2 to $14. Open daily, 11:30am to 2am. Liquor. Credit cards accepted; reservations required for parties of eight or more.

Joseph's, 279 Dartmouth St. (266-1502). T-Copley. Grand old French restaurant. One of Boston's most famous. Dinners are all à la carte and start at $5. Major credit cards accepted; reservations advisable. Open Mon-Sat, 11:45am to 11pm. Liquor. Jackets required.

Ken's at Copley, 549 Boylston St. (266-6149). T-Copley. Large deli-restaurant on Copley Square, known for its blintzes, pastrami, cheese pie, pastries and combination sandwiches. Good for breakfast or brunch. Meals go from $1.75 to $5.95. Beer and wine available; no reservations or credit cards. Open daily, 7am to 3am.

Newbury's Steak House, 94 Mass. Ave. (536-0184). T-Auditorium; free parking at 341 Newbury St. Steaks (filet mignon, sirloin, London broil) and fresh seafoods. Large sandwiches served for lunch and dinner. Salad bar. Lunches range from $1.95 to $2.75, dinners from $3.25 to $5.75. Liquor. Open daily, noon to midnight.

Ritz Carlton Dining Room and Cafe, 15 Arlington St. (536-5700). T-Arlington. Considered one of Boston's finest restaurants, the Ritz offers excellent continental and New England cuisine in dining rooms overlooking the Public Garden. Reservations are required in the dining room but not in the cafe. Liquor. Dinners in the cafe range from $5 to $7.50, lunches $4 to $6. Prices in the dining room are from $10 to $15 for dinner, and $7 to $10 for lunch. Open daily from noon to 2:30pm, 6pm to 9pm. Cafe closed Sun afternoon. Jackets and ties required.

Top of the Hub, Top of the Prudential Tower (52nd floor) (536-1775). T-Prudential. If it is a clear day, the Top of the Hub will give you a superb view of the city. The food is American, with prices ranging from $6 to $11. A cocktail lounge, featuring music and dancing, is open every night until 1am, Sun and Mon until midnight. Restaurant hours are: Mon-Sat, 11:30am to 3:15pm, 5:30pm to midnight; Sun, buffet brunch, 11am to 2pm, dinner, 4:30pm to midnight. Credit cards accepted, reservations not required. Liquor. Jackets and ties required for dinner.

Trader Vic's, Statler Hilton Hotel, Park Sq. at Arlington St. (426-2000, X354 or 355). T-Arlington. Part of the famous national chain, known for its steaks, lobster, curry, Cantonese food and exotic cocktails. Meals from $5 to $11. Children's portion priced accordingly. Reservations advisable; all major credit cards accepted. Open for lunch, Mon-Fri, 11:30am to 2:30pm; daily for dinner, 5pm to 11:30pm. Jackets and ties preferred except for lunch during summer.

SOUTH END

Bob the Chef, 604 Columbus Ave. (262-9773). This is "the home of soul food." Chicken, fish, ribs, black-eyed peas, and rice pudding are among the many recommended specialties. The meals are filling, and the prices are low ($2.75-$3.60). No credit cards, liquor, or reservations. Open Tues-Sat, 11am to 9pm.

Premier Restaurant, 1130 Washington St. (426-2218). T-Dover; ample parking. Billing itself as the "last of its kind in Boston," this large Jewish-style delicatessen serves dinners from $3 to $4. Hot pastrami, and home-made soups are the house specialties. Seating 150, it was rated best deli by *Boston* Magazine. Open Mon-Sat, 5am to 9pm.

Red Fez, 1222 Washington St. (338-8446). T-Dover. A Lebanese-Middle Eastern restaurant with primarily a family and couples appeal. Reservations are required; wine and beer available. Lunch, $2.50, dinner, $3.50 to $6. Open daily, 11:30am to 10pm.

CAMBRIDGE

Averof Restaurant, 1972 Mass. Ave. (354-4500). T-Harvard, then take bus to North Cambridge, Porter Square; plenty of parking. Averof's fare is primarily Greek and Middle Eastern —shish kebab, moussaka, kalamaria. The atmosphere is casual and frequently the Middle Eastern entertainment includes a belly dancer. Prices range from $1.10 to $5.50. There is a children's menu. Liquor. Open Mon-Sat, 11:30am to 1am; Sun, 1pm to 11pm.

Bartley's Burger Cottage, 1246 Massachusetts Ave. (354-9830). T-Harvard. For hamburgers, try one of Bartley's 25 varieties. The burgers are *large*; salads and sandwiches, too. Prices from 60¢ to $2.25. Open Mon-Sat, 8am to 6pm. No credit cards or liquor license.

Casa Mexico, 75 Winthrop St. (491-4552). T-Harvard. This cheerful basement offers authentic Mexican cuisine: chiles rellenos (a spicy appetizer), guacamole (avocado salad), enchiladas verdes, and much more. A la carte meals range from $5.50 to $7. Open Mon-Thurs, noon to 2:30pm, 6pm to 10pm; Fri-Sat, noon to 2:30pm, 6pm to 11pm; Sun, 6pm to

10pm. Bring your own liquor or wine; reservations possible Sun-Thurs. No credit cards.

Casa Portugal, 1200 Cambridge St. (491-8880). T-Harvard Square, then take Lechmere bus. Portuguese-style pork and seafood dishes are the specialties: marinated pork with clams, bacalhau (cod fish). Liquor. Reservations recommended on Fri and Sat. Children's minute steaks are $2.50. Regular meals are from $3 to $5. Open Mon and Tues, 5pm to 9:30pm; Wed-Sat, noon to 9:30pm. Closed Sun during June, July and Aug.

Elsie's, 71 Mt. Auburn St. (491-2842). T-Harvard. Quick sandwiches, subs, hamburgers and frappes—a favorite hangout of Harvard students. All items are under $2. Pinball machines in an adjoining room. Open Mon-Fri, 6:30am to midnight; Sat, 8am to 4pm; closed Sun during summer.

The Hungry Persian, 14A Eliot St. (354-9015). T-Harvard. This homey place features Middle Eastern sandwiches in Syrian bread, costing from 70¢ to $1.50 (for the special sandwich: beef, ham, turkey, lettuce, tomato and cheese in a special sauce). Seats 75; phoned-in take-out orders are accepted. Popular with the Harvard Sq. crowd. Open Mon-Sat, 11am to midnight; Sun, noon to midnight.

Iruña, 56 Boylston St. (868-5633). T-Harvard. Authentic Spanish food in Harvard Sq. Iruña offers paella (shrimp, chicken, rice), filete (filet mignon), carzuela (seafood), salads, omelets, sangria, and more. Lunches up to $2, dinners to $5.50 (à la carte). Open weekdays, noon to 2pm, 6pm to 9pm; Fri-Sat, noon to 2pm, 6pm to 10pm. No credit cards; no reservations. Liquor.

Joyce Chen Restaurant, 302 Mass. Ave. (492-7272) T-Harvard, then Dudley bus; or (expected to open in late 1974) 390 Rindge Ave. (492-7373) T-Harvard, and bus to North Cambridge and shuttle up Rindge Ave. The Boston area's most famous Chinese restaurant. Specializes in Mandarin and Szechuan food but has dishes from all major Chinese cuisines. The new Rindge Ave. restaurant will offer a menu with a wider variety of Chinese food and will also feature cooking demonstrations and exhibits of Chinese culture. Prices about $3 to $6 per person. Special buffets Tues and Wed 6pm to 8:30pm. Credit cards accepted. Liquor. Open Sun-Thurs noon to 10pm, Fri and Sat noon to midnight.

Legal Seafoods, 237 Hampshire St. (547-1410) T-Harvard, then take Lechmere bus. Restaurant offers fresh seafood from its own fish market. Julia Child, chef of TV fame, likes it, as do students, families and business people from the Harvard/MIT communities. Meals run from $2.50 to $6.95. When the Chinese delegation visited the U.S. in 1973 they chose to eat here. Open Mon-Sat 11am to 9pm, Sun 1pm to 9pm.

Natalie's, 1672 Mass. Ave. (547-9081). T-Harvard. Italian restaurant with primarily student clientele. Meals priced from $2 to $5. Liquor. Open Mon-Thurs, 11:30am to 10pm; Fri, 11:30am to midnight; Sat, 5pm to 11pm.

Natraj Indian Restaurant, 419 Mass. Ave. (547-8810). T-Central; parking behind the restaurant. Combine an evening at the Central Square Cinema with a moderately-priced authentic Indian meal at Natraj. Full dinners range from $2.75 to $4.95 (à la carte items, too). The hot curry is very hot, but the menu provides many milder items to choose from. There's a special $12.75 dinner for 2, but a "minimum advance notice of 8 hours is required for this dinner." Dinner: Mon-Thurs, 5:30pm to 9pm; Fri-Sat, 5:30pm to 10pm. Lunch: Tues-Fri, 11:30am to 2pm. Reservations required on Fri and Sat. Master Charge accepted.

The Underdog, 6 Bow St. (661-0388). T-Harvard, or Dudley bus along Massachusetts Ave. Specializes in Hebrew National kosher franks, pastrami and hot combination sandwiches. No sandwich over $1.60 at this writing (underdogs, 60¢). Seats only 20, but you can phone take-out orders. Promises best pinball in Harvard Sq. Will supply food for hot dog barbecues and picnics (2-day notice for large groups). Open daily, 11:30am to 1am.

Wursthaus Restaurant, 4 Boylston St. (491-7110). T-Harvard. One of the oldest restaurants in Harvard Sq., the Wursthaus features German-American food at prices from $1.65 to $7. The Wursthaus carries 112 kinds of imported beer (and non-alcoholic beers for minors). The desserts are the best of the Wurst: try the cheese cake or apple strudel. Clientele includes business people, families, and students with cash to spare. Open Sun-Thurs, 8am to midnight; Fri-Sat, 8am to 1am. No credit cards; reservations not required.

ALL OVER TOWN

Bailey's, 26 Temple Place (T-Park St.); 74 Franklin St. (T-State); 392 Boylston St. (T-Arlington); 21 Brattle St. (T-Harvard); 1330 Boylston St., Brookline (T-Kenmore Sq., then bus to Chestnut Hill). These old-fashioned ice cream parlors are a Boston institution, famous for large, sloppy sundaes and cones. The firm is 100 years old, and with due respect to the past, candy is made by hand at the 26 Temple Place store in Boston. Price range is 25¢ to $1.25.

Brigham's is another Boston institution that has now spread to the suburbs and surrounding areas. It is a chain of ice cream and candy parlors which usually also offer sandwiches and often hamburgers (though not all Brigham's stores have grills). Most locations seat 60 at counters and tables, and also fill take-out orders.

Friendly's is a reliable ice cream chain that also serves burgers, sandwiches, and luncheon platters. There are dozens of locations throughout Massachusetts, often near main roads and in shopping plazas. Lunches run from 50¢ to $1.59. Free-standing shops are open from 7am to 11pm daily; Friendly's located in shopping malls are open at 9am, and closed Sundays. Boston locations are Charles River Plaza (T-Charles) and the Museum of Science (T-Science Park).

Howard Johnson's, Exec. Office: Howard Johnson Plaza, Dorchester, (848-2350). Howard Johnson's has 21 restaurants in the Boston area. For the location nearest you check the phone book, a Boston 200 Visitor Information Center or call the executive office. The two Boston restaurants are at 500 Boylston St. (262-8914), and 196 Stuart St. (338-8349). Moderately-priced food of middle-quality served in identical fashion in restaurants across the U. S. Daily specials.

Pewter Pot Muffin House, 164 Tremont St. (Boston Common) (423-6288) T-Park St.; 741 Boylston St. (near Prudential Center) (536-4470) T-Prudential; 3 Brattle St., Cambridge (547-5376) T-Harvard. Open daily, 7am-midnight, serving a variety of inexpensive breakfast, lunch and dinner foods. Muffins are the specialty—the 12 varieties include blueberry, cranberry, corn, chocolate chip, and banana nut. No credit cards, reservations or liquor.

THEATER, MUSIC AND DANCE

After New York City, Boston offers more cultural activity than any other city on the East Coast. New shows often run in Boston before opening on Broadway, the Symphony Orchestra is world-famous, and the many universities of the area provide talent and stimulation for repertory companies, dance groups, and choruses. Community participation is high-level too; Elma Lewis' National Center of Afro-American Artists (NCAAA) has been selected by the American Revolutionary Bicentennial Administration in Washington as the "national symbol of the arts made meaningful in current history."

To underline the city's position as an important cultural center, Boston 200 has instituted a program called **Festival American** (see Calendar p. 215) designed to enlighten and entertain Boston residents and visitors. A major aim is to make the arts available to a maximum number of people and to focus attention on the significant contributions of American artists. Festival American will incorporate Summerthing, a nationally known program of the Mayor's Office of Cultural Affairs, which brings a wide variety of performing artists to Boston's parks and neighborhood centers.

The following listings divide Boston cultural organizations into three groups: Theater, Music, and Dance. For the major organizations, those that perform frequently and regularly, a short description has been provided. To find out about the current activities of these and other groups, the best sources of information are the daily Boston *Globe* and Boston *Herald American*, the Boston 200 Newspaper, and the weekly *Real Paper* and Boston *Phoenix*. Additionally, call Boston 200 Information (338-1975) or ARTSLINE (261-1660), a recorded message from the Mayor's Office of Cultural Affairs describing the day's cultural highlights.

THEATER

Boston Center for the Arts, 539 Tremont St., Boston (426-5000). Supported by the City of Boston and private foundation grants, the BCA provides office, rehearsal, and performance facilities to a variety of Boston cultural organizations. By 1976 the Center, whose nucleus is the Cyclorama building, will consist of five theaters, three restaurants and an art gallery. For more information on groups affiliated with the BCA consult listings for the Boston Philharmonia Orchestra, the Associate Artists Opera, the Theatre Co. of Boston, the Boston Ballet, Stage I, the Theater Workshop Boston—OM Theater Workshop, the American Center for Performing and Creative Arts, the Mass. Center Repertory Co., and the New England Regional Opera.

Boston Repertory Theater Inc., One Boylston Place, Boston (423-6580). T-Boylston. A year-round repertory company which presents varied forms of traditional and modern theater. Performances are at 8pm and tickets are $1-$4.

Cambridge Ensemble, 1151 Mass. Ave, Cambridge (876-2544). T-Harvard. A new theater group presenting both original and scripted plays. A special show for the Boston Bicentennial, "The Calvin Coolidge Follies," will open in 1975.

Caravan Theater, Harvard-Epworth Church, 1555 Mass. Ave., Cambridge (868-8520). T-Harvard. A political and sociological review featuring original material and music. Performances are Wed, Fri, and Sat at 8pm and tickets are $2-$3. Open Oct-June.

Charles Playhouse, 76 Warrenton St., Boston (423-2255). T-Boylston. A highly active 2-theater complex which presents classic and contemporary drama and an occasional musical review. Tues-Fri performances are at 8pm; Sat and Sun there are two shows. Tickets are $3-$6.50.

Colonial Theater, 106 Boylston St., Boston, Mass. (426-9366). T-Boylston. Broadway, pre-Broadway and repertory theater featuring national companies. Evening performances are at 7:30pm and there are Sat and mid-week matinees. Tickets are $3.50-$10.

Past and Presents.

Boston 200 presents some revolutionary gift and souvenir ideas to commemorate your visit to Boston—where it all began. The Boston 200 seal is your assurance that the items you choose have been approved by the city's official Bicentennial organization.

First, picture this. Specially prepared Bicentennial postcards, slides and a souvenir photo book, all depicting old and new Boston, are available throughout the city at prices ranging from 10 cents to $1.25.

Now, as you recall, there was a group of "Indians" during our Revolution that went slightly overboard in the eyes of King George. And you can toast their success with the fine Oolong tea that fills the Boston Chinese Tea Party Tea Chests. These sturdy replicas of the crates that were heaved into Boston Harbor cost $3

The Boston 200 group of ceramic and glassware products is your chance to put history to good use. Any of these high quality mementos of your trip to Boston—America's home town—will begin working as soon as you reach home. All ashtrays, coasters, tiles, glasses and mugs carry the Boston 200 seal and are priced from $1.95 to $8.95 for the handsome Revere Tankard.

Of course, if you're interested in making a little history on your own, these Bicentennial Needlepoint Kits in a variety of designs — Boston scenes, historic flags, colonial dolls — are the perfect choice. It's your own effort that completes the kits that range in price from $9.50 to $19.50.

And there's a lot of colonial charm and quite a few colonial charms in the Boston 200 collection of Bicentennial jewelry. The attractive Boston 200 seal has been reproduced on bracelets, brooches, necklaces and rings. And the charms? The charms depict many of the most important themes of our Revolution. All items, in a wide range of prices, are available at all official Bicentennial outlets.

Speaking of revolution, the model citizens that got America off to that great start left part of their legacy in brick and mortar. If you're out to build a record of the past, any one of these heirloom quality Landmark Models — of The Old State House, The Old North Church or Faneuil Hall — is the best way to get started. Each model has been carefully researched and comes with complete historical notes. They're an entertaining and educational experience at $2 each.

A gift collection of truly historic proportions. From Boston 200.

Boston 200™

Official Boston 200 gift and souvenir products are available throughout the city at these locations:

Boston 200 ™

The Boston Stone Gift Shop
Marshall Street

Howard Johnson 57 Motel
200 Stuart Street

Old North Church
193 Salem Street

London Wax Museum
179 Tremont Street

Statler Hilton Pharmacy
60 Arlington Street

Elson, Inc.
Statler Hilton Newsstand
Park Square

Zell's Inc.
Treasure Masters Corp.
(Top of Pru.—Souvenir Stand)

NU 5-1.00 Store
352 Hanover Street

Center Plaza Pharmacy, Inc.
One Center Plaza

F.W. Woolworth Co. #2
Washington Street

The Boston Tea Party Ship
27 State Street

East India Trading Co.
10 Marshall Street
Creek Square

North Station Bookstore
North Station

Archer Kent Stores
174 Tremont Street
733 Boylston Street
Washington Park Shopping
  Center, Roxbury

Bunker Hill Monument
Souvenir Shop
Monument Square
Charlestown

Jordan Marsh Co.
450 Washington Street

Filenes
426 Washington Street

Zell's Inc.
Top of Hancock Tower

Hollis Drug
Faneuil Hall

Old South Meeting House
Washington Street

Kennedy Prints
40 Joy Street
Beacon Hill

Sheraton Boston Hotel
Newsstand
Sheraton Boston Hotel
Prudential Center

Delphi Gift Shop
Hotel Bradford
273 Tremont Street

Liggett Drug Store
375 Washington Street

Mondello's
279 Hanover Street

House of Hurwitz
569 Washington Street

Card Carousel
238 Boylston Street

Hasty Pudding Theatricals, 12 Holyoke St., Cambridge, Mass. (495-5205). T-Harvard. A Harvard tradition. A sophomoric, scatological musical featuring an all-male cast. Probably the oldest drag show in the country. The season runs from March to early April in Cambridge. Tickets are $3-$7.

Loeb Drama Center, 64 Brattle St., Cambridge (864-2630). T-Harvard. Harvard University's theater. Presents both student drama productions and a variety of professional offerings.

Massachusetts Center Repertory Co., 541 Tremont St., Boston (262-0340). T-Park St., then Tremont St. bus. A versatile equity repertory company which has performed Shakespeare, musicals and avant garde theater. Six evening performances and two matinees per week in a season which runs Oct-June. Part of the Boston Center for the Arts. Tickets $2.50-$4.50.

National Center of Afro-American Artists Drama Program, 122 Elm Hill Ave., Roxbury (442-8820). T-Egleston, then bus. Major performing components are the National Center Theater Co. and the Elma Lewis Children's Theater Co. Actors are drawn from programs for college, secondary, middle, and preschool students as well as a theater training program at Norfolk Prison. The companies perform works not only from black literary tradition, but also from the body of world literature. For the Bicentennial, productions will focus on the material of eighteenth- and nineteenth-century black poets and writers. A newer company, the Wuhabi Mime Co., is also expected to contribute. Performances are at the National Center as well as theaters, schools and universities in the Boston area.

Peoples' Theater, 1253 Cambridge St., Cambridge (547-4930). T-Central, Harvard or Lechmere, then bus to Inman Sq. An interracial dramatic group which has been in existence for more than 10 years and performs in a storefront theater renovated by members of the company. Major productions, generally of contemporary material, are done in the winter and spring. Performances are Fri and Sat evenings at 8pm, Sun at 7pm. Tickets are free-$2.

Pocket Mime Theater, Church of the Covenant, 67 Newbury St., Boston (247-9000). T-Arlington. French Classical mime with emphasis on American themes. Performances are Thurs, Fri, and Sat evenings and there is a Sat matinee. The season is Oct-Apr and tickets are $3.

The Proposition, 241 Hampshire St., Cambridge (876-0088). T-Central, then Central Sq.-Porter Sq. bus line. Light improvisational revue is offered year-round. The focus is generally political and social. The Proposition Circus for Children, also an improvisation, features games and stories and performs Sat afternoons from June-Sept. A special Bicentennial show, a political cabaret entitled *The Boston Tea Party*, will be presented in 1975 at theaters in the Boston area. Wed and Thurs evening performances are at 8:30, Fri and Sat at 8pm and 10pm., and Sat afternoons at 2pm. Tickets are $3-$4.

Shubert Theater, 265 Tremont St., Boston (426-4520). T-Boylston. Open Sept-June, presenting Broadway and pre-Broadway musicals, dramas and comedies. Evening performances at 7:30pm, matinees at 2pm. Tickets are $3-$15.

Stage I, 539 Tremont St., Boston (426-8492). T-Park St., then Tremont St. bus. An experimental theater company specializing in drama concerning myth and ritual. Often classic works are adapted to incorporate dance. Performances Thurs, Fri and Sat at 8:30pm at the Boston Center for the Arts.

Theatre Co. of Boston, 551 Tremont St., Boston (423-7193). A resident professional equity group specializing in abstract drama and theater of the absurd. Evening performances are Tues-Sun, matinees are Wed and Sat. Tickets run $3-$6.

Theater Workshop Boston—OM Theater, 539 Tremont St., Boston (482-4778). A professional company and school associated with the Boston Center for the Arts which creates original works and develops new forms of dramatic expression. Programs for children and adults are performed at the BCA and other Boston area theaters. Tickets are $2-$3.50.

Tufts Arena Theater, Tufts University, Medford (623-3880). T-Harvard or Lechmere, then Medford Sq. bus. Sept.-June the Arena Theater is the vehicle of the Tufts University Drama Department. In the summer a repertory company of young professionals and advanced students performs Wed-Sat at 8:15pm. For the summers of 1975 and 1976, in honor of the Bicentennial, a special program, "This Boston Tumult," has been scheduled. Four playwrights, including Englishman David Forsyth, have been commissioned to write historical plays dealing with occurrences between 1760 and 1775. Tickets to the Arena Theater are $2.50-$3.50.

Wilbur Theater, 252 Tremont St., Boston (426-9366). T-Boylston. Broadway and pre-Broadway material in a season running rom late Aug to middle June. Performances are Mon-Sat evenings at 7:30pm with matinees on Sat and occasionally midweek. Tickets are $3-$9.

MUSIC

Associated Artists Opera, 551 Tremont St., Boston (542-0308). T-Park St., then Tremont St. bus. Affiliated with the Boston Center for the Arts. All performances are held at the Center's National Theater. The season runs Nov-Feb and includes operatic adaptations of modern plays as well as classical works. Talent is drawn exclusively from the New England area. Performances are at 8pm and tickets cost $4-$8.50.

Boston Pops, Symphony Hall, 251 Huntington Ave., Boston (266-1492) T-Symphony. The world-famous Pops, founded in 1885 and directed by Arthur Fiedler since 1930, plays Mon-Sat at Symphony Hall in May and June. Additionally, free evening concerts are given during the first half of July at the Hatch Shell on the Esplanade. Viennese waltzes, show music, and marches are the basis of the program, and there are frequent guest performers representing all branches of the musical world. At Symphony Hall the audience can sit around tables where refreshments are available during the concert. Show time is 8:30pm and tickets cost $1.50-$8.

Boston Philharmonia Orchestra, 551 Tremont St., Boston (536-2950). T-Park St., then Tremont St. bus. Six to eight programs annually with performances on Sun evenings in the National Theater of the Boston Center for the Arts. The music is classical, although assisting artists are sometimes modern stylists. Performances are at 8pm and tickets cost $2-$5.

Berklee College of Music, 1140 Boylston St., Boston (266-4322). T-Auditorium. 90 free performances during the academic year in the Recital Hall. The fare ranges from soloists to big band sounds and many of the students have had extensive professional experience with big name bands. Additionally, several major concerts are given at John Hancock Hall.

Boston Symphony Orchestra, 251 Huntington Ave., Boston (266-1492). T-Symphony. The Boston Symphony, with Seiji Ozawa as Music Director and Colin Davis as Principal Guest Conductor, is one of the nation's finest. The repertoire varies, but always consists of superbly performed classical music. About 75 performances are given Tuesday, Thursday, and Saturday evenings and Friday afternoons in a season which runs from late September to late April. In addition, there are Wednesday evening open rehearsals and a children's series under the direction of Harry Ellis Dickson. The bulk of tickets for all series are sold to subscribers who come regularly throughout the season, but seats for single performances are often available. Most evening concerts begin at 8:30pm, afternoon concerts at 2pm. Tickets are $1.50-$8. During the summer the Orchestra is in residence at Tanglewood in Western Massachusetts. Trips to Tanglewood for concerts are available through Peter Pan Bus Lines.

Camerata Players, Museum of Fine Arts, 465 Huntington Ave., Boston (267-9300). T-Huntington Ave. line. Renaissance and baroque music utilizing instruments from the Museum of Fine Arts collection. Concerts are free every Tues night Oct-May at the museum and four performances per year are given in larger halls.

Chorus Pro Musica, 645 Boylston St., Boston (267-7442). A 100-member chorus active Oct-June. Performs at Symphony Hall, Sanders Theater at Harvard University, and local churches. Programs usually incorporate contemporary and little known works with traditional material. For the Bicentennial the Chorus will focus on early American music and its European origins. Tickets to performances range from $2-$6.

Civic Symphony of Boston, 12 Ellsworth Ave., Cambridge (566-0367). A community orchestra made up of amateurs and students which concentrates on unusual and eccentric interpretations of great masterpieces. The season is Dec-May, performances are at Jordan Hall (T-Symphony), and tickets are $1-$3.50.

Concert Cruises, Water Music Inc., 21 Sherman St., Cambridge (492-3667). T-Aquarium. Classical music on board a Bay State Line boat touring Boston harbor. Performers are local choruses, chamber groups and ensembles. Two sailings, at 5:30pm and 7pm every Mon and Thurs, June-Sept. Embarkation is from Long Wharf at State St. and Atlantic Ave. Tickets are $2-$3.50. Water Music also runs the Jazz Boat on Wednesdays at the same times; tickets are $3. Cocktails may be purchased on board.

Handel and Haydn Society, 140 Boylston St., Boston (266-3605). T-Symphony. America's oldest choral group, founded 1815. Five concerts of classical choral music each year between Oct and late May. The *Messiah* is performed at Christmas. Ticket prices are $3.50-$7.50 and the concerts are held at Jordan Hall and Symphony Hall.

Masterworks Chorale, Box 312, Lexington (235-6210). Excellent choral group with members from more than 40 Greater Boston communities. Most performances are at Cary Hall in Lexington, but there are occasional Boston and Cambridge concerts. The Chorale will be especially active during Bicentennial. Admission free.

National Center of Afro-American Artists Music Program, 122 Elm Hill Ave., Roxbury, Mass. (442-8820). T-Egleston, then bus. A variegated program celebrating the treasures of black musical tradition: African, Afro-Cuban, gospel and jazz. Gospel is performed by Black Persuasion and the Children of Black Persuasion, choral music by the 35-year-old National Center Chorus, opera by the National Center Opera Workshop, and contemporary music by the National Center Jazz Orchestra. The Bicentennial will be a period of expanded activity featuring exchanges between American and international music groups and performances in theaters throughout the Boston area as well as at the National Center.

New England Conservatory of Music, 290 Huntington Ave., Boston (536-2412). T-Symphony. America's oldest conservatory, founded 1867. Involved in all major musical areas except rock. 200 free concerts per year, Oct-June, at Jordan Hall and Recital Hall featuring students and a distinguished faculty. Performances generally begin at 8:30pm. Call for current information.

New England Regional Opera, 539 Tremont St., Boston (423-7853). T-Park St., then Tremont St. bus. Affiliated with the Boston Center for the Arts. Operas, each performed six times during a season running from Nov-May. A production of *Hansel and Gretel* is done annually. Performances are at the National Theater and tickets are $6-$8.

Opera Company of Boston, 172 Newbury St., Boston (267-8050). Four operas, three performances each, during a season which runs January-May. The company is well known for its spectacular productions and inventive presentations of new or seldom-performed operas. Internationally renowned guest artists frequently complement local singers. Sarah Caldwell is the nationally known director, and performances are at the Orpheum Theater (T-Washington). Tickets are $4-$20.

SPEBSQSA INC., 52 First St., Cambridge (547-2700). The Society for the Preservation and Encouragement of Barbershop Quartet Singing in America performs at the Hotel Lenox every Tues night at 8:30pm. The show is free, and choral music often accompanies the traditional quartet *a cappella*.

DANCE

Boston Ballet Company, 551 Tremont St., Boston (542-3945). T-Boylston. Considered one of the nation's finest companies. Performs chiefly at the Music Hall Theater under the direction of E. Virginia Williams and presents a balanced repertoire of classical and contemporary ballet by American and European composers. The main season runs Nov-Mar, including the traditional *Nutcracker Suite* at Christmastime. During the summer the company presents a free series at the Hatch Shell on the Esplanade. Tickets at the Music Hall run $4-$12.50.

National Center of Afro-American Artists Dance Program, 122 Elm Hill Ave., Roxbury (442-8820). T-Egleston, then bus. The Dance Co. of the NCAAA, the Children's Dance Co. of the NCAAA, and the Primitive Dance Co. of the NCAAA, three distinct performing companies, are the heart of the program. Modern and jazz dancing are performed by the Dance Co. and the Children's Dance Co., while the Primitive Dance Co. specializes in African and Afro-Caribbean dance. During 1975 new ballets celebrating aspects of black life from pre-Revolutionary days to the present will be premiered. Performances are at the National Center and at theaters and schools in the area.

NIGHTLIFE AND SINNING

If drinking, dancing, and listening to music are your idea of how to spend an evening, Boston can be most accommodating. The problem, as always, is to match your tastes with those of local establishments. Boston abounds with loud singles bars because of the burgeoning population of young, unmarried people, but also has elegant cocktail lounges (located mainly in hotels) and smoky jazz spots with nationally known performers. For those not interested in drinking there are coffee-houses that specialize in traditional blues or folk music and serve espresso, sandwiches, and pastries. The following listings should give you a rough idea about where to go, as well as where not to go. Whatever your choice, enjoy yourself.

BOSTON BARS

Athens After Dark, 3 Appleton St., Boston (423-3652). T-Arlington. Greek supper club with continuous entertainment. Belly-dancing, Greek folk music and dancing tunes. Cover charge $1.50 weekdays, $2.50 weekends. No credit cards. Open 8pm to 2am nightly.

Bachelors III, Park Square, Boston (266-0200). T-Arlington. Young businessmen's restaurant and nightclub. Live band every night with shows starting 8pm or 8:30pm. No cover. All major credit cards accepted. Restaurant open daily, bar open Mon-Fri 8am to 2am; Sat till 1am; Sun 5pm to 2am.

Boston Club/The Garage, 969 Commonwealth Ave., Boston (542-1550). T-Commonwealth Ave. line. Dancing place for younger crowd. $1 cover. No credit cards. Live music.

Bunratty's, 186 Harvard Ave., Allston (254-9820). T-Commonwealth Ave. line. Casual young dating bar with top commercial bands. Small cover on weekends. Open 2pm to 2am. Restaurant during day. Nightclub after 9pm.

Burke's Place, 15 New Chardon St., Government Center, Boston (723-4746). T-Government Center. "Boston's showcase for fine new bands." Largest nightclub downtown. Live music. Nightly specials at the bar like couples night, or beer splash. All major credit cards accepted. Weekend cover. Open 11am to 2am. Restaurant upstairs.

Cafe Budapest Bar, Copley Square Hotel, 90 Exeter St., Boston (734-3388). T-Copley. Elegant European salon with velvet furniture and chandeliers. Cocktails and crepes to the strains of piano, violin, and Hungarian love songs. Open noon to midnight daily.

Copley's, Copley Plaza Hotel, Copley Square (267-5300). T-Copley. The bar and restaurant occupy the state suite of a 19th-century gentleman, complete with Edwardian prints and antique books. Unobtrusive piano or ensemble. Very popular with young professionals. Snacks available at the oyster bar. Open daily 11:30am to 2am.

Daisy Buchanan's, 240 Newbury St., Boston (247-8516). T-Copley. Dating bar where many professional athletes hang out. Lively jukebox and a simulated English pub atmosphere. No cover charge or credit cards. Open 11am to 2am daily.

Diamond Jim's, Hotel Lenox, 710 Boylston St., Boston (536-5300). T-Copley. Piano bar with guest singers. Customers often sing along. Adjacent to Delmonico's restaurant. Major credit cards accepted. Open Mon-Sat, 5pm to 2am.

Dunfey's Last Hurrah, The Parker House, 60 School St., Boston (227-8600). T-Park St. Eating, drinking, dancing and listening in turn-of-the-century atmosphere. Dixieland band. A well dressed crowd, though no particular age group predominates. Major credit cards. Open 10:30am to 2am daily. Entertainment in the evening only.

The Groggery, 14 Franklin St., Allston (corner of Harvard and Cambridge Sts.) (254-3642). T-Commonwealth Ave. line. Raucous freak haven. Dancing nightly to live rock music. Cover charge on weekends. No credit cards. Lots of street-parking. Very casual. Open daily 8pm to 2am.

Hillbilly Ranch, 27 Eliot St., Park Square, Boston (338-7147). T-Arlington or Boylston. Country-and-Western music bookings from Nashville. No cover, no credit cards. Performances begin at 9pm. Dancing. Open 9pm to 2am.

Jazz Workshop, 733 Boylston St., Boston (267-1300). T-Copley. Boston's prime jazz cabaret. Nationally known artists. Very popular. Sets at 9:30pm and 11:30pm. Cover varies. Call for details.

Lucifer's, 533 Commonwealth Ave., Boston (536-1950). T-Kenmore. Singles nightclub with name entertainment like the Platters, Happenings, Brooklyn Bridge. Weekdays no cover, weekends $2. Major credit cards. Open 7:30pm to 2am daily.

Medieval Manor, Massachusetts and Commonwealth Ave., Boston (262-5144). T-Auditorium or Kenmore. Zany medieval theater restaurant with singing and dancing minstrels, acrobats, and court jester. Major credit cards accepted. Nightly "banquets" at 8pm except on Mon.

Merry-Go-Round, Sheraton Plaza Hotel, Copley Sq., Boston (267-5300). T-Copley. A relaxed cocktail lounge with a revolving bar in the center, music, and a small dance floor. An older crowd generally. Credit cards accepted. Open Mon-Thurs 5pm to 1am, Fri and Sat 2pm to 1am.

Oliver's, 62 Brookline Ave., Boston (536-4840). T-Kenmore or Fenway. Parking on street. Dance bar with live rock music by well-known groups. Mostly early twenties. Cover charge varies. No credit cards accepted. Open noon to 1am daily.

Paul's Mall, 733 Boylston St., Boston (267-1300). T-Copley. The best nightclub in Boston. Top artists nightly at decent prices. Crowded. Cover charge. Call for details. Open Sun-Fri, 9pm to 2am, Sat 8pm to 1am.

Persian Lounge, Sheraton Boston Hotel, Prudential Center, Boston (236-2000). T-Auditorium or Prudential. Quiet piano bar frequented by couples and businessmen. All major credit cards. Open Mon-Sat, 11am to 1am; Sun, noon to 1am.

Scotch 'n Sirloin Lounge, 77 N. Washington St., Boston (723-3677). T-Government Center. Traditional New Orleans jazz and dancing atop an old factory building overlooking the harbor and downtown Boston. Fashionable crowd. Cover charge $2 per person. Major credit cards. Entertainment begins at 8 pm weekdays, 9:30pm weekends Open till 2am. Sunday jam sessions 4pm to 8pm in winter, 6pm to 10pm in summer.

Sugar Shack, 110 Boylston St., Boston (426-0086). T-Boylston. Parking at Common Garage. Boston's finest soul showcase. Top black acts in country. Mainly singles. Liquor. Cover varies from $1-4. No credit cards. Performances at 10pm and 1am. Open daily 8pm to 2am.

Tommy's Point After, 271 Dartmouth St., Boston (536-6560). T-Copley. Not a young person's place. Dancing nightly to bands playing pop, jazz, and sometimes rock music. All major credit cards. Open Mon-Sat, 11:30am to 2am. Closed Sun.

Top of the Hub Lounge, Prudential Center, Boston (536-1775). T-Prudential or Auditorium. One of the nation's loftiest drinking spots. Inexpensive drinks, dancing music, and a romantic view of the city's lights. All major credit cards except Carte Blanche. Open Mon-Sat, noon to midnight, Sun, noon to midnight.

The Townhouse, 84 Beacon St., Boston (227-9600). T-Arlington. Combination restaurant/nightclub on Beacon Hill. Up-and-coming young professionals. Bull and Finch Pub. All major credit cards accepted. No cover. No dancing. Open daily 11:30am to 1am.

Trader Vic's Bar, Statler Hilton Hotel, Park Sq., Boston (423-2549). T-Arlington. A branch of the international chain serving exotic rum drinks. Dim and quiet with bamboo hut decor. All major credit cards. Open 11am to 1am daily.

Upstairs Pub, Sheraton Boston Hotel, Prudential Center, Boston (236-2000). T-Auditorium or Prudential. Dancing and songs in a "Colonial tavern" with dartboard. All major credit cards. Open daily 1pm to 2am.

Zelda's, 1194 Commonwealth Ave., Boston (731-0271). T-Commonwealth Ave. line. Parking Fashionable singles discotheque. Cover on Wed, Fri-Sun. No credit cards. No jeans. Mainly mid-twenties. Lunch served. Open daily noon to 2am.

Casablanca, Brattle Street, Harvard Square, Cambridge (876-0999). T-Harvard. Dark, split-level cabaret. Kinky wall murals from old movies. Jukebox. Downstairs: students and young businessmen, folk-rock and piano music Sun-Thurs. Upstairs: Harvard preppies. No dancing. Open Sun-Thurs noon to 1am, Fri-Sat until 2am.

Molly's Bar, 33 Dunster St., Harvard Square, Cambridge (354-0508). T-Harvard. Drinks and food in the basement of "The Garage." No cover or minimum. Major credit cards accepted. Young professionals and older students. Open daily 4pm to 1am.

Jacks, 952 Massachusetts Ave., Cambridge (491-7800). T-Central. Probably the most popular dating bar in Cambridge. Wall to wall people. Dancing to live rock and country rock. Food served until 9:30pm. No cover. No credit cards. Open daily 11:30am to 1am.

Kings, 30B Boylston St., Harvard Square, Cambridge (354-9352). T-Harvard. Club in basement of "The Garage". Country-and-Western, bluegrass, and soul live (Thurs-Sat) or on jukebox. Food during day. Mixed crowd. Dancing. No cover. No credit cards. Open 8am to 1am.

Orson Welles Bar, 1001 Massachusetts Ave., Cambridge (868-3607). T-Harvard. Restaurant-bar attracting young working people, artists and assorted other Cambridge types. American Express accepted. Special rate on movies at Orson Welles Theater if you eat here. Bar open daily 11:30am to midnight.

Oxford Ale House, 36 Church St., Harvard Square, Cambridge (876-5353). T-Harvard. Loud and lively cruising place for college students and young workers. Live rock music nightly except Monday, Jazz Night. Food served during day. Friendly atmosphere but crowded. No cover. Open Mon-Wed 11:30am to 1am, Tues-Fri 11:30am to 2am, Sat-Sun noon to 1am.

Speakeasy, 22 Norfolk St., Cambridge (354-2525). T-Central. Nationally known small blues nightclub. Some jazz and soul. Prohibition bistro decor. Casual. No credit cards. $1 cover on Fri and Sat. Open 7:30pm to 1am.

BOSTON COFFEE HOUSES

Stone-Phoenix Coffeehouse, 1120 Boylston St., Boston. T-Auditorium. Huge cafe with Egyptian-style decor. National and local folk artists. Performances at 9:15pm and 12:30am. Cover varies. Open 8pm to 1am.

Sword-in-the-Stone, 15 Charles St., Boston (523-9168). T-Charles. Boston's oldest coffeehouse. Small with Arthurian candle-lit atmosphere. Live folk, pop, and blues music nightly by local artists. Performances at 9:15pm and 12:30am. Cover varies from 75¢ to $1.50. Open 8pm to 1am.

Turk's Head, 71½ Charles St., Boston (227-3524). T-Charles. Small continental cafe on Beacon Hill. Live entertainment nightly. Gourmet continental food. Meals from $2 to $10. No credit cards. No cover. Open 8am to midnight. Dinner served until 8pm. Jackets and ties required in the evening.

CAMBRIDGE COFFEE HOUSES

Algiers, Brattle St., Cambridge (547-9112). T-Harvard. Smoky cafe with North African flavor. Arab guitarists. Foreign and student crowd. No cover. Weekend minimum. Food served. Open 11am to midnight daily.

The Blue Parrot, 123A Mt. Auburn St., Cambridge (491-1551). T-Harvard. Restaurant/coffeehouse with continental cuisine, beer and wine. Mainly students and other Cambridge types. No cover. Minimum on Fri and Sat nights.

Cafe Pamplona, 12 Bow St., Cambridge. T-Harvard. Tiny, low ceilinged basement cafe serving continental coffees, sandwiches, and ice cream concoctions. Outdoor tables in warm weather. No credit cards. Open Mon-Sat 11am to 6pm and 8pm to 1am; Sun 3pm to 6pm and 8pm to 1am.

Cambridge Folk and Tale House, 863 Main St., Cambridge (492-2900). T-Central. Very informal all-night coffeehouse and bar. Different program every night. Jazz. Classical. Women's issues. Theater. Movies. $1.50 cover. Opens at 8pm.

Nameless Coffeehouse, 3 Church St., Cambridge (864-1630). T-Harvard. Intimate performance center for local folk, blues and jazz professionals. 18+ college crowd. Snack food. Donation only. Open Fri-Sat 7:30pm to 10pm.

Passim, 47 Palmer St., Harvard Square (492-7679). T-Harvard. Best of nationally-known folk music in a uniquely casual setting. Combination coffeehouse/gallery. No credit cards. Cover charge and performance times vary with artists. Open Tues-Sat noon to 5:30pm. Coffeehouse from 7:45pm.

SINNING

"You can sin in Boston, too, but you've got to do it early."
—*Businessman on Washington Street, 1/74*

The Combat Zone on lower Washington Street is not-so-Puritan Boston's center for adult entertainment. Not as garish as Times Square, but just as educational. Where else but in Boston would "The Pilgrim" be a burlesque house? And "The Mayflower" a porno showcase? T-Essex, Boylston.

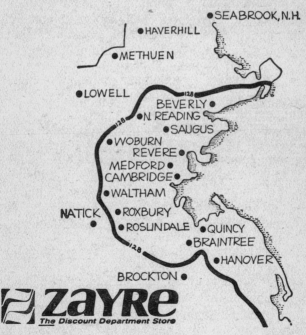

INDEX

311

313

FOR FURTHER READING

The following books were invaluable to the editors in researching and writing the trail descriptions, and we recommend them to anyone interested in learning more about Boston.

Cleveland Amory, *The Proper Bostonians*

Eleanor Early, *And This Is Boston!*

Richard Frothingham, *History of Charlestown, Massachusetts*

Harvard Student Agencies, *Cheap Eats* (edited by Paul Silver and Katherine C. Haspel)

James F. Hunnewell, *A Century of Town Life; A History of Charlestown, Massachusetts (1775–1887)*

George F. Weston, Jr., *Boston Ways: High, By, and Folk*

Walter M. Whitehill, *Boston: A Topographical History*